POLICE ETHICS

THE CORRUPTION OF NOBLE CAUSE

JOHN P. CRANK / **MICHAEL A. CALDERO**
BOISE STATE UNIVERSITY   BELLEVUE COMMUNITY COLLEGE

anderson publishing co.
2035 Reading Road
Cincinnati, OH 45202
800-582-7295

Police Ethics: The Corruption of Noble Cause

Copyright © 2000
Anderson Publishing Co.
2035 Reading Rd.
Cincinnati, OH 45202

Phone 800.582.7295 or 513.421.4142
Web Site www.andersonpublishing.com

Library of Congress Cataloging-in-Publication Data

Crank, John P.
    Police ethics : the corruption of noble cause / John P. Crank, Michael A. Caldero.
        p.   cm.
    Includes bibliographical references and index.
    ISBN 1-58360-504-5 (pbk.)
    1. Police--United States. 2. Law enforcement--Moral and ethical aspects--United States. 3. Police ethics--United States. I. Caldero, Michael A. (Michael Anthony), 1943-   . II. Title.
    HV8138.C6728 1999
    174'.93632--dc21

99-38850
CIP

Cover design by Tin Box Studio, Inc.
Cover photo credit: © Brad Smith/PhotoSmith

EDITOR Gail Eccleston
ASSISTANT EDITOR Sharon L. Boyles
ACQUISITIONS EDITOR Michael C. Braswell

Table of Contents

Introduction

Officers stroll into the room and take seats. In the back of the room, there are the usual coffee dispensers for decaf and regular, and a tray of doughnuts. Today the command staff is attending a lecture on police ethics, and the speaker, Michael Caldero, is from a northwestern city. The chief walks in, chats briefly with a couple of the officers, and takes a seat in the back of the room. In the minds of the officers is a single sentiment.

Who in the heck is this person telling *me* about police ethics?

That's what the audience thinks when Mike begins his presentation on police ethics. This sentiment is expressed in several ways.

- What does education have to contribute to police work?
- Forget everything you learned in a book – here's how we do it on the street.
- An outsider can never understand police work.
- Why do I have to waste my time listening to this crap?
- His experience is with another agency. We don't work that way here.

Mike has heard it all. When they don't say it, they are thinking it. No one wants to hear a discussion on ethics. Ethics is learned in the streets. It's about victims and the assholes that prey on them. Mike organizes his materials and prepares to begin. He has talked to commanders before. They're accustomed to leaving a lot unsaid.

He begins. *Why are you people here today?*

A commander responds. "Same reason you are."

Mike laughs at this comment. It's the laugh of a cop. It's a half-second late. Like he's heard something hidden in what you said that even you don't know.

We put the question to you, reader. Why are you reading this book?

Chances are that if you're reading this book it's because you have to, so you might as well grin and bear it. You can bet that your instructor will test you on the material!

More importantly, we have something to say. Something that we think is important. Something we believe in. Our message is vigilance. The danger here, though, is not from predatory offenders or dangerous, unknown circumstances. The question central to our inquiry is – how well do you know yourself?

This is a different kind of book on police ethics. We'll discuss clear ethical dilemmas such as accepting free gifts and the like, but only as a secondary issue. If you're a police officer, you have department policies that clearly state what you are permitted to do and what is illegal or inappropriate. Whether or not you accept gratuities, you know when you are doing right or wrong by your department. In this book, we have our sights set on a different kind of ethical issue, one less clear but more important.

This book aims squarely at noble-cause corruption. What do we mean by noble cause corruption? It is corruption committed in the name of good ends, corruption that happens when police officers care too much about their work. It is corruption committed in order to get the bad guys off the streets, to protect the innocent and the children from the predators that inflict pain and suffering on them. It is the corruption of police power, when officers do bad things because they believe that the outcomes will be good.

Some readers will no doubt feel betrayed by our approach to ethics. At times, we will seem too quick to criticize the police, to make them out to be bad guys. Without a doubt, we are raising moral questions about police officers who see themselves as warriors against evil, the guardians of the thin blue line between order and disorder. Noble-cause corruption is a difficult topic to write about, because we are committed to the police, and because we also carry the beliefs that drive the noble cause. Yet, in today's world of intricate social and legal complexity, we recognize that there has to be a limit on the zeal police show for their work. All too often, as you will see in this book, there is not.

The time for discussing the ethics of police power is long overdue. It is a neglected topic, though a few researchers are beginning to acknowledge its importance in today's world (Carter, 1999; Barker & Carter, 1999;

Kraska & Kappeler, 1995). We live in a country where the authority of the police to intervene in the affairs of the citizenry is on the ascent. Traditional due process restrictions on police authority are being relaxed. Citizens sometimes encourage illegal police behavior to "do something about crime." And with these changes, opportunities for noble-cause corruption are increasing. Consider the following three examples.

The first example is drug interdiction activity, where we encounter such tactics as "drug-courier profiles." Routine automobile stops aimed at the interception of drug couriers are conducted in many states, and permitted by the Supreme Court, without the prior requirement of probable cause for stopping the vehicle. A "profile" based on a vehicle's and occupant's similarity to known drug-courier activity can provide the basis for a stop, and cars that are profiled are routinely searched in some states. Profiles, however, create easy opportunities for what has been called race-profiling – stopping vehicles based on the race or ethnicity of their occupants. Cops know, for example, that they can stop Latinos in old, beat-up cars in farming areas and sharply increase the production of statistics for license, registration, and insurance violations. Some observers call the practice of profiling "DWM" – driving while minority. Given the nature of profile stops, it is extremely difficult to determine whether race-profiling occurs, thus increasing opportunities for noble-cause corruption.

Second, the courts are relaxing the circumstances under which confessions are admissible. Under *Arizona v. Fulminante*, the Supreme Court provided a basis for permitting coerced confessions under certain circumstances. What is the impact of such decisions on the police? In this decision are the seeds of noble cause corruption. As Skolnick and Fyfe, 1993:65) observe, "If courts allow the police to deceive suspects for the good end of convicting criminals, can we really expect the police to be truthful when offering testimony?"

Third, we witness the expansion of police authority in various versions of "community policing." Some reformers argue that police should be able to intervene even when a law has not been broken, on behalf of community civility (Wilson & Kelling, 1982; Kelling, 1985; see also Klockars, 1985). It is argued that the police have become too concerned with the rights of individuals and detached from the needs of local communities. Police, it is suggested, need the authority to intervene in ordinary problems of public order on behalf of their local communities. Bums need to be rousted out of parks. Skateboarders create fear and need to be controlled. In short, the police should have the authority to do something about problems that do not involve the breaking of the law, but are disruptive to local ideas of public order.

In the United States today, police power is an awaking leviathan. The power of the police to intervene in citizen's lives stems directly from the courts, whose legal opinions are in turn driven by public opinion favorable to stern justice. It is a power that can be used for good or evil. It has enormous power to corrupt.

To understand how police can be corrupted by their work, we need to first recognize that they strongly believe in the "core" activity of their work: doing something about crime. Sometimes the public thinks of the police as automatons in blue, without feelings, dispensing law. This is called the "just the facts, ma'am" approach to police work. The police, however, believe in their work, and they carry it out passionately. They care about getting bad guys off the streets. They are morally committed to their work. Their morality carries simple ideas of right and wrong, good and evil. For the police, good and evil is a concrete notion practiced in the day-to-day work of policing. The police see themselves on the side of angels. And they deal with bad guys and assholes, who they firmly believe are associates of the non-angelic crowd. But it is precisely this – the nature of good and evil, and who decides which is which – that is up for grabs in the current era.

This book is about the power that police use. It is meant as a way to think about that power – not only in the street-level sense of getting bad guys off the streets and dealing with assholes, but in terms of how it can corrupt the police as individuals, as organizations, and as a profession. This book is intended to provide students of policing with a realistic understanding of the kinds of corruption that can envelop police officers. We recommend that students carefully consider what we have to say – the problems we describe are in their future, and they must be prepared for it if they wish to undertake a career in police work, as well as in other careers. This book is also designed to be an exercise in ethical tuning-up to street officers, a call from us to them to act from an ethically alert frame of mind. And it is a wake-up call to administrators as well, to remember what street life was like and to recognize that noble-cause corruption can happen, and likely does, in their organization.

There are many public voices, including respectable citizens and legislators who should know better, that encourage the police to be tougher than the bad guys, to step over the line if that's what it takes to do something about crime, to do what it takes to win the war on crime. We're here to steer recruits and students interested in a policing career away from that path of stepping over the line. We're here to provide a different view, maybe not so simple in its good-guy/bad-guy imagery, but a view more consistent with the kind of work that the police do. Our ethics come from the way the police and the public share similar dreams, struggle through ordinary problems, and seek peace and happiness in their daily lives. We believe in the noble cause, but we believe that noble-cause corruption breaks the bond that links the police to those they are sworn to protect.

When police reformers talk about corruption, they are mostly concerned with the illegal use of police authority or power for economic gain. A review of any of the many police ethics books shows that, with a few important exceptions, they seem to be more concerned with grafting and illegal economic gain – a free cup of coffee, for example – than with violence and corruption in the name of law and order. There are several reasons for this. Economic corruption is more tangible – it is easier to identify. If someone accepts a free meal from a restaurant, there is a clear-cut, identifiable act. An illegal search of an offender to find drugs is much more difficult to explain, and putting someone in jail for a weekend for COC – contempt of cop – is intangible. These latter types are noble-cause corruption, more difficult to deal with because they are closely aligned with the morality of the police – they serve purposes that the police tend to support. But they are far-reaching in their consequences. When they happen, the damage to the object of a police officer's scorn is substantial – a beating, jail, or prison time and a criminal record – hopes for a return to a normal life damaged beyond repair. The department becomes vulnerable to liability. And perhaps most importantly, the legitimacy of the police is undermined.

It is more politically expedient to talk about economic corruption than noble-cause corruption. Economic corruption is usually explained in terms of criminal acts and described in terms of a slippery slope – small crimes (for example, taking a bribe from a motorist), provide the justification for more serious ones such as shaking down a drug dealer for cash. When we look at economic corruption, we can explain everything in terms of "rotten apples" (an aphorism for bad cops) and we don't have to ask the deeper, harder questions about the nature of police work. Even when many officers in the same agency are involved in economic crime, we think about their criminality in terms of economic temptations and their impact on individual weaknesses. It is the explanation that departments most frequently use to explain corruption problems.

Noble-cause corruption is different. When we look for explanations of noble-cause corruption, we have to look for an explanation for crime in the nature of police work and the kinds of people who are drawn to policing. We begin to recognize how our values themselves contribute to our corruption – how we become that which we most dislike. When an officer makes a questionable arrest, or when an asshole is thumped, the police are acting out of strongly held moral beliefs. Both of these are noble-cause corruption – corruption in the name of the moral rightness of good ends. Ethics aimed at economic crime will not help us understand these kinds of corruption. Noble-cause corruption is about how we can be corrupted while we are carrying out our most highly held beliefs. In a dark way, it is our strongest desire to protect the innocent from the cruel that sometimes carry the seeds of our own undoing.

We believe that the noble cause is something of which the police can be proud. The noble cause enables police to celebrate their special craft, to find meaning in the day-to-day activity of their work. Without the noble cause, police work would lose its meaning, and police officers would lose their sense of humanity, their concern for the innocent, and their dislike of bad people. This makes it difficult to write about the noble cause corrupted, about how our own values can corrupt us.

Where do we draw the line between where we act on behalf of the noble cause and where we encounter noble-cause corruption? The line is fuzzy, indistinct. It is a gray line, worked out in the day-to-day world of police work. There is not an absolute rule an officer can memorize from his or her department's Standard Operating Procedure or some school's academic textbook to distinguish this line. But we will discuss many examples of it in this book.

Although the line may be fuzzy and indistinct, there are real consequences for the corruption of the noble cause. For an individual officer, it is paid in terms of stress, sleepless nights, and the possibility of lawsuits, criminal charges, unpleasant media attention, alienation from the public and from former friends, friction with supervisors, increasing difficulty in gaining promotion, and maybe a visit from the internal affairs officer. A few officers will commit noble-cause corruption and be unable to reconcile it to their sworn obligations to uphold the law. These officers will suffer a great deal of job-related stress. Sometimes the price is a retirement spent justifying what they did. For managers, it is stark disbelief, a denial followed by loss of esteem and frustration. For departments, the cost is a loss of legitimacy in the eyes of the public, an inability to get witness and victim testimony because ordinary people are afraid of the police, a change of executive leadership, corruption scandal in the headlines, and civil litigation. For all of us, it is a threat to the democratic values we cherish.

We're not asking police officers to believe in their work any less. To paraphrase Skolnick and Bayley (1986), we think that the answer for police officers – for us all, for that matter, certainly the public no less than the police – lies in understanding the petty problems and frustrations that overwhelm everyday people. It is in the problems of life that the struggle between good and evil is fought with the greatest intensity. And that is a struggle we all share.

In this book we will discuss noble-cause corruption, how to think about it, its different forms, what it can do to street cops, and how it affects police administrators and the department. We will discuss how police can protect ourselves against it. The topic is difficult, but we hope the reader will bear with us. The goal is worth the work it takes to think and act on this important topic.

We're not going to provide absolutes. If you are a police officer or recruit, we can't tell you that you'll never encounter situations in which ends outweigh means. What we're telling you is to be very, very careful. There are many people out there – prosecutors, the public, legislators, even colleagues – who will make it easy to justify corrupting the noble cause. They will lead you down the garden path. They won't tell you what you are getting into. Or if they do, it'll be like a footnote in a book, the kind of footnotes you never paid attention to in school. You thought ethics was about accepting a free cup of coffee. If you read this book you'll know what you're walking into. Forewarned is forearmed. Now you're warned.

Purpose of this Book

We have written this book in accordance with Sherman's (1999:310) admonition: that instead of being ethically disinterested "fence-pole sitters," as academics tend to be, we benefit from examining police problems in the light of basic moral principles and from a moral point of view (See Figure I.1). If we want to live by principles of personal responsibility, a moral foundation and ethical sense may well be the only road that will get us there.

Figure I.1

> ### Learning Ethics Differently
>
> Many issues in police ethics are in fact clear-cut, and hold little room for serious philosophical analysis. One would have a hard time making a rational defense of police officers stealing, for example.
>
> But what may be wrong with the way police ethics is now taught and learned is just that assumption: that all police ethical issues are as clear-cut as stealing. They are not. The issues of force, time, discretion, loyalty, and others are all very complex, with many shades of gray. To deny this complexity, as the formal approaches of police academies and police rule books often do, may simply encourage unethical behavior. A list of "do's" and "don'ts" that officers must follow because they are ordered to is a virtual challenge to their ingenuity: catch me if you can. And in the face of a police culture that already has established values quite contrary to many of the official rules, the black-and-white approach to ethics may be naive.

Source: Lawrence Sherman (1999). *Learning Police Ethics*, p. 310.

The purpose of this book is to provide a way of thinking about police ethical dilemmas and for police officers to think ethically about their work. It is a product of our understanding of the police, what they do, and why they do it. In the text, we challenge contemporary ways of thinking about the police on a variety of issues. Sometimes we are intentionally provocative.

The narrative in this book is developed from an ethics presentation Dr. Caldero developed for police commanders. The presentation is a one-day event, a condensation of the information presented here. Our tone is a blend of academic and conversational styles, emphasizing key points of the presentation. Quotes from Dr. Caldero are italicized. The presentation is expanded by additional material intended to clarify particular points of emphasis.

This book is about who police officers are and who they should be. For those of you that are or will soon be police officers, it's about your moral self. It's about how to think about the communities where police do their work. And it's a way to think about how communities should be policed in the face of the profound changes our country will encounter in the twenty-first century.

This book is intended primarily for students studying police issues and for police recruits. The issues presented in the book are useful for studying ethical issues in policing and for understanding the everyday world street officers inhabit and in which they work. Sections in the book are also written for police managers and commanders. Too often, in the ranks of management, commanders forget about the constant temptations of the street. When things go sour (and here's a rule of thumb – they either just have or are about to) it's always a surprise for managers. It shouldn't be. We explain why.

We think that general criminal justice students will also have much to gain from this book. It provides a perspective on police work not often discussed openly in the classroom. Today, too many college instructors take sides – they either know nothing about real police work and distrust police altogether, or they are cheerleaders for the police regardless of what the police do. This book aims at an ethical balance between these two viewpoints.

The narrative of the book flows back and forth between its twin audiences of university or college students and police officers. This is intentional. Many students who read the book will become police officers and will be informed by the discussions. And many police officers who read the book are, or will become, students.

What can we hope to accomplish by ethics education and training? We make ethical decisions every time we use some value or moral basis to decide how to act. Ethics training enables us to think about why we make the decisions we do. But ethics training, to be useful, has to be about more than lofty, academic thinking about why we act the way we do. Ethics has to be practical, that is, be useful in the kind of decisions we make in our daily work routines. When confronted with a routine situation, an officer has to decide the right way to act and avoid doing the wrong thing. A practical ethical standard is the standard we bring to bear when deciding what is right and what is wrong.

Our view, stated simply, is that police work is too "ends" focused. Our police sense of identity is bound up in the achievement of law and order. We tend to believe that there are ends so noble, so right, that sometimes it's okay to bend the rules a bit. Sometimes we end up bending the rules a lot.

Ends-oriented thinking is pervasive in traditional policing. The challenge to community policing is to prevent it from becoming central there as well. An officer who believes that he or she is the guardian of neighborhood order is simply exchanging ends-oriented law enforcement for ends-oriented order maintenance. The problems of noble-cause corruption are left unaddressed and may in fact increase.

We argue for a means-oriented ethic of negotiated order that will prepare police for America's future. The United States is in the midst of profound demographic changes, in rural as well as urban areas. The population of the United States is radically diversifying its ethnicity and racial character, and growth is creating crime and disorder pressures in traditionally rural areas. The reality we confront in the United States is a polyglot of ethnic, religious, racial, age, and income groups. For the most part, citizens don't live in ethnic enclaves but mix and mingle in heterogenous neighborhoods. Policing's future, in order to adapt to the needs of the twenty-first century, requires a refocusing from moral ends to negotiated ends. Order is not to be asserted, but negotiated.

Today, the police are responding to changes in the urban and rural American landscape by implementing what is commonly called community policing. What will the role of a community police officer be? The idea that the future will be full of neighborhoods of like-minded individuals is false. We don't need police to be guardians of some sort of moral order that exists only mythically in neighborhoods and certainly doesn't describe the way in which the United States is diversifying along religious, ethnic, and income lines. To respond to the dramatic internationalization of American society, we need police to be *negotiators of public order*. Skills at negotiating order will be the tools police use to enable people to get along. Ends-oriented thinking can't get them there. Means-oriented thinking, we believe, can.

Overview of Chapters

Part 1 addresses the ethical issues of accountability. The first chapter poses the dilemma of accountability – how can we hold the police responsible for their behavior? In this section we distinguish between noble-cause corruption and other types of ethical problems. Noble-cause corruption, we argue, is particularly difficult to deal with because it involves behaviors consistent with beliefs carried by many police officers. Police officers' identification with victims and stern determination to get criminals off the street are powerful and admirable elements of police work, and they provide the core elements of the noble cause. But they also foster a psychology that justifies noble-cause corruption. We present a review of the literature on the police that has dealt with noble-cause and its corruption. Part 1 concludes with a analysis and discussion of police values, what they are, and where they come from.

Part 2 looks at the way in which noble cause is subverted. We begin this section with a discussion of the historical relationship between economic and noble-cause corruption. We then describe how the hiring process reinforces the noble cause, and how it is instrumental in sustaining noble-cause corruption. The corruption of noble cause, we argue, is at the core of many entrenched police problems. Where noble-cause corruption is widespread, police culture acts as a shield to protect officers from oversight. The consequences of noble-cause corruption include insularity, secrecy, and loss of legitimacy. Many elements in this section are particularly aimed at commanders. We encourage commanders to recognize how traditional police hiring and training practices intensify noble-cause corruption.

Part 3 presents noble-cause corruption as a form of what ethicists call a means-ends dilemma. Herbert Packer's justice model is used to describe how the justice system creates pressure to de-emphasize police concerns over the due process laws and administrative guidelines and emphasizes criminal justice "ends" such as the accumulation of arrest statistics. A means orientation to police work, we suggest, provides an alternative ethic that can protect officers and agencies against the corruptive effects of the noble cause. We suggest that it is the "golden apples," sometimes the best officers in the department, those most committed to their work, that are the most vulnerable to noble-cause corruption.

Part 4 considers ethical dilemmas we think will face the police in the twenty-first century. Through various examples, we try to show how community policing fits with a means-oriented ethical outlook. Through an analysis of demographic patterns and population changes in the twenty-first century, we construct a role for the police in terms of the "negotiation of order." By this we mean that the responsibilities of the police will increasingly be to help different and often conflicting groups coexist in a society increasingly divided along status, religious, racial, and ethnic lines. An ends-oriented ethic, we argue, will be ineffective and out-of-touch, contributing to growing internal strife and a breakdown of internal security. By viewing their work in terms of a means-orientation to the co-production of community order, police can help us deal with the profound social changes that even now are occurring.

Prologue

> *A man hears what he wants to hear and*
> *disregards the rest.*
> Simon and Garfunkel, *The Boxer*

Mike looks over his audience. All the participants are command officers. He begins. *Do you understand your officers? Do you really understand them? What they're about?* The commanders look at him. The
question has no meaning to them. He looks at his watch. It will have
meaning in about seven hours.

*I'm going to read something. It's called the Law Enforcement Code
of Ethics. It's the model of ethics developed by the International Association of Chiefs of Police. You all know what it is.* The Law Enforcement
Code of Ethics is widely used by police organizations in the United States
as a standard for police ethics.[1] All books on police ethics discuss the
code. It's printed in Figure P.1.

*What does this code tell us? Is it a statement of law? No. Is it a
moral statement? Yes. Listen again to the opening sentence.*

My fundamental duty is to serve mankind; to safeguard lives and property; to protect the innocent against deception, the weak against oppression or intimidation, and the peaceful against violence or disorder; and to
respect the Constitutional rights of all men to liberty, equality, and justice.

Mike continues. *Okay, picture this. A police officer has testified
against a bad guy. He arrested the felon for drug possession and sales.
It was a good arrest, plain sight. He didn't mention the part where his
partner had taken the drugs out of a bag found illegally and scattered
them in plain sight so he could see them. His partner will back up the*

arrest in court. This good officer thinks about the code. He remembers "My fundamental duty is to serve mankind...to safeguard lives and property . . . the peaceful against violence or disorder . . . the weak against oppression." He has done his moral duty. Tonight society has one less creep out on the streets. The officer will sleep well tonight.

Figure P.1

Law Enforcement Code of Ethics

As a law enforcement Officer my fundamental duty is to serve mankind; to safeguard lives and property; to protect the innocent against deception, the weak against oppression or intimidation, and the peaceful against violence or disorder; and to respect the Constitutional rights of all men to liberty, equality, and justice.

I will keep my private life unsullied as an example to all; maintain courageous calm in the face of danger, scorn or ridicule; develop self-restraint; and be constantly mindful of the welfare of others. In thought and deed in both my personal and professional life, I will be exemplary in obeying the laws of the land and the regulations of my department. Whatever I see or hear of a confidential nature or that is confided to me in my official capacity will be kept ever secret unless revelation is necessary in the performance of my duty.

I will never act officiously or permit personal feelings, prejudice, animosities, or friendships to influence my decisions. With no compromise for crime and with relentless prosecution of criminals, I will enforce the law courteously without fear or favor, malice or ill will, never employing unnecessary force or violence and never accepting gratuities.

I recognize the badge of my office as a symbol of public faith, and I accept it as a public trust to be held so long as I am true to the ethics of the police service. I will constantly strive to achieve those objectives and ideals, dedicating myself before God to my chosen profession . . . law enforcement.

Finish reading the code. It's a moral statement from start to finish. This is why, when you hire a new recruit, you're hiring an authorized representative of a moral standard, a person who absolutely believes in his or her work, who will use the law to advance the noble cause. What you need to understand is the morality of your officers, and how it affects every single decision they make. It's your organization, and you need to know why your street officers make the decisions they do.

One of the commanders responds to this. "You can take the first paragraph that way, but the ethics code says a lot more than that. It says to be honest in thought and in deed. To consider the welfare of others, and to enforce the law fairly."

Mike responds. *No. It doesn't say enforce the law fairly. It says to enforce the law courteously. In other words, smile when you make an arrest. And this cop, the one that bent a teenie weenie law, well, he's considering the welfare of victims, and he's being honest to his values. You've got to realize that this good officer is acting squarely from the ethics code. Maybe he's hearing what he wants to hear. But what he hears fits his sense of the noble cause – get the crud off the streets. If he doesn't make the arrest, well, then he's violating his ethics and as he sees it the law enforcement code as well. Today I'm here to explain what this kind of ends-oriented ethics means for him, and for you and the department as well. And at the end of the day, I'll show you a different way to think about police ethics.*

Accountability and the Ethics of Noble Cause

Few problems have been as perplexing as holding the police accountable for their behavior. What consensus there is over the control of the police has to do with clearly defined illegal behavior. Almost everyone thinks that the police shouldn't steal, rob, or commit murder – the same rules that they apply to citizens. And citizens expect police to be punished the same way for these crimes that they are.

The police also have responsibilities that require assertive, authoritarian rather than negotiating, democratic skills: they are expected to stop, detain, sometimes seize, and if necessary injure or kill citizens when they are engaged in wrongful behavior. There are many complex rules that surround each of these responsibilities. These rules are carried by civil law, criminal law, and police department policy. And there is a great deal of confusion and lack of agreement when it comes to holding police accountable for these rules.

Consider, for example, an illegal search of a suspect in order to find out if he or she's carrying drugs. Is this wrong? It's certainly illegal. How about when an informant calls the police to tell them they know of a suspect that has drugs in their house. Should the police use the informant's information and raid the house? And what if the informant is himself a police officer who believes that the suspect is a drug dealer and wants to look around the house. Is that all right? And what if the police officer crashes the door, the suspect defends himself with a weapon and is killed, and there are no drugs in the house, only a homeowner defending his or her property. Is that all right?

All of the activities described above are acts committed on behalf of a good end – getting bad guys off the streets. And they are all also illegal. They represent noble-cause corruption – when an officer breaks the law in order to achieve a good end.

The topic of noble-cause corruption, like the examples above, frequently involves behavior that cannot be easily defined as good or bad. Sometimes trying to define what is wrong with it is like grasping at smoke. If an officer smashes a felon's fingers to get information about a serious crime, is she a "rotten apple" or a "golden apple" – a bad cop or a good cop? It is sometimes difficult to tell what is wrong or right behavior, particularly when an officer is committed to a good outcome. It is easy to be blind in the service of good ends. Yet noble-cause corruption goes to the heart of democratic process in the United States. Noble cause corruption represents the authority of the sovereign to intercede with impunity into the affairs of the citizenry, and there is no democracy in that.

Chapter 1 discusses the central problems of accountability. It is a somewhat theoretical discussion, and presents a perspective on the profound difficulties encountered when we hold public servants accountable for their behavior. It concludes that there is a limit on the extent to which accountability is a reachable goal. Chapter 2 frames the accountability issue for police officers. This chapter provides a description of the noble cause and the central values that motivate it. The chapter concludes with a discussion of the literature that has developed elements of noble-cause corruption. Chapter 3 assesses efforts to measure police values. It argues that police values are not learned on the job but are fully in place when officers are hired. And discretion – discretion has been the stuff of police studies for 20 years. This chapter concludes with a re-consideration of police morality and discretion, arguing that discretion among the police is highly overrated. Given our knowledge of police values, how can we **not** know how they will act?

Accountability: Why We Teach Ethics

1

There go my people: I must rush to catch up with them, for I am their leader.

Mahatma Ghandi

Key Terms

Central ethical dilemma	internal ethics
external accountability mechanisms	Pascal's wager
	police accountability
external ethics	scandal cycle
internal accountability mechanisms	standard operating procedure
	stealth driving

The quote above is an apt description of administrators' efforts to control the behavior of street-level officers. Police chiefs provide both administrative and moral leadership for their departments. A chief, to survive and flourish as the head of his or her organization, must acquire the loyalty of the rank and file (Bordua & Reiss, 1986). They are expected to be moral leaders on issues of departmental responsibility and the ethical behavior of their officers, as well as to provide managerial leadership on administrative and command tasks. Yet the reasons for which they were hired are often intimately tied to the reasons for which they will be ultimately removed – an inability to control line officers' behavior. In spite of a variety of efforts to control line-level behavior over the past century, accountability problems persist. Executives often find that they are a step behind what their officers are doing on the streets.

This chapter focuses on dilemmas of accountability. By accountability, we mean efforts to control the behavior of line officers. This chapter is somewhat abstract, because issues of accountability are difficult to resolve. We argue that accountability is paradoxical, in that efforts to hold police officers accountable tend to backfire and undermine the very goals they seek – controlling police behavior. Both the nature of the police craft and the command structure of organizations limit in important ways efforts to hold officers accountable for their behavior. Two kinds of accountability procedures are discussed, oversight mechanisms and personal morality. The chapter closes with a discussion of reasons for focusing on ethics as an accountability mechanism.

> Mike begins his presentation to the commanders. *You manage an organization that is about doing law enforcement, but is also about controlling your lower-ranking officers. What you need to understand is that these two goals, law enforcement and controlling line officers, can conflict with each other. I'm going to show you why the values that your officers carry, the same values that you hire them for and in which you take personal pride, get in the way of your efforts to control them.*

Scandal and Accountability Cycles

We live in a country where personal responsibility is highly valued. We believe that people should be held accountable for their behavior. We want the police to hold citizens accountable when they step over the line and engage in criminal conduct. And we hold the police to a higher standard. We not only expect them to enforce the laws of the land but want them to hold to a strict standard of ethical conduct. They not only have to act legally, they are expected to stand above any hint of moral and legal impropriety.

Unfortunately, like the rest of us, the police do not always act legally. The daily papers are sometimes filled with accounts of police scandal. And it always seems to come as a surprise to police departments in which the scandal is found. A person could look at almost all instances of police misconduct and find that other officers in the departments where they worked expressed surprise and denial, followed by outrage if the charges were sustained.

Police departments sometimes seem to be caught in **scandal cycles**. They become involved in a scandal, hold hearings, act to rid themselves of corruption, pass through a "professionalizing" period under the guidance of a new chief, and then witness the emergence of scandal all over again. If a scandal is severe enough, and if there is sufficient clout among municipal leaders, the chief will be forced out of office. And a new chief will be selected with a new mandate: to sweep with a new broom, to clean up the graft, to control his or her officers. Like the character in Ghandi's quote above, the chief (or Sheriff) takes charge of a runaway organization. He or she will put new policies into place and institute command-level reviews that overhaul the image of the department. A few police officers will be branded as rotten apples and invited to participate in the department's early retirement program.

Within a short period of time the department will begin making information publicly available about how things have changed. Newspapers will discuss how the new chief's policies have cleaned up the department, how arrests are up and how the agency is coming down *hard* on real crime. And, like hail over a field of young corn, corruption of all types returns with a vengeance, to destroy the professional image of the department. There is new scandal. The cycle repeats itself.

Police accountability refers to efforts to control police behavior. Since the founding of modern policing in Britain, accountability has been a significant problem for police administrators. Since the turn of the twentieth century, it has been one of the central problems of policing in the United States (Walker, 1977) (See Figure 1.2). At the center of almost every police reform movement has been an effort to develop new strategies to hold the police accountable for their behavior.

Figure 1.1

Police Reform and Controlling Police Officers

The law enforcement strategy, as envisioned by early twentieth century reformers, contained two elements. The first was a narrowing of the police function to law enforcement. The second was controlling officers. Kelling and Bratton describe this second function as follows:

> At first this assertion (the officer control function) seems strange – control of officers should be a means of improving police performance, not an end in itself. Yet, one has to put oneself in the position of the reformers. For them, political meddling, corruption, and abuse were so rampant in policing that it was impossible to direct effectively efforts to any desired goal; therefore, control was in the forefront of all their innovations. Concern for means overshadowed ends. Control became the strategy. Thus, it is no surprise that even as recently as the 1970s in New York City, patrol officers were constrained from making low-level drug arrests because administrators feared they would be corrupted. (Kelling & Bratton, 1993:2)

Consider the works of the International Association of Chiefs of Police in 1893, the Wickersham Commission in 1931, the President's Commission on Law Enforcement and Administration of Justice in 1967, and the

Christopher Commission in 1991. All these commissions were convened in part or in whole because the police were charged with corrupt practices, and the public – or at least important legislators- were outraged. All commissions submitted recommendations about how to improve problems. And police departments responded! Police agencies throughout the century have intensified accountability procedures, added new agency units, created more paperwork, assigned new supervisory responsibilities, and in some cases have permitted citizen oversight. These changes, though well-intentioned, were largely ceremonial, which means that they changed the structure of the police organization. On the street, where the bullet hits the bone, organizational changes have had less of an effect. Police confront the same issues today that they did 100 years ago. And aside from some amazing technological innovations and more complicated oversight mechanisms, what police officers do today is surprisingly similar to what their predecessors did 100 years ago (See Figure 1.2).

Police and Accountability Procedures

Today, we have immersed the police in accountability procedures. Let's review the various ways that the police are held accountable for their behavior (Walker, 1990). There are **external accountability mechanisms** for police organizations: these include the Supreme Court decisions concerning due process, civil litigations against the police at the federal level, civil litigations against the police at the state level, criminal charges against the police at the state level, criminal charges against the police at the federal level, citizen review boards, ombudsmen, mayor and city councils, and of course, the newspapers and national press for major scandals. Within the organization, police organizations try to hold their officers accountable with **internal accountability mechanisms** such as the chain of command, internal affairs, written standard operating procedures (as one police wag put it, written accounts of "100 years of departmental f___-ups"), video cameras mounted on the patrol car dash, dispatch notification when an officer leaves the patrol car, and citizen complaint files. Are you a police officer? Do you have the feeling someone is watching you? Today, police officers have to submit to random drug tests in their own department. This means that they have to pee in a cup and then give the cup to a technician. Degrading? You bet it is.

And no one is satisfied. American citizens are as concerned about protecting democratic rights against a standing militia – and that's what the police are – as they were 150 years ago when the first police department was founded in the United States. Perhaps this is a healthy attitude for Americans, existing as we do in a world where democracies are rare and notoriously unstable. But it makes the police perhaps the most scrutinized occupation – after the Presidency of the United States – in the Unit-

Figure 1.2

Police Commissions and Police Brutality: An Historical Overview

The National Commission on Law Observance, also known as the Wickersham Commission, was established by President Hoover in 1929. In 1931, it published 14 volumes, two of which were about the police. One of these volumes focused on police lawlessness, and identified widespread police abuses to obtain coerced confessions.

As the result of the commission findings, Hopkins (1931) wrote Our Lawless Police. Hopkins developed what he called a "war theory of crime control." He suggested that police believe they are waging a war on crime and that any means are justified to win that war. The police perceive themselves pressured by the public to get results, and the consequences of that pressure include a tendency to settle matters "in the streets," by applying "back alley" or "curbstone" justice. In effect, these officers believed that illegal behavior (police brutality) was necessary if law and order was to be maintained (Roberg & Kuykendall, 1993:164).

Subsequent commissions found evidence of police brutality. The President's Commission on Civil Rights, appointed by President Truman in 1947, expressed deep concern about police brutality. In 1961, the U.S. Civil Rights Commission stated that police brutality continued to be a serious problem throughout the United States (Wagner & Decker, 1997).

In 1967, the President's Commission on Law Enforcement and the Administration of Justice (also known as the Crime Commission) again noted problems of police brutality. The Crime Commission recommended a wide variety of controls over inappropriate and illegal police behavior, including emotional stability testing, judicial review, and the use of civil liability.

Have these commissions been successful in their advocacy of external and internal controls over police behavior? The answer is "yes and no." By "yes," we mean that external and internal oversight of police officers has expanded, and has done so dramatically. For example, civil liability against the police is commonplace today, and many departments have video cameras installed in patrol vehicles in order to monitor police-citizen interactions during routine stops.

By "no," we mean that it is far less clear that these oversight mechanisms have had an impact on police behavior. As recently as 1991, the Independent Commission on the Los Angeles Police Department, also known as the Christopher Commission, observed significant problems of brutality and excessive force committed by Los Angeles police officers. Importantly, these problems were occurring in spite of the presence of a highly regarded internal review mechanism for police accountability. The Human Rights Watch (1998:27) observed that police brutality was "persistent" in the 14 major U.S. cities they evaluated, and that both internal and external oversight mechanisms designed to deal with brutality were ineffective.

ed States. We continue to seek ways to control the police, to make sure that no wrong is done, to insure that they conform to standards of public and private conduct the rest of us would heartily and righteously resist.

So, when we've done all we can to control them, and we still aren't satisfied, what's left? Teach 'em ethics! That'll do it! Increasingly, as we confront the moral and practical limits of accountability in terms of punishment-based oversight mechanisms, we seek accountability from within a person – an individual who wants to act right, who knows how to make the right choices. Ethics is the current curative, elixir against bad cops.

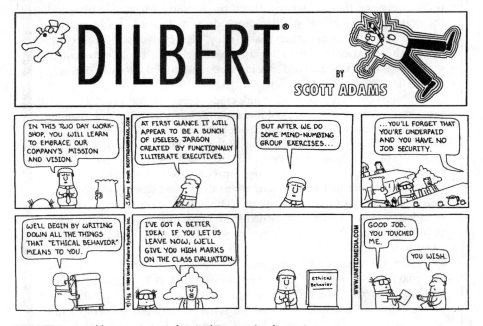

DILBERT reprinted by permission of United Feature Syndicate, Inc.

Ethics as Accountability:
Why Managers Can Only Do So Much

The primary work of police departments is carried out by street-level officers. Street-level officers conduct the work of the organization in its most practical sense – they make concrete decisions about how to deal with everyday human problems. They exercise wide latitude when deciding to intervene, how to intervene in citizen affairs, whether to make an arrest, what level of force to use, and how to exit situations. Very little of this latitude can be brought under administrative control for two reasons. First, officers are charged with uncovering that which many people do not want to reveal – criminal wrongdoing – and who will sometimes resist being seized if the wrongdoing is uncovered. Police consequently have to adjust their behavior to changing circumstances in which the outcome is neither known nor predictable. Second, the independence of officers in their day-to-day work enables them to follow their moral predispositions to deal with crime and public order problems. Officers are, for the most part, out of direct administrative supervision when they are on patrol. And their encounters with citizens are initiated and concluded with discretionary decisions about whether and how to intervene and whether or not to invoke criminal sanctions.

The nature of line-level police work – its unpredictability and discretionary nature, coupled with the moral predispositions of police officers, create profound accountability problems. In this section, we're going to discuss the two types of efforts to control street accountability – through external oversight and through ethics training aimed at providing an appropriate moral sense.

In their efforts to control line officer behavior, administrators confront a **central ethical dilemma**. The dilemma is two-pronged. The first dilemma stems from the use of external oversight to control behavior. If administrative oversight mechanisms are used to control the behavior of street-level officers, then they will resist, disguise, or obscure their behavior under the secretive protection of line-level culture. The second dilemma stems from the use of internal, moral controls over behavior, and is enacted by efforts to hire the right kind of officer. If managers try to control behavior by hiring morally righteous officers, their morality will undermine subsequent administrative efforts to control their behavior.

Consider administrative, oversight-based accountability. Under administrative means of accountability (e.g., chain of command, internal review), the police organization uses written policies, which are codes of conduct. These policies are the department's **standard operating procedure**. Individual policies sometimes tell officers what to do and sometimes tell them what not to do. For example, policies identify the appropriate dress code for a police officer. However, policies also are written to tell police officers what not to do. Most typically, policies identify inappropriate behavior. Violations for inappropriate behavior may involve a mild, informal chastisement, verbal reprimand, removal from promotion eligibility for a fixed period of time, or suspension.

Figure 1.3

Stealth Driving and Departmental Policy

Officer J was frustrated with his inability to catch prostitutes and crack dealers on his night-time beat. He knew that they avoided the streets and conducted their work at night inside a large park next to a busy city street. He also knew that the park was unlit at night except for lights around a central fountain, adding to opportunities for victimization. Small-time criminals such as potential drug buyers and "johns" were occasionally robbed and beaten entering and leaving the park. He was also concerned that children, playing in the park in the daytime, would prick their finger on a used syringe and contract AIDS. So he began the practice of **stealth driving**. He would turn off the lights of his squad car and, narrowly passing through the wrought iron gates at the entrance of the park, drive his vehicle through all its dark areas. He continued the practice for a couple of months. A complaint to the chief's office, however, abruptly changed his pattern of "stealth" driving. Concerns were voiced that the "stealth" patrol might accidentally run over a drunk or homeless person sleeping in the park. A formal policy was posted, and commanders announced at all shifts, that officers were not to drive their automobiles through the parks. Officer J also was assigned responsibility for all "ride-alongs" as an informal punishment. However, he did not wholly abandon the practice of "stealth" driving" but confined the driving to the principal sidewalks in the park where drunks were unlikely to sleep.

In the example provided by Figure 1.3, we can see how the police organization develops a policy – in this instance forbidding "stealth" driving in the parks – to control the behavior of its line officers. It is an administrative solution to accountability. However, efforts at administrative control over what street officers do can create conflicts between line officers and administrators, as it did in the example of Officer J above. In this example, a departmental policy was used to prohibit an officer from doing what he thought was "good" police work – stealth driving to suppress criminal activity and protect children.

Police organizations also make use of formal ethical codes. The prologue to this book contained one such code, the Police Officers Code of Conduct. These ethical codes, together with the department's policies, represent an organization's ethical principals. Ethics, under an administrative model of accountability, are **external** to police officers, in the sense that they are administrative codes produced by police managers to inform officers about organizationally correct behavior. They are a standard that officers can use to learn about appropriate behavior. The moral psychology of an officer is of secondary importance – the department tells them what is right and wrong.

On the other hand, ethics can be **internal**. This means that officers carry within themselves a sense of ethical or moral responsibility about what constitutes "correct" behavior. If officers are ethical and moral, they do not need external oversight. Their morality is greater than their commitment to the organization itself, coming from their moral conception of "goodness" and "badness." Indeed, a great deal of pre-hiring screening is devoted to insuring that officers think a particular way about police work, and that police are committed to a particular way of looking at the world. "Internal" ethics consequently seems to be a perfect solution to the problems created by external oversight.

The internal solution to ethical accountability hides a problem that is very difficult to solve. It is the problem of good ends. If officers are committed to a moral way of viewing the world, then efforts by managers to control their behavior are profoundly limited. If officers are committed to morally good ends, that is, they absolutely believe in what's right and what's wrong, organizational control over their behavior is limited. If police officers believe that policing is a just cause, policies that interfere with their work will be viewed as immoral. And police officers may circumvent the organizational rules in order to do what they believe is right. This is precisely what Officer J did in Figure 1.3.

The reader might ask, "Don't all officers share a 'common' way of looking at police work, a similar sense of right and wrong?" There are two important reasons why the ethics of line officers and managerial policies conflict with each other. The first reason is the unpredictable nature of police work, and results in Accountability Dilemma 1 described below. The second reason is the ethics that officers themselves carry – a commitment to the noble cause, and a willingness to circumvent due process and administrative protocols to carry out the noble cause – getting bad guys off the streets, and results in Accountability Dilemma 2.

Accountability Dilemma 1: Unpredictability. Harmon (1995) describes Accountability Dilemma 1 below:

> Even if managers were able to eliminate sources of unpredictability within their organizations, such actions would be incompatible with dealing sensibly in the face of the unpredictable environments they are committed to changing. This is because organizational success (that is, effectiveness in the broader sense of the word) requires continuous innovation, adjustment, and problem- and goal-redefinition that are directly at odds with controlling and making predictable subordinates' behavior in order to achieve predefined goals. (Michael Harmon, 1995:183-184)

What does this accountability dilemma mean? Consider the day-to-day work carried out by line officers. Provided an automobile or other means to cover their assigned beat, they are expected to move from situation to situation, resolving problems of all kinds. When wrongdoing is suspected, they investigate. Wrongdoers, however, do not normally admit illegal behavior to a police officer, and few people want to be arrested. Consequently, police seek to penetrate the reality presented to them in order to uncover hidden culpability. This work – trying to find hidden guilt – makes patrol-citizen interactions unpredictable.

Line officers are consequently presented with work that may be uncertain and is unforeseeable from one moment to the next (Manning, 1989). Their work is characterized by powerful cultural themes of unpredictability, the unknown, danger, and edge control (Crank, 1998). What an officer is doing any one minute may provide no clue about what's going to happen the next. Chance encounters play a surprisingly high role in daily police work, and can undermine police efforts to control behavior.

Themes of uncertainty are central to the street officer's working personality. Consider the following comment from a street officer:

Figure 1.4

Survival on the Street

Ever notice two police officers talking to each other on the street? They never look at each other. One is always looking behind the other. They very seldom look each other in the eye. It's a survival mechanism. They want to know what's coming up at them. (Fletcher, 1990:12)

Police organizations, on the other hand, are bureaucracies, and bureaucracies do not deal very well with unpredictability. Bureaucracies like their organizational parts to be well-oiled, all functioning together. They work best when all the parts combine their efforts to achieve some clearly defined goal or goal cluster. Managers try to control unpredictability through bureaucratic procedures, by developing standard operating procedures, chain-of-command, internal affairs, written objectives, goals and standards, and policies. The logic behind many of these complex bureaucratic procedures is to identify inappropriate behavior and to provide penalties for violations of appropriate behavior.

Accountability Dilemma 1 states that, if managers were to be successful at eliminating unpredictability among line officers through the use of bureaucratic procedures – that is, if line officers rigidly followed bureaucratic protocols – they would be incapable of dealing with their day-to-day work environment. The work environment of the police involves dealing with people in unpredictable situations in which the "truth" is deliberately obscured, and adapting to changing situational circumstances. If we were to make the police perfectly regimented, true automatons of bureaucracy, they would be perfectly unsuited for their work.

Managers, concerned over the control of line behavior, tend to elaborate the body of policies already in place. Bureaucratic accountability consequently grows, but does not increase in effectiveness (often increasing managerial frustration with their line personnel as a consequence). Is the reader a manager? Does this sound familiar?

Accountability Dilemma 2: Line-Officer Morality. If bureaucracy is unable to adequately deal with line-officer accountability, then how can we insure that officers act right? An alternative in today's world is to instill a sense of order and morality through ethics training. If, the logic goes, a person has internal or "psychological" checks for inappropriate behavior, then there will be no need for external controls. By instilling ethics as an internal value system to guide their conduct, it is believed that individuals will act responsibly. Their ethical training should serve as an accountability "anchor" for the moral responsibilities that they carry as a public servant.

Ethics training, however, does not occur on a moral "blank slate." Recruits already have strong moral commitments to the occupation of policing – that's why they became police officers. Through socialization processes they fine-tune their crime-control focus to developing the tools and skills needed to control their assigned territories. In other words, police have an ethical way of looking at the world fully in place before they are hired, an ethic that is honed during pre-service training and assignment to a training officer. Police are morally predisposed to seek what they consider to be good ends. They are surrounded by audiences that encourage them to seek the morally good end. In short, they are moral creatures, acting in an uncertain world to bring about a noble end.

In Figure 1.5, Buerger (1998) describes the value predispositions carried by police recruits.

The issues Buerger describes in Figure 1.5: the pre-existing views of recruits about police work, the similarity of views regardless of personal racial or ethnic differences, a familial background in policing, and an environment that celebrates a view of police work as law enforcement, are central to understanding the ethical predispositions of police. Ethics training cannot act as if police are insufficiently ethical or that they are not yet ethical – they are indeed ethical, but in ways that bewilder reformists.

The problem for ethics training is not that police are ethical, but that they are ethical in a way that can confound administrative efforts to control their behavior. Street officers are committed to a noble end, and that commitment sometimes justifies violating administrative protocols and principles of due process. Consider again the example of stealth driving described previously. An officer was engaged in behavior, stealth driving, aimed at encountering or suppressing criminal activity. Administrative protocols, in the form of a written policy, prohibited this activity. Informally, the officer ended up "eating the s___ end of the Sergeant's stick" by having to do the ride-along detail. Yet he did not stop doing stealth driving, though he changed the driving patterns to the principle sidewalks in the park. In short, the officer's commitment to the good ends of policing justified violation of administrative protocols.

Figure 1.5

The Ethical Predispositions of Recruits

Far from being *tabula rasa*, candidates for police employment present themselves with (and perhaps because of) an already developed idea of what constitutes police work. Recruits expect to do "law enforcement," not "problem solving" or "community service." Some are "legacies" from police families, the second or third generation to enter policing: A *New York Times* study of recent New York City Police Department (NYCPD) academy class indicated that one-half of the white recruits, almost one-half of the black recruits, and one-third of the Hispanic recruits had a relative who was a current or former member of the NYCPD (Kilborn, 1994). Almost all will have had an exposure to media police work, whether reconstructions like *Top Cops* or the live-action displays of *COPS*. Many recruits already have an ingrained idea of what police work is supposed to be; among legacies, that conceptual framework and belief system will likely have been shaped by family members and friends whose viewpoints embody exactly the attitudes that reform training hopes to eradicate.

Source: Michael Buerger (1998). "Police Training as a Pentecost." *Police Quarterly,* 1-1:31.

A book on police ethics, we believe, has to address these twin accountability problems. We believe that a psychologically interior, moral basis for accountability is a more effective way to control behavior than external, punishment-based administrative protocols. However, the ethic that is carried by many police officers today, a commitment to good ends or what we call the "noble cause," can result in a moral way of thinking about police work that conflicts with principles of law and administration. Further, current hiring and training protocols, a political environment that encourages "efficient" prosecution, and promotion criteria based on the production of crime control statistics, further encourage a focus on good ends. Too frequently, the result is the corruption of "noble cause," where the police violate the law and administrative procedure in order to do what they think is morally right.

The two accountability dilemmas characterize police work today. The two dilemmas, which are the unpredictability of police work and the moral commitment many police officers have to the noble cause, are dynamically related in a way that both undermines accountability and encourages noble-cause corruption. Our concern is twofold: that these accountability dilemmas are endemic to police organizations, and that they have been largely unaddressed in a systematic way in literature on police ethics.[2] This book addresses the twin accountability problems in four ways:

1. Remind managers of their line-level roots. Police managers chafe and carp at the reluctance of line officers to follow administrative directives. In all departments in which we have talked to middle managers and commanders, there is a stated belief that young officers aren't "committed" to the traditions of the department. Yet these same managers all were previously line officers, and all at one time were likely as resistant to administrative direction and oversight as the officers now under them. What accounts for this inconsistency?

Part of the inconsistency, of course, is that managers were not "average" line officers but rather represent that small group of officers who were administratively adept. For whatever reason, they had the "right stuff" to achieve administrative success. Another part, though, is that administrative work focuses on linking budget and strategy, both long-term concerns. Managers also are responsible for liaison activities, regularly meeting with community notables and media representatives. They interact with community "good guys" rather than "bad guys." They consequently tend to forget how they thought through day-to-day enforcement and public order problems when they were line officers. As they move up the chain of command, reasons for resisting administrative rules in order to do "good" police work are replaced with efforts to promote long-term success through strategic planning.

One of the goals of this book, consequently, is to remind managers about how line officers think through problems. We focus on how the noble cause justifies the violation of administrative protocols and due process elements of the procedural law. By understanding the ethical bases of line officer behavior, managers can more clearly understand the limitations of existing policy and become more effective in their efforts to develop meaningful administrative protocols.

2. Illuminate the consequences of noble-cause corruption. Officers in many departments are socialized into a local departmental culture that justifies low levels of noble-cause corruption. Although it is officially discouraged, most officers believe that other officers will protect them and that they are in fact only "bending the rules" in order to do good police work. Another purpose of this book is to provide a sense of the potential consequences of noble-cause corruption for officers, for the agency, and for the public. By illuminating consequences of noble-cause corruption – without engaging in silly "scare" tactics – we hope to provide police officers and recruits with a practical sense of what noble-cause corruption can do to them.

3. Provide recruits with a practical sense of moral issues. Ethical training in police department today tends to focus on economic corruption. Officers are taught that they shouldn't accept small "gratuities."

If they do, they will have started down the "slippery slope" and will be dealing drugs before they realize what they've done with their lives. Of course, many officers take gratuities and will never become serious grafters. The slippery slope, although capable of explaining some instances of police corruption, does not realistically apply to most officers, including some very good officers who accept perks. We believe that the ethical perspective presented in this book, by focusing on noble-cause corruption, is practical and applies to circumstances confronted by almost all police officers. It will consequently be useful for understanding the ethical dilemmas facing recruits and experienced officers alike.

4. Provide an ethic for a community policing environment. Police agencies across the United States are increasingly adopting community policing elements. These elements include a broadening of the decision-making authority of line officers. Community police officers carry wider authority to develop tactical responses to public order and crime problems than officers working in more traditional organizational settings (Mastrofski, 1999).

Our concern is with a way of thinking about police ethics in a discretionary environment expanded to facilitate broad line-level decision-making. Under a traditional model of law enforcement, line-level decisionmaking was subject to chain-of-command review, and violations were punished. As we move into an age of community policing, departments are relaxing controls on police officers in order to let them make important decisions about the well-being of the communities and neighborhoods they serve. Traditional administrative controls on line behavior don't work very well in a community policing environment – the job is too unstructured and unpredictable to control behavior. Managers consequently need to shift their focus from the regulation of line-level behavior to granting line personnel the means for self-regulation.

If officers are provided wider discretion and fewer bureaucratic controls on their behavior, what moral or ethical standard will direct their behavior? We don't yet know how well internal ethical controls will work in an environment of expanded police discretion. Many observers of the police are hesitant to widen the discretion of the police (See the exchange between Kelling and Klockars in Geller, 1985). Yet there is a sense of inevitability to change in the police today. As agencies shift to a community policing organizational platform and philosophy, police will increasingly be expected to act on their own sense of right and wrong, to let them make practical judgments about their day-to-day work. And with ethics training we try to fortify their sense of moral *responsibility* so that they will make good decisions.

Forewarned Is Forearmed

We are both optimistic and pessimistic about the ability of ethical training to prepare police officers for the world of tomorrow. On the one hand, we think that the ethical approach presented here will provide a way of thinking about difficult ethical problems. The ethical perspective presented in this book is a way to think about police work that furthers fundamental ideas of fair play. It also aims at what we think will be a central role of the police in the future – as negotiators of public order. We believe that this ethic will make individual police officers and the departments they represent more effective in maintaining order in a pluralistic, multi-religious, and multicultural society.

On the other, we recognize that some police officers or college students who read this book will be suspicious about ethics training, will view it as too bookish and against the grain of the daily work of the police. If this is you, think about ethics training as a police version of **Pascal's wager**. Pascal offered that it was impossible to know with certainty the existence of God. However, the wise man won't take the chance and live a sinful life. If he gambles, and bets on the wrong side, he might suffer an eternity of brimstone and damnation.

You can consider letting ethical decisionmaking control your passions. There will be many opportunities to mess up – it goes with the territory. With so many people tracking you, it's impossible to do right all the time, and there will be times when you will need your colleagues to stand by you. But what does the wise police officer do?

If you think there's no brimstone and living hell for a police officer, you might be surprised. There are video cameras everywhere, waiting to put your face on national news. And no matter how good at being bad you think you are, there's always the chance, the thin chance, that one day you'll wake up to the tap-tap-tapping of an internal affairs officer at your door. Believe me, these things will ruin your life. Do you know for certain that you aren't being watched? If you don't, here's a simple experiment. Find your name and address on the Internet. I'll bet you that I can do it in two minutes.

Take Pascal's wager. Bet wisely.

Framing the
Ethical Problem

Key Terms

asshole
cynicism
Dirty Harry problem
just means
maturity
means-ends conflicts
noble cause

passion
perspective
power of self
subcultural trait
street justice
value-based decisionmaking

The purpose of this book is practical. We discuss the power that police have and routinely use in their daily activities. The power carried by a police officer defines the limits of freedom in a most immediate sense: the authority of the state to seize someone's body or to initiate a process that can end in prison or death. It is a power that can be used to achieve goals a police officer *knows* are morally right. To get the scum off the streets. To wheel and deal with informers. To be tougher than the bad guys.

Some readers are police officers and have already been on patrol for a few years. If you are one of these readers, you may be certain, as certain as you can be about anything, that giving rough shift to troublemakers is the right thing to do. Legislators clamor about how the courts are too lenient, a sentiment you likely wholeheartedly agree with since you've had to deal with the courts and you know how they work. You know that there are many times when colleagues engage in questionable behavior and that some superiors, prosecutors, and judges wink and look the other way. You need to pressure suspects so that you can find what they're up to and so that they will not cause problems on your beat. What alternatives do you have? What happens in your sector is your responsibility. If you don't take control, no one else will. And here's something no other ethics book will tell you – you're right.

Being right, of course, is not the whole story. We all get punished for doing the right thing – it is an axiom of bureaucratic life, as true for teachers and business people as for police officers. Police officers, like employees in other occupations, frequently encounter disagreeable opinions about their work. Unfortunately, there comes a time when an officer finds his or her name in the newspaper or internal affairs comes knocking at the door. This is always bad. And what is it about police work that is so hard on an officer's health? All departments carry stories about how their brethren don't live long after retirement (now you know why you've been having those chest pains since your mid forties). Many police officers have been stressed for their entire adult life, preoccupied with control, unable to relax.

The ethical dilemma faced by many police officers is reconciling their personal morality with the clear recognition that they have a lot of power, the power to really hurt people, by asserting physical control of course, but far greater power by starting the legal process that will put them in jail or prison. Most ethics books will tell an officer to turn off the power, that police are creatures of the law and that due process and administrative protocols are rules that must be followed. We have a different perspective. We don't tell police to turn it off – it can't be done. We counsel instead that it be wisely used.

We have a different way of thinking about ethics. We call it **value-based decisionmaking**. The values carried by police officers determine their decisions to intervene in the lives of citizens, what they do when they intervene, and the way in which they bring interventions to a conclusion. And the most important values that mobilize officers are embodied in the noble cause. The noble cause is, for most officers, the touchstone from which value-based decisionmaking occurs. Indeed, values are the cornerstone of the work police do – they dispense justice by controlling people. So we'll start this chapter with a discussion of the noble cause and what it means to police work.

Values and the Noble Cause

Get a room full of police officers together and ask them why they wanted to become cops. It doesn't matter if they're from New Mexico or Alabama. It doesn't matter if they're senior staff or probationary officers. If you think that they'll say that it was for the money, then police work is not for you. The answer is the same everywhere, variations on a theme.

"I believed in it." "I wanted to contribute to society." "I wanted to do something important with my life." This is the noble cause, larger than any one person's life. The cause motivates them to join, and it stays with them throughout their careers.

What is the **noble cause**? The noble cause is a profound moral commitment to make the world a safer place to live. Put simply, it is getting bad guys off the street. Police believe that they're on the side of angels and their purpose in life is getting rid of bad guys. They are trained and armed to protect the innocent and think about that goal in terms of "keeping the scum off the streets." It is not simply a verbal commitment, recited at graduation at the local Peace Officer Standards and Training (POST) academy. Nor is it something police have to learn. It's something to which they are morally committed. Those that don't feel it are not destined for police work and will be quickly liberated from the hazards of a career in blue.

The noble cause is practical and immediate. It's about an officer's conduct in day-to-day police work. It motivates an officer's behavior with citizens and mobilizes a great deal of police solidarity. Two noble-cause themes help explain why police feel it so strongly – the smell of the victim's blood, and the tower.

The Smell of the Victim's Blood

Cops are acutely aware of victims. This is an aspect of policing that scholars overlook. Yet it is one of the central components of the noble cause.

Mike looks across his audience, trying to find the words to explain the emotions that underlay the noble cause.

Cops can smell the blood of victims.

The first time Mike refers to the smell of a victim's blood, it puts off listeners. But he explains. Victims motivate cops in a way no other cause does. Police are resolutely focused on the consequences of crime for victims. It's an aspect of our democratic heritage that is deeply ingrained in the sympathies of contemporary police. Guyot (1991) describes how police work forges a bond between police officers and victims.

> The relationship that can develop between an individual victim and an individual responding officer is a personal tie between one who is suffering and one who understands suffering. The officer's calm helps the victim to recover some measure of calm; the officer's concern gives emotional and psychological support. (Guyot, 1991:133)

Delattre (1996:273) captures this sentiment in his discussion of the child abuse death of six-year-old Eliza Izquierdo in New York City. New York police detective Nancy Farrell led the investigation into Eliza's death. Expressing her pain, Farrell stated, "I'm very angry that this was allowed to happen in the greatest city in the world, and nothing in my job makes me angry. I've been wanting to hug and kiss every child that walks past me because of how I've spent the past few days."

Figure 2.1

Victims and the Noble Cause

Consider a deputy in Nampa, Idaho, who patrols and lives in an area that is a Hispanic labor camp. The camp is home to two groups of Latinos. The first group is made up of families whose roots extend to the highlands of Central Mexico, and who were invited to farm in Idaho during the Second World War labor shortage and subsequently settled in. The deputy was born to a family from this group. The second group is represented by contemporary migrants who work in Idaho during the summer and return to Texas during the winter, a tougher crowd that is characterized by young men whose work separates them from their spouses regularly.

The deputy is particularly concerned about the children in the labor camp because they are often unattended and play out of doors. He is profoundly concerned that one of the children will be kidnapped by a stranger. He worries that the parents don't sense the potential danger to them.

An outside observer might observe that the chances that one of the children will be kidnapped by a stranger is somewhere between minuscule and non-existent; that if a child were kidnapped, it is most likely that the kidnapper would be an estranged spouse. That observer, however, would be displaying his or her ignorance of the passion police carry for victims. To understand the police, one has to recognize that the fear and concern carried by this officer is unrelenting – it goes with the emotional territory and is central to the noble cause.

When we think of police brutality, we sometimes imagine it as the unreasoned, vicious power of the state acted out against an individual citizen. Part of the reason we haven't learned how to control it is because we have failed to understand how it can be rooted in the way in which police relate to victims – protecting the public, doing something meaningful for other people. The violence described by McDonald in Figure 2.2 emerges from profound beliefs in the wrongness of victimization. What reformers have failed to realize is how this kind of police violence is deeply rooted in our democratic traditions.

Figure 2.2

Getting Even with Victimizers

The relationship between concern for victims and noble-cause violence has been powerfully described by Cherokee Paul McDonald (1991). The following quote from his book expresses the sheer emotional power of victim concerns.

> With my left I keep pounding his face, my fist crashing into his mouth his eyes his throat, while he screams.
>
> "I ain't bad, man. Oh *please*, mister. I ain't bad."
>
> But you were so bad back there on the sidewalk, weren't you? You so bad and you so cocky. Yea, knock that old woman down . . . old woman, only lives a couple of blocks from you, shit head. Knock her down and run off with her sorry little Social Security check. . . .

Source: Paul McDonald (1991). *Blue Truth*, pp. 28-29. New York, NY: St. Martin's Paperbacks.

To overlook this dimension of violence is to fail to understand the roots of much of what is called brutality. If we fail to recognize that police smell the victim's blood, we have no hope to control the use of violence by police officers. The victim's blood mobilizes them. The more we want our street officers to reflect a democratic ethos, to be committed to the poor and care about the downtrodden, the more we open the door for noble-cause violence.

The Tower

Mike continues. *Imagine that there's a shooter. He's in a tower. It's at a university campus. The shooter has several rifles, and he has already killed 12 students. What are you going to do?* Ask a room full of officers what they'd do, and they'll tell you. Take him out. Call for back-up. Bring in a sniper. In all of their responses the underlying theme is the same. They will run *toward* the tower.

Now ask them what a sane person would do. They'll think a minute. Then someone will say "they'll run *away from* the tower." They'll chuckle, recognizing the obvious difference between themselves and ordinary citizens. Ask them what a lawyer would do. They'll chuckle again. But they understand now. They are talking to a brethren, someone who knows what the noble cause is. It's at the core of their being. The true nature of police work, they believe, is in the service of the noble cause.

Mike looks across his audience. *When a police officer is killed, what happens?* Think about it for a minute. Do citizens discover the event it in the obituaries? No. They hear about it on the news, no matter who the police officer is. There's a parade. Do doctors get a parade? No, not even if they're excellent doctors. But police officers do. They do so because they risk their lives for strangers. The police run toward the shooter; they risk their lives for the sane person who runs away from the shooter. When they are killed, they are mourned publicly. More than any civilian occupation, police are embedded in the moral fabric of the nation. Their life is dedicated to the noble cause, the protection of the innocent, in service to mankind. It is a standard that is for most officers higher than the law. It is why being a police person is not simply a job, it is a calling. It is why police run toward the tower.

Noble Cause, Victim, and Tower as Subcultural Traits

The noble cause, concerns over victims, and the tower are **subcultural traits**. They represent values that are imported from broader American life and accentuated in police work. Consider the noble cause, with its focus on good ends. The intense, consuming focus of the police on morally good ends is not a cultural aberration, somehow making the police different from the rest of us. It's an ordinary trait, American as apple pie. We "want the bottom line." We believe it is a question of "moral fiber" to "not let anything get in our way." We have our "eyes on the prize." It's important to "give our all." We think we should "have it your way baby." "Don't look back." "Winning isn't everything – it's the only thing." "The race isn't run until you reach the finish line." "It ain't over till it's over." "Never say die." "Go the distance." It's a "run for the roses." "Perseverance wins the day." You've got to have "true grit." And on, and on. The focus on moral outcomes is ingrained in us from birth. As sociologists put it, for the police it's a subcultural trait, imported from the broader cultural milieu and intensified in police work. Put plain, it's bred in the bone. To deflect the police away from their resolute focus on good ends is as unlikely as convincing football players that their team should go for a tie when victory is within reach. It's an impossible goal – it goes against their sense of moral worth as a police officer, and against their grain as Americans.

Concern with victims represents a similar subcultural pattern. A concern with victims is as American as cheering for the underdog, hoping that even an ordinary citizen can have a chance at success. The bully that brings about pain or suffering is punished in kind; it is the just and ordinary ending to many a story and movie line. The storming of the tower represents the ultimate conclusion – that no one shall stand above the law. The tower is a parable as corny as a WWII movie: Good shall prevail, whatever the cost. Yet it is a parable acted out by the police, and for which the public celebrates them as heroes and gives them parades when they are killed in the line of duty.

Literature Related to the Noble Cause

Some writers have recognized the importance of the noble cause to police work. We will briefly discuss their contributions to this important idea.

Van Maanen and the Asshole

Van Maanen's brilliant essay titled "The Asshole" (1978b) is a study into the morality of the noble cause. Under what circumstances, he asked, do police officers find themselves in confrontations with trouble-makers and why do police sometimes end those confrontations violently? To answer this question requires that we examine the moral roots of police work.

Van Maanen noted that the moral mandate felt by police as their responsibility at the societal level, protecting people and preserving order, is transformed at the street level into controlling assigned territory and the people in it. Challenges to police control of their territories are sometimes corrected with acts of **street justice** – violence or rude treat- ment carried out against citizens. Under what conditions, he asks, is street justice acted out? He argued that street violence was more likely to occur when police officers thought that they were dealing with assholes.

Who are **assholes**? According to Van Maanen, assholes were not nec- essarily law-breakers. They were citizens who challenged police efforts to control police-citizen interactions and, by implication, a threat to an offi- cer's responsibility to control their assigned beat. Consider the example provided by Van Maanen (1978b:228).

Policeman to motorist stopped for speeding:

"May I see your driver's license, please?"

Motorist:

"Why the hell are you picking on me and not somewhere else look- ing for some real criminals?"

Policeman:

"Cause you're an asshole, that's why . . . but I didn't know that until you opened your mouth."

The term *assholes* takes on significance only if you understand the way in which police morality is wedded to their occupationally defined sense of territory. Anyone who disputes the police right to control their territory is likely to receive a rude pronouncement to the contrary. Consequently, as Van Maanen recognized, to a large degree assholes are what policing is all about. We will return to Van Maanen later.

Niederhoffer and Police Cynicism

In 1967, Arthur Niederhoffer published a book titled *Behind the Shield*. Niederhoffer, then recently retired from the New York City Police Department, was profoundly concerned about a pervasive cynicism that he thought affected many police officers he knew. By **cynicism**, Niederhoffer meant a loss of commitment to the ideals of police work, a brooding belief that perhaps the police didn't really make much of a difference, perhaps the wrongs of the world couldn't be righted after all. Cynicism, he argued, was the inevitable outcome of work on the street, particularly contact with criminal and disorderly people. Cynicism was not only important for its jading effects on officers' spirits. It was, he thought, a midpoint in the process of police corruption. A cynical officer, Niederhoffer argued, was vulnerable to corrupting influences. Cynicism was prevented by a renewal of commitment to police work.

A variety of scholars have subsequently assessed cynicism. They have shown that the way Niederhoffer measured cynicism actually masked several different kinds of cynicism. Police cynicism is not a single sentiment but can be experienced with regard to the courts, toward the police organization, toward education, and toward dedication to duty (Regoli & Poole, 1978; Regoli, 1976). Cynicism, these researchers concluded, was a complicated emotion with many facets, all important to the daily lives of police officers.

Cynicism is closely tied to the noble cause. Cynicism's different facets tap specific ways in which the noble cause becomes jaded. One cannot, for example, fully understand cynicism toward the courts unless it is also recognized that many police view the courts as too lenient, morally bankrupt, overrun with lawyers, and without the courage to actually do something about bad guys. In other words, the courts, when viewed cynically, are seen as hindering police efforts to carry out their commitment to the noble cause. And herein lie the seeds of noble-cause corruption.

As cynicism toward the courts increases, officers sometimes decide that they will have to act on their own to insure that criminals are arrested, booked, and found guilty. Cynicism toward the courts thus leads to noble-cause corruption in the form of testimonial deception and lying. And cop's cynicism toward their own organization – we will have much to say about police officers' attitudes toward their organization later.

Delattre and the Noble Cause

Delattre (1996:190-213) was one of the few writers to specifically use and discuss the ethical implications of the term "noble cause." Delattre wrote that the way we think about our own worth is in terms of the "causes" that we take on. We are frequently judged and often judge ourselves, he observed, by whether our goals are admirable or despicable. Commitment to a noble cause can lead us to believe that some ends are so important that any means to achieve them is acceptable.

Noble-cause commitment troubled Delattre. Ends in themselves, Delattre warned, were insufficient to justify all behaviors needed to achieve them. Delattre quoted Camus (1974:5):

There are means that cannot be excused.

In other words, no matter how noble the end, and no matter how worthwhile the goal, some ways of acting are unacceptable to reach that goal. The question that confronts police officers when they are committed to a good end is where and how to draw the line between acceptable and unacceptable behavior to reach the noble end.

When Camus made the statement above, he was trying to convince a young friend that the need for justice outweighs the greatness of country. He was talking to a young friend who had become a Nazi and was subordinating all his values to a Nazi cause that was soon to sweep across Europe. The German people carried a great bitterness for the way the Versailles treaty had subjugated their homeland after World War I, and the Nazi movement represented for many young Germans the resurgence of homeland independence and patriotism. To his young friend, the highest value was patriotism. Justice, according to Camus, was a higher standard – a means that was more important than the brutal ends sought by the Nazi movement.

A belief in justice, Delattre stated, was why American traditions have embodied the principle of fair play into the high law of the land, the constitution. He argued that means embodied in legal due process – conforming to the dictates of the law – must be carefully weighed against any end, no matter how right the end seems at the time. We call this perspective **just means**, by which we mean the ethical concern that means used to achieve ends should conform to broad considerations of human values, particularly as those values are embodied in legal and administrative due process.

Figure 2.3

Delattre: Managing Noble Cause

Delattre framed noble-cause corruption as follows: In law enforcement, are illegal actions that violate the rights of citizens ever morally right or excusable? Is there such a thing as excusable police
wrongdoing? The answer is difficult, not clear. Yet, from Delattre's
thoughtful musings, a few important principles come through.

1. Lower-ranking personnel should never have the authority
    to make such decisions. The decision is so inherently grave
    and so important that only a commander should make it.
    The decision to use illegal means should never be left to
    the discretion of line or even middle management person-
    nel in a police organization.

2. If a commander were to initiate the use of the third degree
    or other illegal police tactic to acquire information in order
    to deal with a compelling circumstance, he or she should
    immediately order an inquiry into the incident, to avoid the
    stigma of cover-up. He should avail himself of constitu-
    tional protections, and at the same time resign immediate-
    ly from his position "to make clear that no one who has vio-
    lated the standards of a position of authority should
    continue in it." (Delattre, 1996:213)

The reader is invited to read Delattre's excellent discussion of
noble-cause corruption – it discusses with clarity the many ethical
problems associated with noble-cause corruption. It is particularly
useful to commanders who may have to make such decisions or
who have the courage to deal with noble-cause problems faced by
their lower-ranking officers.

Carl Klockars and the Dirty Harry Problem

Carl Klockars (1983) presented the noble-cause dilemma in terms of
what is widely called the **Dirty Harry problem** (see also Klockars, 1985).
When should an officer commit a dirty act to achieve a good end? Klockars
(1983:429) presented a thought experiment. He described a then-popular
movie titled *Dirty Harry*. Klockars described the following scene:

A 14-year-old girl has been kidnapped and is being held by a psycho-
pathic killer. The killer, "Scorpio," who has already struck twice,
demands $200,000 ransom to release the girl, who is buried with just
enough oxygen to keep her alive for a few hours.

"Dirty" Harry gets the job of delivering the ransom money. Scorpio reneges on the deal and lets the girl die. Scorpio escapes, but Harry tracks him down. He confronts Scorpio on the 50-yard line of a football field. Harry shoots him in the leg while Scorpio is trying to surrender.

> As the camera draws back from the scene, Harry stands on Scorpio's bullet-mangled leg to torture a confession of the girl's location from him.

In the incident, there is a good end, an effort to save the life of an innocent victim of kidnapping. There is also a bad means, extorting a confession using third-degree torture tactics. There is also the connection between the end and the means – as Klockars (1991a) notes, a means that can be justified if "what must be known, and, importantly, known before the act is committed, is that it will result in the achievement of the good end."

Klockars presented a compelling argument that the "Dirty Harry" problem is at the core of the police role. He identified four elements of police culture that predispose police to believe that they are dealing with guilty people, even in the absence of evidence, and thus justify the corruption of noble cause:

Figure 2.4

Klockars: Elements of Police Culture that Predispose Guilt

The operative assumption of guilt. The police tend to assume guilt as a working premise of their craft. Officers believe that any questionable or furtive behavior they witness is evidence of some concealed offense.

The worst of all possible guilt. Police, Klockars observed, are obliged not only to make an operative assumption of guilt but also to think that the person is dangerously guilty. ". . . the premise that the one who has the most to hide will try hardest to hide it is a reasonable assumption for interrogation" (1983). Consequently, it is imperative that police rapidly find out the underlying truth. This perspective justifies the use of the third degree.

The great guilty place assumption. Police are exposed to highly selective samples of their environment. Places are criminogenic, and the wise policeman sees danger where there might be none apparent to less suspicious eyes.

The not guilty (this time) assumption. When a random stop of a motorist proves unwarranted, a vehicle search finds nothing, or an interrogation fails, police do not conclude that the person is thereby innocent. Most people have committed numerous crimes for which they have not been caught. Sometimes a little additional pressure will bring out an undisclosed truth that is being hidden by a seemingly innocent citizen.

Police officers, according to Klockars, tend to think that they are dealing with people that are factually guilty, even if they can't prove it in the
current instance. Police think that they must use tricky means to find the
guilt that people have. Bad guys know the ins and outs of the law, and
must be tricked or forced into telling the truth. Legal restrictions on
police behavior consequently have a backfiring effect, intensifying the
need for officers to use dirty means to uncover wrongdoing.

> . . . Dirty Harry problems can arise wherever restrictions are placed on
> police methods and are particularly likely to do so when police themselves
> perceive that those restrictions are undesirable, unreasonable, or unfair.

The presumption of guilt can extend beyond illegal behavior. Our
concern is that the police, convinced of the guilt of a suspect, may fabri-
cate evidence in order to convince a jury of what officers already "know."
This concern is demonstrated in Figure 2.5 below.

If Klockars is right, if the Dirty Harry problem is a dilemma frequently confronted by police officers, how should it be resolved? Is it acceptable for police officers to set aside legal means for good means?

His answer is frequently misunderstood by readers. On the one hand
he seems to be supporting the use of dirty means for good ends. Observe
the following frequently cited quote in his article: "I know I would want
him (Dirty Harry Calahan) to do what he did, and what is more, I would
want anyone who policed for me to be prepared to do so as well."
(Klockars, 1983:429). Yet, as Pollock (1998:189) observed, Klockars was
making a more subtle point: "we all are guilty in a sense by expecting certain ones among us to do the 'dirty work' and then condemning them for
their actions." In other words, when police commit moral wrongs, when
they ignore the constitution, use too much force, or lie to convict a bad
person, they are doing exactly what we want them to do. We just don't
want to know that they're doing it.

Klockars' conclusion, however, is that police who use dirty means to
achieve good ends must be punished.

> . . . it is, in fact, only when his wrongful acts are punished that he will
> come to see them as wrongful and will appreciate the genuine moral –
> rather than technical or occupational – choice he makes in resorting to
> them. (1983:429)

Klockars is aware that the punishment of police shifts the burden of
using dirty ends to the public. "We recognize," he observes, "that we create a Dirty Harry problem for ourselves and for those we urge to effect
such punishments." He concludes (1983:429) that:

> It is a fitting end, one which teaches once again that the danger in Dirty
> Harry problems is never in their resolution, but in thinking that one has
> found a resolution with which one can truly live in peace.

The strength of Klockars model is threefold. First, he shows that the actual occurrence of good ends can never be known for certain. We can never know outcomes. Our faith in good ends is sustained by hope, not fact. Obviously, the person Dirty Harry tried to save died. Second, the Dirty Harry problem reveals the way police officers think about their work settings, that is, as places of unknown dangers and dangerous people. Third, though it may not have been his intent, Klockars showed how the public is implicated in the pressures for police to use dirty means to achieve good ends.

Mike is troubled by Klockars' conclusion to the Dirty Harry problem. *Listen to what he says. He leads officers down the primrose path. He seems to tell them that the ends are the most important. That he wants officers to have the courage to make the right decision. But what are the recommendations? Read the last page of the article. They end up sacrificed on the altar of just means.*

Figure 2.5

Police Perjury in Homicide Cases

The presumption of guilt is a pervasive characteristic of police work, and can result in perjury on the witness stand in order to convince a jury of that which an officer is certain. It can even come into play in homicide cases. Because the stakes are so high, one would think that cases of murder are the most carefully handled by the criminal justice system. However, homicide cases tend to be highly visible and emotionally charged – they amplify many police officers' concerns over victims and outrage over brutal criminal conduct. Problems of police perjury can haunt these cases. Consider the following three examples.

Case #1. On February 5, 1999, Anthony Porter was released from prison. He was held 16 years on death row. Porter was blest – he had been scheduled to be executed in the previous February, but his lawyers argued that he should not be put to death because of his mental condition and he won a stay of execution. Subsequently, the main prosecution witness stated that he had been pressured by the police to implicate Mr. Porter. Another man has since admitted to the murders, and a corroborating witness has been found.

Case #2. Betty Tyson was at one time New York's longest serving female inmate, in prison for 25 years. She had been convicted for murdering a white, well-to-do middle-aged businessman. Witnesses had placed Tyson at the scene, and she also confessed. It appeared to be an open-and-shut case, even though no physical evidence tied her to the scene. She received a 25-life sentence for the murder. However, a reporter would later find that much of the case was falsified. The "confession" occurred from a severe beating she received at the hands of the police. One of the witnesses stated that "Detective Mahoney had actually put a revolver to his head and forced him to lie on the witness stand." And, in another document, one of the witnesses had stated that

Figure 2.5, *continued*

he had never seen Ms. Tyson at the murder scene, the opposite of what he stated at her trial. On May 25, 25 years after her arrest, a prosecutor announced that Ms. Tyson was free and would not be retried. She has since been paid $1 million for false imprisonment.

Case #3. This case is in some ways the most troubling because it displays collusion between the police and prosecutors in the prosecution of an innocent person. Two men were convicted of murdering and raping a 10-year-old girl in Du Page County in Illinois. A law professor at Northwestern University subsequently assigned the case to his students as a classroom project. Their research, however, led to substantial evidence that the individuals did not commit the crime, and they were subsequently freed. Another individual has since confessed to the murder, and an investigator admitted he had falsely testified about evidence central to the case. At the present time, three prosecutors and four sheriff's deputies are facing charges of conspiracy, perjury, and obstruction of justice.

These cases are troubling. Many advocates of capitol punishment contend that, with the substantial safeguards available for defendants, mistakes will rarely be made. Yet this logic does not account for the noble cause, the tendency of the police to presume guilt, and vengeful sympathies for the victims, and the evidence suggests otherwise. Since Illinois has reinstated its death penalty, 11 individuals have been convicted, but 10 have been found to have been wrongly convicted and have been freed. It may be that, because of their emotionally charged atmosphere and police-prosecutorial presumptions of defendant's guilt, death penalty cases are the most likely, rather than the least likely, to result in mistakes.

Sources: Adapted from Belluck, 1999, "Convict Freed After 16 Years on Death Row," New York Times National Report, Saturday, February 6: A6; Klein, 1999, "A Free Woman, Finally," ABC-NEWS.com, February 8.

Muir: The Tension Between Means and Ends

Muir (1977) argued that all police officers face a fundamental conflict. No matter what you do, he cautioned new police recruits, you will find yourself in situations from which you cannot escape without corrupting yourselves.

The corrupting situations he was talking about were **means-ends conflicts**. There were situations that police officers find themselves in, he cautioned, that presented a profound moral dilemma. If officers are committed to achieving good outcomes, they will at some point in their careers encounter situations where the good ends cannot be achieved by legal ends. If they break the law to pursue those outcomes, they will have corrupted themselves by breaking the law that they are sworn to uphold. There is no way, Muir argued, to avoid being corrupted in one way or another. For example, officers have sometimes perjured their testimony, flaked drugs, and even put someone behind bars they *knew* was a bad guy in spite of a lack of compelling legal evidence. Muir called this way of thinking **passion** and police officers that thought this way "enforcers." Passionate officers were those so committed to good ends that they ignored just means.

On the other hand, if officers failed to pursue those ends that they knew were right, if they became too obsessed with the rules of the game, they corrupted themselves by abandoning that in which they believed. He called this view **perspective** and labeled cops that thought this way "reciprocators." Officers with too much perspective were so committed to just means that they lost their sense of noble ends.

Inevitably officers encountered circumstances with means-ends conflicts. When they did, the dilemma was complete. If officers didn't use those bad ends, they corrupted themselves by refusing to get outcomes that they knew were morally right. If they did, they corrupted themselves, only in a different way, by violating the law they were sworn to uphold. Muir's advice? He presented the argument originally stated by Weber in an earlier time. He had two recommendations.

1. If you are uncomfortable with moral dilemmas, you probably don't belong in police work.

2. If you are committed to a career as a police officer and are willing to brave its ethical dangers, be prepared to temper your passion with perspective.

Police had to be prepared for situations where force might be used and had to learn to act even when all choices were difficult. Officers that balanced perspective and passion were what Muir called "professionals." The ability to balance the two perspectives revealed maturity in police decisionmaking (see Figure 2.6).

Muir Reconsidered

Both authors of this book have lectured on Muir's ideas of *passion* and *perspective* every year to policing students. It's a great lecture – interesting to police officers, non-police students, and instructors alike. Yet, Muir's intent is often misunderstood by students. What instructors want to convey is that the use of coercive force is ethically complex, that a police officer should not act hastily in the use of force even when force is legally authorized.

This is not what students hear.

Figure 2.6

> ### Power and Wickedness
>
> "Are there ways to prevent the person in power from becoming wicked? In his essay "Politics as a Vocation," the German social theorist Max Weber (1864-1920) probed the question. He framed the problem of personality and power as follows: 'He who lets himself in for politics, that is, for power and force as a means, contracts with diabolical powers and for his action it is not true that good can follow only from good and evil from evil, but that often the opposite is true. Anyone who fails to see this is, indeed, a political infant.
>
> The secret to avoiding corruption by coercive power – i.e., wickedness, banality, or cowardice – was to combine passion with perspective. Once again, to resort to Weber's language, the 'good politician' was defined by an ability to forge together "warm passion and a cool sense of proportion . . . in one and the same soul."

Source: William Ker Muir, Jr. (1997). *Police Street Corner Politicians*, pp. 49-50.

Our experience as educators is that students hear their instructor telling them that, if they believe strongly enough, it's okay to break the law to get the bad guys. This may sound very old fashioned. Yet we have experienced it repeatedly in classes. Because students are preparing for a career in the field of law *enforce*ment, they tend to identify with someone called an *enforcer*. And – make no mistake – they are passionate about enforcement. In discussions on Muir's ideas of police ethics, they "hear" their instructor justifying noble-cause corruption. It's the worst lesson they could learn.

We will reconsider Muir's message for three reasons: (1) we believe that there is a need to communicate more clearly what Muir intended, (2) Muir and Weber's audience were different in ways fundamental for thinking about police authority and use of force, and (3) one of the terms, *perspective*, that Muir adapted from Weber has another meaning that, when recognized, subtly but importantly changes the way Muir's writings might be interpreted by police recruits.

First, Muir's ideas have, we think, been widely misunderstood. Muir nowhere suggested that illegal means were appropriate for the achievement of good ends. What Muir sought to convey in his discussion of Weber's political model of ethical decisionmaking was:

1. Why coercion is necessary for legitimate police work. Muir does not discuss illegal coercion. He is trying to explain the necessity for police use-of-force in a democratic society.

2. Why legal coercion should be balanced with perspective, by which is meant the capacity to understand the way in which tragedy is interwoven with action.[3] An enforcer is not someone that uses illegal force. It is someone that too rapidly uses legal force to solve problems when other strategies might be more effective.

An officer that sometimes feels compelled to use so-called **dirty means** to achieve good ends, and by dirty means we mean illegal means such as testilying,[4] manipulating evidence, using unnecessary force, or the like, is acting in a way inconsistent with Muir's notion of a mature officer. It is not even close to Muir's idea of an enforcer, who Muir described as a person who can't integrate his or her use of violence into a broader moral point-of-view.

Second, there are limitations in the extent to which Weber's political model can be used as a scale to measure police morality. Weber's speech was directed to future politicians, individuals who would be legislating law. Politicians make the law. Police do not. There are many of us who sometimes wonder if this is an unfortunate turn of affairs. But it is how things are and how they will remain. Muir recognized the limited applicability of Weber's message to the police and, consequently, narrowly defined passion to acted or threatened physical coercion. There is no suggestion in Muir's work that police had the authority to violate the law on behalf of good ends.

Third, if one reads Weber, it can be observed that in some interpretations he also used the word "responsibility" to convey the idea of perspective. Substituting terms appropriately, police balance passion against responsibility rather than perspective. This subtle difference is important: responsibility is a term with a great deal of meaning to the police. The notion of personal responsibility is at the core of the police craft – it is one of the fundamental themes of policing. So if we substitute the word responsibility for perspective, we can restate Muir as follows: passion needs to be balanced with responsibility. This is a statement with a lot of meaning to the police. It is clear and straightforward. Officers are responsible for their personal behavior. Use of force should only be carried out in a responsible way. Within this definition, there is no place for illegal use of force.[5]

What is the ethical lesson provided by Muir to which we should attend? Police officers have three ways to get people to do what they want them to do. The first is the ability to trade something of value to get someone to go along. The second is truth. Sometimes people will act, not because they are coerced, but because they are convinced of the rightness of the action. These ways are what Muir (1977:48) calls the "power of the purse and the word." Third is coercion – the threat or application of force.

The dilemma Muir described was whether or not police should use coercive means when such means seem to be the most reasonable way to solve a particular problem. It was about the process of adapting oneself to the use of force in order to achieve compliance, yet recognizing that other means might be more suitable. **Maturity** was in the ability to balance the use of force with power of the purse and the word and to integrate the three into a moral perspective that reconciled the use of force with a belief in just means.

Consider the following quote from Weber. It brings home the idea of a balanced perspective consistent with the way police think about their work.

> It is immensely moving when a mature man – no matter whether young or old in years – is aware of a responsibility for the consequence of his conduct and really feels such responsibility with heart and soul. He then acts by following an ethic of responsibility and somewhere he reaches the point where he says "Here I stand. I can do no other." (Weber, 1981:426)

The Power of Self

In the quote above is a dimension of power not discussed by Muir; nor to our knowledge is it discussed in the works of Weber.[6] It represents a powerful ethic central to many of the world's religions. It also provides a basis for thinking about the responsibility of authority in a democracy. We call it the power of self. And we believe that it is an important part of police work, a part frequently overlooked in police training.

The **power of self** is the power to show others right behavior through example, to pass values on to others because one acts as a representative of the best of those values. It is different from the power of the word, which can be camouflaged in deception. It is different from the power of the purse, which can represent no value at all. And it is different from force, which is the enactment of the will of a sovereign over his or her minions. The power of self is that which we expect from our leaders – to lead through example as well as talent, to provide a role model appropriate for the rest of us to follow.

The power of self, we believe, is central to governance in a democratic environment. The morals and ethics we expect of our leaders are the ethics we also expect from each other. These are ethics acted out by all of us in our everyday lives, striving to do better than we can sometimes, but as well as we must. We look to the police, as we look to other public servants, as models for what we should be. We recognize the moral role carried by the police in society, and we expect them to behave in a way that reflects a democratic ethic – fair play, honesty, perseverance. The power of self is the power of the police to lead through example, to encourage people to treat each other fairly because their behavior is fair. It is the power to encourage peaceful resolutions to problems because they maintain public order through peaceful means. It is the power to approach conflicts not from the perspective of asserting some vague idea of public order, but to seek a negotiated end to disorder. It is the power to work with the policed, particularly the poor, to help them resolve the petty problems that overwhelm their daily lives but are rarely seen and not understood by well-heeled legislators and policymakers.

We believe that the power of self is an important though neglected power that the police have. Moreover, the power of the self will have to be developed in order for the police to successfully deal with the profound demographic and social changes that will characterize the twenty-first century. The power of self – to lead by example, to negotiate order, and to act on behalf of the policed – are important and overlooked dimensions of the police today. In the last section of the book, we will describe the re-emerging role of the power of self and its contribution to twenty-first century policing.

When Weber wrote "Here I stand: I can do no other," he asserted a standard of behavior. This should be the police standard, one that they can display to the public, one that holds their behavior as an exemplar to be carried by the public as a model for their behavior as well.

Measuring Cops' Values

3

Key Terms

hypothesis	occupational socialization
instrumental values	representativeness
matched groups	value systems
terminal values	values

Mike: *Would you be surprised if I told you that the values your line officers have were in place before they were hired, that your local police culture had almost no impact on them, and that it didn't make any difference if they were men or women, or if they were black, green, yellow, or white, and they probably haven't changed in the past 30 years?*

The commanders look at him in disbelief. They have been taught that the principal source of resistance to their command was police culture, or whatever word was used to describe line officers who acted on their own. They also know that the occupation of policing has changed a great deal in the past 30 years. And they have been told that a way to reform policing is through the hiring of women and minority group members. Mike's observation contradicts these views.

This chapter is about the values police carry and where they acquire those values. We will review measures of police values. The purpose of the chapter is to provide the results of measures of police values and assess what those values mean to reformers. In the previous chapter, we described how the noble cause, concerns about victims, and the tower were subcultural traits, imported from outside groups and refined in police work. In this chapter, we look at some of the research that had been conducted on police values. A review of our research and pertinent findings reveal both patterns and sources of values carried by the police. Our discussion will draw heavily on the work of Milton Rokeach in the early 1970s and follow-up research in the 1980s and early 1990s. At times, the discussion will be a bit technical, and we ask that readers bear with us. It is important, we think, that readers understand the nature of the research that was conducted.

Rokeach and the Value Survey

In 1971, Milton Rokeach and his colleagues published a paper on value differences between the police and citizens, whom they called the "policed." Their work had two purposes. The first was to determine the extent to which the values carried by police officers matched values of other American citizens. The second was to evaluate whether police officers' values resulted from the nature of police work or if they were already in place when officers were hired. Rokeach and his colleagues' work, because it focuses on values, is important in understanding the powerful pull the noble cause has on the police.

Rokeach suggested that values carried by individuals tended to be relatively few in number, and all individuals tended to carry similar values, though they varied in the degree and pattern. **Values** were defined as "an enduring belief that a specific mode of conduct or end-state of existence is personally or socially preferable to (its) opposite" (Rokeach, 1973:5). An example of a mode of conduct was "loyalty" and an end state was "equality."

Values, Rokeach et al. continued, were organized into **value systems**. He defined value systems as "an enduring organization of beliefs concerning preferable modes of conduct or end-states of existence" (Rokeach, 1973:5). In all behavior worth understanding and investigating, Rokeach contended, one could see the workings of human values and value systems.

The police, Rokeach et al. observed, maintain public order, control people, and provide important services in needy circumstances. In all of these activities, police officers act in such a way to insure that orderliness prevails. Consequently, we should expect that they will carry values that stress the "desirability of maintaining the status quo," particularly values of obedience and conformity to laws and norms of society (Rokeach et al., 1971:156). The authors suggested that police were likely to be drawn from politically conservative groups where such values were prized, and within those groups recruitment would favor individuals with a high desire for police work.

Figure 3.1

Rokeach and the Importance of Values

Rokeach's research on values emerged from his efforts to identify the way in which citizens engaged in political decisionmaking (1973). Rokeach observed that values are central to human decisionmaking. A person's values, he argued, provided a standard for understanding their decisions and actions. This can occur in seven ways:

1. They lead us to take particular positions on social issues.

2. They predispose us to favor one particular or religious ideology over another.

3. They guide representations of self (the image we want to portray) to others.

4. They allow us to evaluate and judge, to heap praise and fix blame on ourselves and others.

5. We employ values in order to assess morality and competency.

6. Values are used to persuade and influence others, to tell us which beliefs, attitudes, values, and actions of others are worth challenging, protesting, and arguing about or worth trying to change.

7. Values . . . tell us how to rationalize . . . beliefs, attitudes, and actions that would otherwise be personally and socially unacceptable so that we will end up with personal feelings of morality and competence, both indispensable ingredients for . . . self-esteem.

Finally, values do not act independently of each other, but operate together as clusters. When individuals are confronted with decisions, they will actuate a cluster of values in deciding how to act. These value-clusters undergird our major political orientation. Rokeach identified particular value clusters that uniquely identified communism, socialism, capitalism, and fascism.

Source: Adapted from Milton Rokeach (1973). *The Nature of Human Values*. New York, NY: The Free Press.

The authors tested the following four hypothesis sets, or ideas they had about important relationships concerning police values. An **hypothesis** is a statement of relationship between two variables. Hypothesis 1 on the next page, for example, states that the importance of a value carried by the police will be different from its importance among the policed. If we measure an end-state such as "equality," for example, and find that the scores of police officers are different than they are for the policed, then we have support for Hypothesis 1.

Figure 3.2

Rokeach: Research Hypotheses

Hypothesis 1.   Police have distinctively different values from other groups in American society.

Hypothesis 2.   Police values are highly similar to the values of the groups from which they are recruited.

Hypothesis 3.   Police values also are determined by particular characteristics of their personality.

Hypothesis 4.   Police values are "fine tuned" by their occupational work.

To measure values, the authors used the "Rokeach Value Survey," a set of scales that provided information on 18 terminal and 18 instrumental values. **Terminal values** were defined as "preferred end-states." **Instrumental** values were defined as "preferred modes of behavior" (Rokeach et al., 1971:158). Put differently, terminal values represent ends that we think are meaningful, and instrumental values are the means or behaviors we think are acceptable.

A survey was distributed to 153 white male members of a mid-sized police department. Participating officers were given a list of values and asked to rank them from the most important to the least important. By comparing recruits to officers that had been in the police force for a long time, the authors assessed whether police work had any influence on their values. The same survey had previously been administered by the National Opinion Research Center to the general population. This provided a non-police sample of citizens whose values could be compared to Rokeach's sample of police officers.

When terminal (ends) values were investigated, the researchers found that the police held the following four values to be more important than did the general population: *an exciting life, a sense of accomplishment, family security,* and *mature love*. Five terminal values were less important to the police than to citizens generally: *a world at peace, a world of beauty, equality, national security,* and *social recognition*. These findings meant that the police placed a higher emphasis on personal than social values than did the public generally.

When instrumental values were examined, police consistently ranked higher than the public on the following values: *capable, honest, intellectual, logical, obedient, responsible,* and *self-controlled*. They consistently placed a lower value on *being broad-minded, cheerful, forgiving, helpful,* and *independent*. The authors observed that:

Together these differences suggest an image of the policeman as a person who sees himself performing his occupational functions in a pro-

fessionally competent and responsible manner. . . . But this professional orientation. . . . has a special quality to it. . . . The data also suggest
that police place a relatively higher value on professional fulfillment that
takes place within the framework of an authority-dominated and rule-
oriented social organization that provides a framework for dealing with
people in an impersonal manner and according to previously formulat-
ed bureaucratic rules. (Rokeach et al., 1971:163)

These findings provided support for the authors' Hypothesis 1:

**Rokeach Finding 1: The police, in their survey, had a different
value system than the policed.**

The second hypothesis the authors tested was: did differences in values emerge from the process of occupational socialization, or were they
already in place when the officers were hired? This time the authors compared the police to a sample of white males matched for income, education, politics, and general background. Matching is a common way for
experimenters to measure whether two groups differ in some important
way. **Matched groups** are those in which members of the police department are measured for important demographic characteristics such as
sex, political affiliation, age, and education. They then are matched with
adult males that are similar on these important variables but are not
police. Then the values are compared. The two groups were very similar
in values, suggesting that the values carried by officers were similar to
selected groups of other adult Americans.

**Rokeach Finding 2: The police carry values similar to particular
groups in society.**

Third, the authors found that within the matched groups, "recruitment
is more likely to take place among those who place a relatively lower value
on *freedom, equality, independence* and *a world of beauty*, and a higher
value on *obedience, self-control, a comfortable life*, and *pleasure*. From
this, the authors determined that both social background and personality
factors were important in understanding police recruitment.

**Rokeach Finding 3: Socialization to important police values
occurs prior to, not after, a person becomes a police officer, and
the police are recruited from among individuals in particular
groups with predisposing personality values.**

With regard to the fourth question, the authors asked if occupational
socialization also affected police values. **Occupational socialization** is
the process by which a recruit learns the values, beliefs, habits, and
norms of the organization into which she or he is hired. If this were the

case, then older officers should reveal values different from young recruits. The authors found that there wasn't a single difference between younger and older officers on any of the 36 values.

Rokeach Finding 4: Occupational socialization has no impact on police officers' values.

Rokeach Revisited: Caldero's Re-Analysis of Police Values

Rokeach's research on police values was published about 30 years ago, in 1971. At that time, the United States was in an epoch of social upheaval, marked by inner city rioting over racial equality and student demonstrations against the Vietnam War. In the past 30 years the occupation of policing has undergone profound changes. Education is more important to the police than ever before. Academy training is substantially more lengthy than it was 20 years ago and is required universally. These changes might well have affected the values carried by police officers. Is it not reasonable to speculate that police values have changed in the face of these sweeping occupational changes? What would happen if we were to re-analyze the police today using the Rokeach method? Would their values be different?

Recently, one of the authors of this book, Dr. Caldero, replicated Rokeach's study on police officers in the northwestern city of Tacoma, Washington (Caldero, 1997). Caldero carried out a questionnaire survey of detectives, patrol officers, and sergeants, distributing questionnaires on the principal shifts. Of 166 questionnaires distributed, 128 were completed and returned, for a rate of 77 percent. What he found might be unsettling to police reformers.

First, Caldero was interested in value stability. Were values held by police similar over time, or had they changed? He first looked at terminal or "ends" values and found that the values of the officers he studied were similar to the findings presented in the Rokeach study. This finding suggested that little change had occurred in police values over time and place. He found, for example, that the value "freedom" was the same ranking it had been in the Rokeach study. Recall that the police in Rokeach's survey rated "freedom" comparatively low, when compared to citizens.[7] Dr. Caldero next looked at instrumental or "means" values. When he compared his data to the Rokeach data, he again found few differences. In other words:

Caldero Finding 1: Officers' values were remarkably similar across the two studies. Officers in this study carry the same value system, with values held at virtually equivalent levels, as Rokeach's officers 30 years ago.

Police recruitment practices have also changed over the past 30 years. A greater number of police officers are selected from the ranks of minority members. Police agencies today are also are more likely to hire educated officers. Do these changes in recruitment practices, Caldero wondered, result in substantive differences in values carried by police officers as well?

Caldero's sample included 16 officers who were minority group members as well as 110 Anglo-Americans. He found that there were no significant scoring differences between the minority and Anglo groups among any of the instrumental (means) values, and that there were only three significant scoring differences among the terminal (ends) values – *equality, inner harmony*, and *sense of accomplishment*. And in terms of relative importance of the different ends values, minority group members rated *equality* tenth versus twelfth for Anglos, still substantially lower than non-police citizens in the Rokeach data.

Caldero Finding 2: Whether members of minority groups or white, police officers hold similar values.

Comparisons across levels of education also showed only minimal differences. Caldero compared officers' values across three categories of education: officers with only a high school education, with some college, and with a college degree. No terminal (ends) values showed significant differences. Only two of the 18 instrumental (means) values showed differences. Officers with only a high school education were more likely to rank *courageous* and *responsible* highest, with officers with some college ranking them the lowest. There was no systematic pattern to the differences.

Caldero Finding 3: Education has little effect on the values held by police officers.

Finally, Caldero looked at length of police service. Instead of looking at age as a substitute for *years of service* as did Rokeach (1971), Caldero directly examined the actual years of police work served by police officers, in three categories: 1-5 years of service, 6-10 years of service, and 11 or more years of service. Like Rokeach and his colleagues, Dr. Caldero found that there was no indication of acquired values over time for the police in the survey. In other words, there was no support for the idea that the police socialization process in some way changed police officers' values.

Caldero Finding 4: The police socialization process has no effect on police officers' values.

What do Caldero's and Rokeach's combined findings tell us about the police? To the extent that the police in the two surveys are representative, they tell us a lot.[8] First, over the past 25 years, the values of the police haven't changed much, but instead have been remarkably constant. Second, they indicate that police values are imported from particular groups in broader society. Third, they suggest that neither minority group membership nor education has much of an effect on police officers' values. If reformers hope that the employment of more educated minority group members will change police values, they may be mistaken. Finally, once hired, values don't change much. In other words, efforts to change the values of police officers after they are hired by modifying the socialization or training process are not likely to be fruitful.

Corroborative Research

In 1998, Zhao, He, and Lovrich conducted an investigation into the attitudes and values of police officers in the Spokane, Washington Police Department. They also used the Rokeach values scales, and their findings were similar to those reported by Caldero above. Spokane police officers' rankings on values orientations appeared to be unaffected by their length of employment, again casting doubt on the argument that police cultural or socialization influences change officers' values.[9] They also observed that "police officers ranked value items quite similarly regardless of whether they had college degrees (or beyond) or reported no college experience," suggesting that education did not affect officers' values.

Zhao and his colleagues were particularly interested in the values carried by Spokane police women. The recent history of women, they observe, has been a struggle for gaining equal employment in public service (1998:31). They found that:

> The value distribution . . . indicates that there are generally no significant differences between male and female officers with respect to their value orientations. Only one item, "happiness," out of 18 produces a difference which is statistically significant. (It was rated higher by the men than the women.) In fact, the rank order is remarkably similar for male and female officers in the Spokane Police Department.

Finally, the authors considered the overall ranking of important political values. They found that the ranking of the value of equality, the single strongest predictor of overall value orientation, was virtually identical in all three surveys (Spokane, Tacoma, and Rokeach et al.). In the Spokane survey, it was ranked thirteenth. In the Tacoma and original Rokeach survey it ranked fourteenth overall.

Only three surveys are discussed in this chapter. They are the only three that we know of that have used the Rokeach value system and to which we have access to the data.[10] An observer might comment that there are more than 17,000 police departments in the United States. Are these surveys representative? The issue of representativeness is important: **representativeness** asks whether the findings of our research accurately reflect the entire population of police organizations in the United States. Clearly, that only three surveys have been conducted is not an adequate basis for representativeness. Yet, the evidence we have thus far collected strongly supports, for the departments studied, the argument that values carried by police officers are imported from selected segments of the American population and only change marginally after that.

Reform and Values

Perhaps the best summary statement that describes the Spokane survey is that the authors' findings are remarkably similar to those reported by Caldero in Tacoma and earlier by Rokeach. Zhao and his colleagues observed this similarity: "the type of persons attracted to police work differs little today from what it has been when traditional styles of policing held sway" (1998:32).

These findings are stone soup for reformers who believe that police values can be changed through higher education, minority hiring, by hiring women, or by changing the police socialization process. If values carried by individual officers are in some way a problem, they are likely to remain a problem.

How, then, can value change among police officers be carried out? We believe that change can occur in two ways. First, administrators that want to instill long-term, systemic change in officer's values will have to do it through the general hiring process. Moreover, and here's the significant complicating factor – they will have to hire people that are different from them. People have to be hired who have different values from the people that are hiring them, whose values administrators don't share and probably don't believe in. Unless this improbable task can be accomplished, one cannot have but pale hope for significant long-term change.

The second way is through ethics education. If the goal is not to change police values but to change how police apply their morality to their work setting (a more limited goal), then we can hope for successes without the need to profoundly overhaul agency hiring policies. As we will argue later, some types of community policing programs may provide conditions for subtle changes in some values (Wycoff & Skogan, 1994).

Ethics training, we think, if done right and applied practically to the work setting, can also affect how officers apply the values they have. We seek, in other words, the more reachable goal of incremental change. We are not trying to re-make the police here, and we certainly don't want a police officer who is emotionally unmoved by the morality of the noble cause. We are trying to instill in police the means to think through and understand a difficult ethical dilemma, the dilemma of noble-cause corruption. And we're trying to inform them about what they're getting into when they abandon means for ends.

We want officers who believe in their work. We don't want police departments to hire recruits who "flake off" orders from higher-ranking officers, or who don't believe that there is a place for law and order in democratic society. Yet, as all veteran police reformers know, change is difficult. When it comes to the police, one should approach significant reform with a certain temperament for fatalism. If one can be content with smaller changes, well, with patience, with a lot of patience and a flair for departmental politics, you might be surprised what you can accomplish.

Noble-Cause Corruption

Part 2

When we think of police corruption, graft typically comes to mind. The police, in their day-to-day pursuits, are exposed to great temptations, and there are few observers to watch what they do. Imagine this. You're a street officer. You've just made an incredible drug bust. Your reputation in the department is assured, and you're feeling charged! There's a pile of money on the floor. All you have to do is reach down, scoop up a handful, and put it in your pocket, and you can put your kid through college. Who's going to rat on you, the drug dealer? What're you going to do? This dilemma is the dilemma of economic corruption, and it is a fateful one, full of unintended events and unanticipated outcomes.

Chapter 4 discusses the history of economic corruption and police reform. We argue that the reform of economic corruption among the police has been somewhat successful, and that economic corruption has declined throughout the twentieth century. Reform was accomplished in part by hiring police officers committed to their work, in part by the establishment of more rigorous hiring standards, and in part through more rigorous supervision of patrol and investigative activities. Yet this accomplishment has had an unintended consequence – officers are hired committed to the noble cause and are vulnerable to noble-cause corruption. In many departments today, many police officers have traded economic corruption for noble-cause corruption.

Chapter 5 considers the hiring process. We argue that in most departments, the process is a collection of complicated procedures that converge on a simple purpose – hiring officers that have a particular set of values. Hiring, we argue, is a values-based process aimed at insuring that recruits carry values sympathetic to the noble cause. Early organizational experiences refine and redirect the way in which officers enact their beliefs in the noble cause. Chapter 6 examines noble-cause corruption from the perspective of commanders. Managers have, we suggest, an astonishing incapacity to recognize noble-cause corruption and are always caught by surprise when noble-cause problems emerge. We argue that noble-cause corruption has a variety of unanticipated consequences for police organizations that are often overlooked by managers.

From Economic to Noble-Cause Corruption

4

Police officers out on the street have a perspective that directly influences how they apply morality, and they use the law to enhance that application.

Officers look at Mike like he's from Mars when he says that. They're trying to figure out if it's threatening or supportive. It's threatening.

I spent six years in the L.A. County Sheriff's Office. I never saw individual-level corruption. Putting something that's not yours in your pocket. I never saw that, not once. A little brutality. That happens. Don't do that. I saw noble-cause corruption. All the time. Individual-level corruption, never.

Today we teach ethics in virtually every Criminal Justice Department and training academy in the United States. What do we teach them? Don't take free coffee – it's wrong. It's a slippery slope, we say – soon you'll be shaking down restaurants for free meals. Next you'll be selling narcotics. Review any textbook on corrupt behavior and they inevitably start their discussion with the wrongs of taking gratuities. Our position is that officers need this kind of ethics instruction, but that they also need to be made aware of a different kind of corruption not addressed within an "economic corruption" model – noble-cause corruption.

We'll begin this chapter by reviewing the idea of the "slippery-slope" and the history of efforts to control economic corruption among the police in the United States. We'll close with a discussion of noble-cause corruption and its relationship to economic corruption.

Sherman: Individual-Level Corruption

The slippery slope is a metaphor for a police officer's pattern of involvement in corrupt activities. What is meant by the **slippery-slope model of economic corruption** is that the first illegal acts committed by a police officer are minor, easy to justify. It becomes easier, however, to commit more serious wrongful acts after a person has committed minor acts of corruption. An officer that is presented with a bribe to over-look a traffic violation, for example, will find it easier to justify the bribe if she or he has already accepted small perks or has helped a bar stay open late. The officer has learned how to rationalize illegal and inappropriate behavior, and can rationalize more serious wrongdoing.

Slippery-slope corruption has been described as a process of "becoming bent" (Sherman, 1985). Not all officers become bent; it happens where, according to Sherman, **grafting subcultures** are already in place in police organizations – that is, where some officers are already involved in economic corruption. Grafting subcultures are groups or cohorts of officers that are already "bent" and that socialize new officers into corrupt activities. Sherman observed that officers go through a series of stages during the process of becoming bent, and these stages when considered together constitute a **moral career**. The stages of corruption are presented in Figure 4.1.

The stages in a moral career, Sherman noted, are not fixed and inevitable outcomes for officers already involved in lower levels of corruption. Each stage is qualified by a **contingency**. Contingency means that the subsequent stage is not inevitable, and an officer can decide not to proceed. At each stage an officer makes a moral decision, and each one is accompanied by varying degrees of peer pressure. A recruit may decide at any stage not to continue down the slippery slope of a moral career. However, recruit must recognize that they will likely be shunned by other officers if they decide to make a decision to "go straight."

Figure 4.1

> **The Stages of a Corrupt Moral Career**
>
> **Minor "perks."** An officer accepts free coffee and meals from restaurants on his or her beat.
>
> **Bar closing.** An officer stays after closing and accepts free drinks to keep the bar open.
>
> **Regulative crimes.** A motorist gives an officer $100 to overlook a traffic violation.
>
> **Gambling crimes.** Regular payoffs are paid by a local gambling operation to permit its continued operation.
>
> **Prostitution.** Payoffs are given to police from brothel operations, prostitutes, or pimps to permit continued activities.
>
> **Narcotics.** Police become involved in the distribution and use of controlled substances.

Source: Lawrence Sherman (1985). "Becoming Bent: Moral Careers of Corrupt Policemen."

The slippery-slope metaphor is a powerful way to think about police corruption. It recognizes the importance of police peers in encouraging corruption and the role played by the secretive elements of police culture. And there is no doubt that economic corruption has held a powerful pull over police officers in many American police departments. Finally, the slippery-slope argument resonates well in the moral environment of policing – it allows problems of corruption to be conceptualized in terms of personal responsibility and moral weakness. Individual officers make bad moral judgments and slide down the corrupt path. They made bad decisions, and the culpability is theirs personally. Blame is clear.

But what of corruption committed because officers are absolutely committed to the moral righteousness of their work? This kind of corruption occurs when officers set aside legal principles and organizational policy for the noble cause, the good end. This kind of corruption does not fit within a slippery-slope model of economic corruption. Officers are becoming corrupted for a good reason, not a bad one – to be more effective in the fight against crime.

Using a simplified historical discussion, we discuss a process by which we think that economic corruption has given way to noble-cause corruption. It is our belief that noble-cause corruption is a more widespread and significant problem today than economic corruption in American police departments, and that noble-cause corruption is increasing in United States police organizations today.

Economic Corruption and Police Reform

Police corruption and reform have been intertwined issues in the history of policing in the United States. Grafting and extortion were principal forms of corruption at the beginning of the twentieth century (Walker, 1984), and doing something about them has been central to police reform. Economic corruption took many forms in the late 1800s. Payments of bribes across all levels of police departments enabled racketeering to flourish. Officers received graft from illicit activities such as prostitution, gambling, and illegal liquor sales (Berman, 1987). Corruption flourished inside departments as well. Officers routinely purchased promotions and preferred assignments. Indeed, as Walker (1977) observed, police *were* the crime problem in this era.

Corruption was closely tied to local political machines. Officers were hired for their loyalties to a particular political party. In return, they were sometimes expected to assist in electioneering fraud, assuring that their party was re-elected to office. Party machines, often as intimately tied to local graft as were police, turned a blind eye to problems of police corruption.

The progressive movement emerged in the late 1800s to advocate municipal reform. The progressive goal was to instill efficiency and morality into local municipal governance. Progressives took an active interest in police departments. Police were a primary source of jobs for local political machines (Fogelson, 1977). Progressive reformers sought to reduce political influence by making police agencies more independent of machine politics (White, 1986).

The International Association of Chiefs of Police (IACP), founded in 1893 as the voice of police professionalism, represented the influence of the progressives in police reform. One of the purposes of the IACP was to exert control over the behavior of line officers by removing the influence of party politics from the activities of police departmental employment policies (Fogelson, 1977). The professionalism movement set a reform agenda that included the establishment of hiring standards, hiring outside the local jurisdiction, recruiting chiefs from military and professional backgrounds, and instilling officers with a crime control mission (Walker, 1977).

The early days of the police professionalism movement marked an important beginning for police corruption reform in the United States. Yet, in spite of the efforts of the professionalism movement, reform occurred slowly, in fits and spurts. Consider the words of Fogelson (1977).

> Despite these (professionalizing) changes most departments had only a
> slightly greater capacity to curtail criminal activity in 1930 than in 1890.
> For one reason, many policemen were not inclined to deal with crime.
> As the sensational scandals that erupted in Chicago, Philadelphia, and

New York in the late 1920s and early 1930s indicated, some officers preferred to work with the gangsters. A few grew well-to-do from their
share of the proceeds. Others preferred to pass their time eating, sleeping, and drinking, talking with buddies or visiting friends, and doing
everything possible to stay away from trouble. (Fogelson, 1977:118)

In the 1920s, **August Vollmer**, sometimes called the patriarch of
police professionalism, was emerging as an advocate of police reform.
Working with the International Association of Chiefs of Police, Vollmer
and his colleagues began "spreading the **gospel of professionalism**"
(Fogelson, 1977:155). Departments focused on excellence through hiring
standards, and officers were expected to be committed to the public
interest and believe in what the police had to offer society. Vollmer
believed that officers should view police work as a moral commitment,
not simply a job (see Figure 4.2).

> *Vollmer*, Mike notes, *understood people. And he understood values. He
> knew that if police had a particular value system, they would use
> those values to enforce the law.*

Vollmer believed that the police could carry a commitment to crime
control, and yet remain value-neutral about social issues (Carte & Carte,
1975). Yet, as we saw in Chapter 3, values about crime control are intricately connected to values about social conditions as well. Vollmer was
right about the power of values, though he might have underestimated
the extent to which they would mobilize street decisionmaking.

In no small measure due to Vollmer's reform efforts, the police professionalism movement had a large impact on police in the United States
(Sykes, 1989). The influence of local municipal politics in the daily affairs
of departments declined, and the practice of patronage, whereby officers
were hired and fired based on their political affiliations, was sharply cur-
tailed. The Vollmerian idea that officers should be committed to police
work have increasingly characterized recruitment and hiring practices.
Professional police officers were those who believed in the importance
of their work, who believed in service to their communities and were
committed to a contribution of police to society.

What sort of officer did Vollmer have in mind? Two aspects of the
Vollmerian vision of professional police officers are important to this discussion. First, Vollmer was a harsh critic of even minor forms of graft. He
was reported to have said that any officer accepting so much as a free cup
of coffee would be fired (Carte, 1986). Another element of his legacy is
the idea that officers should be morally committed to the occupation of
policing. Consider the following statement he made in a letter to a friend:

Figure 4.2

Vollmer and Professionalism

My fancy pictures to me a new profession in which the very best manhood in our nation will be happy to serve in the future. Why should not the cream of the nation be perfectly willing to devote their lives to the cause of service providing that service is dignified, socialized, and professionalized. Surely the Army offers no such opportunity for contributing to the welfare of the nation. . . . [Carte, 1986:5].

Consider Figure 4.2 carefully. Vollmer sought an officer that was highly educated, committed to police work, skilled in the latest technologies. This vision of police professionalism is grounded in the moral rightness of the fight against crime. It is a moral commitment of service to the country and to the welfare of the nation.

The Vollmerian vision of police work has had a powerful sway on reformers since Vollmer (Jefferson, 1987). It is a vision of police work that was carried by his influential students such as O.W. Wilson, who became a proponent of scientific police management, and Robert Parker, who later became Chief of the Los Angeles police department. And it is a vision that has changed police work.

By the 1960s, by most accounts, police corruption had substantially declined. As Fogelson (1977:245) noted, they were "fairly honest," or at worst, **grass-eaters**, the Knapp commission's term for officers that passively accepted graft but didn't actively hustle it. We believe that, at least in part, today's relatively lower levels of economic corruption stemmed from reformer's successes in establishing personnel procedures aimed at hiring police officers with integrity and commitment.

Today, we have achieved much of Vollmer's dream of professionalism among the police, though not always in quite the way he envisioned it and not as thoroughly as he had hoped. Since the beginnings of the twentieth century, police reformers have sought a curative for police corruption in officers committed to the ideals of policing. They sought an officer committed to a moral vision. And they have largely succeeded.

In the current age, American officers are morally committed to their work. They believe in enforcing the law. They do not like "bad guys" and take pride in a "good pinch." Central to their beliefs is Vollmer's vision – they believe they contribute to the welfare of the nation, that their work is morally important. And the law is the tool they use to carry out this moral vision. The conversion of police mission over this century – from a public sector job to a profound moral commitment – may have been the most important success of the police professionalism movement. And it is among the least recognized.

The Magic Pencil: Re-Thinking
the Bases of Police Corruption

Many of the outcomes of the professionalism movement, though successful, were not quite as intended (Fogelson, 1977). This includes its success in efforts to stamp out corruption. Except for narcotics, where it is almost impossible to avoid corruption because of its high value, easy availability and lightweight portability, levels of economic corruption known at the beginnings of the twentieth century have sharply declined.

Unfortunately, the door may have been opened for another kind of corruption: the corruption of belief from caring about police work too much. Noble-cause corruption.

Noble-cause corruption can take many different forms. For example, an officer might be tempted to provide some "street justice" to an uncooperative suspect. The magic pencil is more effective. Mike explains this to his audience.

> *I can beat up someone, and they have some marks on them. Maybe a trip to the hospital. Or I can pull out my magic pencil. You guys know what the magic pencil is. I start writing, and he's got a year in jail. Haven't your officers had a class in creative writing? You know what I mean. If you don't, you've been away from patrol too long. Your officers know.*

Figure 4.3

The Magic Pencil

To take the dirt bags to jail I would do anything – illegal searches, illegal seizures, anything, besides, I had the magic pencil. Oh yea. Fantasy on paper. So here I was, Mr. Honor Code, doing what I had to do. Except that one day something happened that changed everything.

The film changes scene. Three officers are discussing what to do about a suspected drug dealer. One of the officers suggests that they stiff in a call (call and report a crime as if a citizen had seen one. In this case, it is a fantasy crime, called in to justify a search of the residence). "You," he observes, "just got to reach out and touch someone." Another officer replies "I'll copy the call."

The officer makes the call. "Yes, I'd like to report an emergency. There's been a guy selling drugs to kids all morning. He just sold them to a little girl. And he drug her inside the house. It's 619 South Sycamore. Please hurry."

Smith describes what happened. "I covered for him. We went in on a stiffed-in call. And as things sometimes happen, things turn to shit. An innocent bystander, a pregnant woman was killed. . . . I started thinking, 'who's the asshole here?'"

Mike plays a training film. It includes a section about the magic pencil. An officer, "Officer Smith," is describing his experiences on patrol.

The **magic pencil** is a form of noble-cause corruption, in which police officers write up an incident in a way that criminalizes a suspect. It is a powerful tool for punishment, and in the hands of a value-based decisionmaker – and that's what the police are – it carries the weight of the United State's massive criminal justice system. It proves the maxim that the pen is mightier than the sword.

Figure 4.4

The Magic Pencil and Police Authority

Consider the comments of one of Fletcher's (1991) Chicago Police Department confidants:

> You want to know what the best brutality is? Stop him, search him, read him his rights, pull out your pen, and smile. You got him. You won.

Source: Connie Fletcher (1991). *What Cops Know*, p. 283.

Today, we've traded economic corruption, or corruption from lack of commitment to police work, for noble-cause corruption, which emerges from an excess of commitment. Yet there are those who will continue to justify noble-cause corruption. "So what," a reader might say, "if an asshole spends an extra weekend in jail. It'll be good for him. Maybe he'll learn a little respect for the law."

Let's see. How can we teach this "asshole" some respect? Let's consider a case in Newark, New Jersey. Vincent Landano was charged and convicted for the 1976 murder of a police officer. In 1998, 21 years later, he was acquitted after being retried. How could this happen? In 1989, the judge, H. Lee Sarokin, became convinced that the state held undisclosed evidence on the murder. He then ordered federal marshals to raid the files of police officers and the prosecutor's office. Evidence uncovered in the raids included information that witnesses were pressured by the police to identify Landano as the gunman. In fact, Landano had been in another state when the crime occurred (Sachs, 1998). Did Landano's experience teach him to respect the law?

Noble-cause corruption is a principle way that public respect for the law is undermined. Mike concludes with a comment on the trial of O.J. Simpson, tried for two counts of first-degree murder in 1996 in a highly publicized trial. The defense had argued that the Los Angeles Police, and particularly the lead detective Mark Furman, were not to be trusted in the collection of evidence and were motivated by racist concerns. The jury, after a short deliberation, acquitted Simpson of all charges in spite of compelling DNA evidence to the contrary.

Mike discusses the Simpson case with the commanders. *Do you understand the jury decision? Do you really understand it? The problems with Furman?*[11] *That's what happens when your department loses legitimacy with the public it serves. Nobody believes you. That's the problem with noble-cause corruption.*

The Mama Rosa's Test

Mike resumes his discussion of noble-cause corruption. *OK, here's a new recruit on patrol. He's all charged up to be one of the guys. Excited. He's out with his training officer and they end up eating at Mama Rosa's café. They are joined by other officers who have been eating there for years.*

At the end of a long meal, all the officers prepare to leave and there is no money on the table. The rookie has his money in his hand and asks how much he should leave. The veteran officers tell the rookie to shut up and put his money away. It seems the cops have been eating free forever and the place has never been held up, unlike other restaurants in the neighborhood. Mama Rosa is very appreciative of this. The rookie insists that he wants to pay for the meal, but he is told to shut up and not jeopardize a good thing.

Here's his test. If the rookie goes along, he is tainted. He loses his virginity. If he doesn't play ball at Mama Rosa's, he won't be trusted as a team player. If he does, the next step is to test him in the field. This might include dropsy testimony, or backing up another officer in court that makes an honest mistake by supporting his partner's version of events. This is how it happens. A test at the restaurant, then a test in the field.

The **Mama Rosa's test** is a loyalty test with a cultural slant – it assesses the willingness of a rookie to go along with other officers when they are acting against the grain of departmental policy. The test shows us how a rookie is learning "what real policing is." It is similar to the slippery-slope image of economic corruption described earlier. But there are important differences.

1. First, the test is not intended to prepare the rookie for a "grafting sub-culture." It's a test of his loyalty to the group. Recall that Mama Rosa is appreciative of what the police do. There's no extortion involved. If Mama Rosa has not been burglarized, although the surrounding restaurants have been burglarized, then the police are preventing crime by eating at Mama Rosa's. They are doing a moral good.

2. The second test involves supporting another officer's version of events. Again, it's a loyalty test. Note that the second test has two components. The first is loyalty – will the rookie go along when the stakes are raised? The second is the good end – officers are trying to do something about crime. That is, it involves a commitment to the noble cause. What the second test shows us is that police loyalty to

each other and commitment to the noble cause are intertwined phe-
nomena. It's part of the reason that police will protect each other
with such passion. Their beliefs and their loyalty are linked together. The brotherhood (and sisterhood) is familial, a bond of loyalty
and morality.

Because low-level corruption involves perks that are so closely tied to
loyalty and to the noble cause, administrative efforts to paint low-level graft
in terms of personal irresponsibility fall on deaf ears. For a street cop, a bad
police officer is a cop that doesn't support another cop. When administrators tell them that being bad involves free coffee, they'll just chuckle and
talk about how far administrators are removed from the real world.

The Slippery Slope Revisited

We are going to present our idea of the **slippery-slope model of
noble-cause corruption**. It differs from Sherman's slippery slope in
subtle but important ways. His concept is germinal to our idea; ours,
however, is designed to describe a process of noble-cause corruption.

Figure 4.5

Slippery Slope of Noble-Cause Corruption

1. **Free meals**. (It always seems to start there.) This is not to test
   willingness to graft but whether an officer is going to be loyal
   to other officers in the squad. This is the Mama Rosa's test.

2. **Loyalty backup**. Here, an officer is tested to see if he or she
   will back up other officers. This is more involved because officers may have to "testily" (give false testimony), dropsy (remove
   drugs from a suspect during a pat-down and then discover them
   in plain sight on the ground), the shake (similar to dropsy, only
   conducted during vehicle stops), or stiffing in a call (discussed
   in Figure 4.3).

3. **Physical violence against citizens**. This is more serious
   because an officer who is violent against a citizen risks death,
   injury, citizen retaliation, or leaving marks that are traceable
   and thus provide evidence of violent police behavior.

4. **Flaking drugs**. This is a much more serious form of noble-
   cause corruption. In this example, cops add drugs to create a
   more serious crime, or they plant drugs on someone to make a
   case. Though some police may get involved in this, it is not
   very common. It is more serious because cops have to be
   engaged in ongoing crime – carrying narcotics – in order to
   commit these acts. Cops engaged in flaking drugs consequently tend to have small loyalty cohorts.

Finally, we believe that noble cause corruption and economic corruption are closely tied to each other. Once started, a police officer may move back and forth across the two lines. In the following section, we will explain this linkage.

Noble-Cause Corruption and Material-Reward Corruption

Noble-cause corruption and material-reward corruption are fundamentally different, though related in practice. Tom Barker (1996:25), defined **material reward corruption** as "whatever the officer receives through the misuse of his or her authority." By material gain, he meant "some tangible object, either cash, services, or goods that have cash value." Noble-cause corruption, on the other hand, is inspired by personally held values of morality rather than material reward. However, we think that there is a relationship between noble-cause corruption and material-reward corruption.

Police reformers have sought to make the police answerable to the law. When police are answerable to the law, they are creations of the law, and are accountable to it. They *do* law enforcement. Consider Pomeroy's (1985:183) comments about police and the law:

> Men and women who are police officers have absolutely no identity or power as police officers outside the law. Police officers are creatures of law, their powers are described and limited by law, and if they operate outside the law, they become criminals just as everyone else and should be punished.

Noble-cause corruption carries with it a different way of thinking about the police relationship to the law from that described above. When officers believe that noble-cause corruption is justified and act on that justification, they are operating on a standard that places personal morality above the law. The police cease being creatures of the law and become legislators of the law. Put simply, police act is if they *are* the law. What the police do is what the law is. Instead, the law becomes one of many tools officers use to act out a moral standard. Pomeroy warned us of the consequences of this possibility:

> If the police are, as a matter of conscious policy, allowed to use force that exceeds what the law allows, the physical freedom and safety of each one of us depend only on the fairness, the political philosophy, the goodwill, and the whim of the person or group that controls the police. (Pomeroy, 1985:185)

Pomeroy recognized the difference between the police as creatures of the law and police as the makers of law. If the police act on their moral predispositions in pursuit of good ends, then whatever they do must be itself good. In such an ethical environment, efforts to control the behavior of police are viewed as disloyal. If police are the law, what they do must be right. If they accept a free dinner in order to safeguard a restaurant, it is because society owes it to them. And if they mistreat suspects, it is because they are the law, and suspects get what they deserve. Noble-cause corruption thus becomes a gateway for material-reward corruption. Where noble-cause corruption flourishes, material-reward corruption cannot be far behind.

When police "become the law," disregard for the well-being of citizens can become a tempestuous problem. Yet the police cannot carry out their task with impunity. As Figure 4.6 shows, the federal government itself may decide to take over a local police department that it thinks is out of control.

Conclusion: I Am the Law

You've got a nice city here, Mike observes. *Would you want the federal government to run the police here? That's what a consent decree is. Would that be a good thing for this city? I don't think so. I don't trust the federal government that much. I doubt if you do, either.*

How does the "I am the law" perspective, described above and in Figure 4.6, fit the perspectives of corruption discussed in this chapter? In his quote above, Pomeroy warned us about a police who use force in excess of the law. The examples of lawless behavior described in Figure 4.6 suggest that the police acted out of a moral standard aimed at identifying potential offenders, not in order to further some illegal economic benefit. It represented a variety of noble-cause corruption on a department-wide basis. And the example reveals how noble-cause corruption, if unchecked, can disrupt fundamental ideas of fair play.

The takeover of a municipal police organization by the federal courts is controversial under any circumstances. The Pittsburgh Fraternal Order of Police (FOP) has actively resisted the consent decree, stating that the premise of the order, that police violence against citizens was a pervasive problem, was untrue. The FOP has likened the Consent Decree to a "witch-hunt," has contended that the department should not be punished for the actions of a few officers, and that transfers will undermine the ability of the police to provide adequate public safety. In the active resistance of the FOP, we can see the profoundly divisive effect a Consent Decree can have on a police organization.

The belief that police are always right, what we call the "I am the law" perspective, can undermine justice in its most elemental sense. In Figure 4.6, we see how it can lead to noble-cause corruption at a systemic level, across a department. In the next chapter, we will look at how hiring practices and early organizational experiences reinforce the noble cause and can sometimes result in noble-cause corruption.

Figure 4.6

A Consent Decree in Pittsburgh

On February 26, the Department of Justice entered into a Consent Decree with the city of Pittsburgh. A consent decree is an agreement by a defendant (in this case the City of Pittsburgh) to cease activities asserted as illegal by the government. If the court approves the agreement, the government's action against the defendant is dropped.

The decree settled a lawsuit brought against the city of Pittsburgh in 1997 by the U.S. Department of Justice, which charged that Pittsburgh police exhibited a systematic pattern of police brutality. The decree grew out of a lawsuit carried out by the American Civil Liberties Union on behalf of 66 city residents. Incidents included the following: Two women stated that police beat them when they stopped to watch officers beat a man. A disabled woman said that police strip-searched her at a traffic stop while her children watched. And a Baptist minister said he was wrongly beaten and arrested while listening to gospel music at home.

The decree established measures for managing the city's police force. If the police conform to the terms of the agreement for five years, then the decree will be dropped. In accordance with the decree, the city of Pittsburgh agreed to undertake the following reforms:

1. Increase training for officers with multiple complaints against them.

2. Monitor all litigation against police officers.

3. Install and implement an early warning system to identify and track problem officers.

4. Require officers to write a report, to be reviewed by supervisors, for any use of force against an individual or when a search and seizure is conducted.

5. Hire an independent auditor to monitor complaint investigations.

Sources: Adapted from: "ACLU Opposes City's Move to Modify Consent Decree Governing Police Spying," www.aclu-il.orgdecree2.html; Marylynne Pitz, "City to Pay Lawyers in Lawsuit," Online Post-Gazette, www.post-gazette.com/regionstate/19980/01bcopso.asp (10/30 1998; Claudia Coates, "Police Brutality Forces Pittsburgh to Start Monitoring P.D." Associated Press, www.web2010.com/marceric/news/nsw93.mm (10/30 1998).

Values, Hiring, and Early Organizational Experiences

5

Key Terms

ethics	value-based hiring
general definition of discretion	value-neutral hiring
low-visibility decisionmaking	value transmission
morality	values are learned on
patronage	job perspective
pre-hiring procedures	value-predisposition
specific definition	perspective
of discretion	

Mike scans his audience and smiles. *You're hiring cops. That means that you're hiring authorized representatives of a moral standard.*

Ethics in criminal justice is one of the most popular topics in current teaching curriculums today. It is impossible to receive a two- or four-year degree in criminal justice without having a class in ethics. Textbooks on the police today typically will have a chapter on police ethics. An increasing number of textbooks are devoted to ethics. All this education and training implies that which is unspoken – that police recruits or officers are not adequately ethical. That somehow their mortal identity is incomplete and training or education can fill in the moral "gaps." The same message is stated repeatedly – shame on officers who take advantage of graft, free coffee, and free meals. Ethics, as taught in college classes and training academies, tends to focus on economic corruption and violence against minority groups.

Our position, however, is that recruits tend to be exceptionally ethical. They are chosen through rigorous hiring standards designed to make sure that they are appropriately ethical. Individuals who express the wrong kind of morality are weeded out during the probationary period. In the early years of employment, an officer's pre-existing morality is finely tuned to the ethical dynamics of loyalty and noble cause as they are played out in local police cultures.

In this chapter, we are going to first discuss the ethical bases of hiring. Officers, we contend, are screened by a value-laden process that seeks to identify those committed to the noble cause. Second, we describe how early training selectively highlights particular experiences and values as ethically meaningful. Early organizational experiences reinforce their noble-cause commitment in a context of officer loyalty. Third, we will discuss how the unique characteristics of police organizations provide an environment supportive of value-based decisionmaking. The police organization, an "upside-down bureaucracy" from the point of view of public decisionmaking, enables officers to make discretionary decisions from a value-based perspective.

Pre-Hiring Procedures

What does it take to become a police officer? Of those who seek a career in policing, only certain ones will make the grade. How are officers selected? **Pre-hiring procedures** assess the qualifications of recruits for police work. The following procedures, common to most departments, are listed in Figure 5.1 with descriptions (Roberg, Crank & Kuykendall, 2000).

The elaborate pre-hiring screening procedures described in Figure 5.1 have been viewed by observers of the police as value neutral. **Value-neutral hiring** is consistent with Vollmer's vision, stated in the previous chapter, that police officers should not carry or act out predispositions about social rights and wrongs. According to this perspective, officers are not screened for their value predispositions, except for honesty and psychological stability, and for evidence of criminal history. The argument in favor of these complex procedures is straightforward: a thorough screening and testing process insures that only the most highly qualified candidates will be hired as police officers. The thoroughness of these procedures matches the public expectations of what police should be.

Figure 5.1

Pre-Hiring Procedures

Application. Applicants must submit an application. The application, listing background and personal characteristics, is the first stage of candidate evaluation. Candidates are expected to conform to certain criteria. The applicant's age is typically restricted to a range of 21 and 35. Height requirements, a traditional hiring criteria, are increasingly challenged in departments for being discriminatory to women and Asian Americans. Some departments have residency requirements.

A criminal record does not automatically disqualify a person for a police position. Many departments will also accept candidates that have used drugs such as marijuana, but only if it was very infrequent, it was youthful, and if a certain quantity of time – 3 to 5 years for most departments – has elapsed. Some departments require that candidates are non-smokers.

Knowledge Testing. Many departments use some sort of standardized intelligence tests to evaluate the intellectual capabilities of candidates. Some departments have moved to make these tests more skills based and job-related. Departments want smart officers but not officers that question procedures.

Physical Agility Testing. Physical testing has traditionally focused on tests of physical strength – push-ups, weight-lifting, chin-ups, and running distance and speed. There is little evidence that these tests have adversely affected either women or minorities, but they screen out candidates that are in poor physical condition or overweight.

Background Check. This is an attempt to assess the character and suitability of candidates. Investigators want to know if the personal history given by the applicant on the application form is truthful. Of particular interest is past experience and lifestyle.

Polygraph. This checks the accuracy of background information, and looks for inappropriate behavior. As important as the polygraph is the pre-polygraph screening, when candidates are advised about the questions to be asked. It is during the pre-polygraph period that examiners find out a large quantity of information about the candidate.

Psychological Testing. Testing assesses emotional stability and maturity. A common testing bank is called the Minnesota Multiphasic Personality Inventory. The California Psychological Inventory is also widely used. Both are called inventories because they test for a wide variety of psychological traits.

Oral Interview. Candidates are measured on communications skills, confidence, interpersonal style, decision-making skills, and demeanor. Questions may include "Why do you want to become a police officer?" Candidates may make decisions about what to do in hypothetical situations.

Source: Adapted from R. Roberg, J. Crank, and J. Kuykendall (2000). *Police and Society*. Roxbury Publishers.

Hiring, however, is not value neutral. Elaborate screening protocols insure that only a particular "type" of person will be hired. This type is squeaky clean (at least for the years immediately preceding the application), has no tolerance for wrongdoing, probably has not been exposed to wrongdoing, and is ready to go out and save America.

If background checks are so thorough, then why has accountability been an ever-present problem in police departments? Does police work, given its tremendous opportunities for graft and abuse, simply encounter the limits of human virtue? In part, yes. Police work provides temptations in the absence of supervision. Do we unwittingly hire a type of officer who is more, not less, prone to some kinds of corruption? In part, yes. Today, officers sometimes act on the belief that the noble cause is a standard higher than the law.

Hiring Is a Value-Based Process

Mike asks the commanders about hiring protocols used in their agency: *With so many hiring procedures, what are you looking for? Why are there so many procedures? Who is it that you are afraid of hiring?*

Administrators will often comment that the different ways of gathering information tend to overlap. In the group Mike is talking to today, answers ranged widely. They're looking for indicators of past or potential problems. They want to know about criminal record. Lifestyle problems. Drug use. Ability to handle stress.

Suppose a candidate comes to the oral interview. He's got a perfect background, checks out, passes the polygraph. But he shows up with hair down to the middle of his back, a peace symbol earring, and a hemp tie. Would he get the job?

No one answers.

Mike singles out one of the officers. *Would he get the job?*

"Well, maybe" the officer responds. The room is quiet for a moment. Then everyone bursts into laughter. Maybe is a good answer when "yes" is unthinkable and "no" is inappropriate.

Would you hire him? He asks another officer.

"Maybe."

The point Mike is making is this. Hiring is value based. In **value-based hiring**, we hire cops for their perspective, we check them out relentlessly to make sure that their values are in order, and then we double check our decision to hire them with values-based tests during their probationary period. They are screened and selected for their values. How do they handle their first arrest? Will they back up another cop without hesitation? These are value judgments. The judgments police make and for which they are screened during recruitment and probation are based more in values than in knowledge of the law. Recruits are tested to see if considerations of loyalty and commitment to the noble cause will override personal safety considerations.

Officers are screened out that don't pass threshold levels of legal history, physical strength and agility, psychological suitability, and weapons training and skills. But these are threshold requirements, necessary conditions to becoming a police officer. They are not sufficient conditions. Values are the glue that unites the elements of the hiring process.

Screening for Values Versus Job-Learned Values

Our value-based image of hiring is *sharply* different from most discussions about the police. As we argued in Chapter 3, when officers are hired, their moral commitments are already in place. Hiring procedures are designed to screen out those who don't have the right way of thinking about police work, who lack the "right stuff" – loyalty and commitment to the noble cause.

This is not a fashionable way to look at values of police officers. The most popular academic view is that a "police perspective" is learned on the job, in the doing of police work.

Academics are fond of asking the question "Why are police different from everyone else?" Of course, the question is biased with its presumption that police are different. But police also see themselves differently, special, members of a select and inwardly focused group (Van Maanen, 1978; Bouza, 1990). It is a bias shared by the police and non-police alike.

The question "Why are police different?" has two answers that have been popular in different times. The first is that a particular type of person is attracted to policing. This perspective was popular in the 1960s but has lost market value. The second is that differences come from the nature of the work that police do, from values learned on the job. This perspective is the most popular in the current era.

Our view, called a **value-predisposition perspective**, is that officers are hired with their values in place, and these values are selectively highlighted and finely tuned during academy and on-the-job training. This perspective is as follows. A person who aspires to becoming a police officer selects policing from a variety of employment options that he or she is thinking about. Recruits are not much different from people that select other careers. A unique set of police values is formed during early organizational experiences in the first few years after hiring. Within a relatively short period of time, a fully framed "police" way of looking at the world is formed. The primary formative influences are the academy (Harris, 1973), the field training officer (Van Maanen, 1978) the police culture (Manning, 1997), the danger and isolation of police work (Skolnick, 1994) internal pressures for the production of arrests (Manning & Redlinger, 1977) and sometimes darker elements of the police socialization process such as corruption (Kappeler, Sluder & Alpert, 1994), to name but a few.

The values-learned-on-the-job perspective is linked to corruption as well. The International Association of Chiefs of Police (1989:53) observed that "there is no guarantee that an individual of good character, hired by a police department, will remain honest. There are a variety of other factors . . . which can erode an officer's commitment to integrity. Many officers face temptation every day" (Kappeler, Sluder & Alpert, 1994:240).

The *values are learned on the job* perspective is not a way of thinking about the police that we share. Chapter 3 shows how important values associated with police work and with the noble cause are already in place at the time of hiring. Training teaches recruits how to apply those values to a police work setting. Prospective police candidates are individuals who already hold a positive reservoir of sentiment for the police. They tend to share the police moral sensibility, dividing the world into good guys and bad guys. They feel good when bad guys are hurt, and they want to be one of the good guys. They already have in place a clear sense of moral justice. They have friends who are police. Long before they have taken their first examination for a position in a police department, they are committed to the noble cause.

Police officers tend to be drawn from a "culture of policing" (Crank, 1998:191-196). This means that police officers come from backgrounds already sympathetic to the police. Their backgrounds include police families, small towns, military personnel, and other similar groups. These groups form a culture of policing because they carry values similar to police, particularly conservative values about the desirability of order in human relations.

Groups that comprise the culture of policing have many elements in common. Economically, they tend to be blue-collar, working class. They are often politically conservative in orientation, though they are slightly less likely to be Democrats than Republicans. Their values are old-fashioned – they do not see the world in terms of competing values and situational ethics. They believe that being American is about moral fiber. And for young people, police work is a way to participate in an important endeavor, to contribute to and maintain the traditions of American society. Police work is one of the primary occupations through which they join the ranks of the middle class in the United States.

Values are carried from broader society to police work by a process called **value transmission**. Pollock (1998:7) provides a way to think about the process of value transmission from early upbringing to the working police environment. **Morality**, she observed, "is used to speak of the total person, or the sum of a person's actions in every sphere of life . . ." **Ethics**, on the other hand, "is used for certain behaviors relating to a profession." Morals, we suggest, represent the values that a person is taught during their upbringing, and are learned from parents, schools, and other important social institutions. Police ethics represent the way those moral values are channeled into specific occupational experiences. Recruits undergo a transition that shapes their moral sense into specific ethical decisions. The underlying ethic that mobilizes police behavior is the noble cause.

New recruits are already committed to the noble cause. They believe in it. It's not something they learn from some dark police subculture. It's not as if a recruit in a POST ethics class watches the instructor draw a stick figure of a suspect with a frowny face behind bars, slaps his forehead, and exclaims "Oh! Now I get it!" The noble cause is an interior, psychological map of the beliefs and morals that characterize their upbringing. Every time they turn on the tube and see a report of a 10-year-old girl that has been kidnapped, the fires of the noble cause are stoked. Each time they hear that some killer has been granted a stay of execution, their blood boils. Abstract ethics discussions will be irrelevant to them.

Early Organizational Experiences

In this section, we argue that early organizational experiences focus the way officers act out their values. First, we examine police discretion, and argue that, from an ethical perspective, many police decisions are not as discretionary as they appear. We then discuss the influence of early organizational experiences on recruits, particularly focusing on the influence of the training officers.

The Myth of Police Discretion

After a break, Mike expands the discussion of value-based decision-making to the topic of discretion. His theme is that police discretion is in part an illusion of how we think about modern bureaucracies. So-called "discretionary" police behavior, he argues, is value-based and predictable.

> *Okay. Imagine this. There's a car full of fat white men in $1,000 suits. The driver's license of the driver is expired. Now, in your mind, imagine slamming these guys on the hood of the car, palms down. Kicking their feet apart. Screaming at them. Can that image, that CONCEPT even enter your mind? It's not even possible. The image doesn't work.*

> *Now imagine doing this to a car full of black teenagers with baseball hats on backwards.*

The audience laughs quietly. Mike laughs too, nodding his head up and down.

> *See. Now that works, doesn't it. You can imagine that. Now you understand that your officers are making value-based decisions about their work. They're not making discretionary decisions. They're making value-based decisions. The issue for many police officers is not what they do. It's whether they're caught.*

Figure 5.2

> ### Discretion and the American Bar Foundation
>
> In 1996, Kleinig observed that "In the American Bar Foundation (ABF) survey of 1956, it was discovered that at each stage of an individual's encounter with the criminal justice system the outcome was determined by a decision that was essentially 'discretionary' in character." This finding was controversial because it suggested that the most important police decisions, those involving the immediate freedom of a suspect, were being made outside formal administrative and legal protocols. (Kleinig, 1996:1)

Discretion Versus "Just the Facts" Policing

The notion that police make discretionary judgments in the conduct of their work, particularly with regard to the decision to arrest, emerged in the 1960s. A discretionary perception of police work represented a sharp break from the then-popular perception of "just the facts" decisionmaking, where police decisions flowed from rational, non-valued judgments of the facts. The ABF survey (noted in Figure 5.2) unleashed a torrent of research on the discretionary nature of criminal justice decision-making (Walker, 1993). Today, police are commonly believed to exercise wide discretion in many aspects of their work that cannot be brought under administrative control. Indeed, a central tenet of the community policing movement is that police officers *should* have wide discretion to act upon their judgments of situational dynamics in police-citizen encounters.

What is discretion? It is commonly defined in two different ways. First, it is generally defined in terms of all decisions made by police in the conduct of their daily work activities. In the **general definition of discretion**, discretion refers to the ability to choose among alternatives when making decisions. In the most general sense, discretion refers to all police decisionmaking. Davis (1969), in a widely cited quote, stated that the a police officer has the "discretion whenever the effective limits on his power leave him free to make a choice among possible courses of action or inaction."

The **specific definition of discretion** is that police discretion emerges in the decision to invoke criminal sanctions. Goldstein (1998) describes discretion in terms of decisions made by police not to make an arrest even when the requisite conditions for an arrest are present. He refers to a decision not to arrest as "non-arrest discretion." Police discretion is a subset of discretion across the criminal justice system.

In this book, we are using the general definition of discretion. We contend that values predispose behavior across the decision-making process, not only in the invocation of a criminal sanction of arrest. When an officer uses force to gain compliance, the officer is by the general definition making a discretionary judgment. The decision to use force may be legal, but the officer is applying his or her judgment to the level of force displayed by a suspect and making an additional judgment about the appropriate force response. Or when an officer makes a decision about when to intervene in a suspicious circumstance, the officer is making a discretionary decision about what is "suspicious" and hence justifies intervention.

Values and Discretion

The administrative response to discretion is to try to bring it under organizational control and regulate it. Policies, rules, and regulations provide a managerial basis for controlling behavior. Administrators operate under what might be called a "value-neutral" vision of police discretion. This means that discretionary judgments of line officers are viewed as a sort of unregulated, uncontrolled form of decisionmaking that, with proper training and guidance, can be controlled by the organization (Cohen, 1996). Officers are held accountable to the law and to policy, and with thoughtful application of discretion they make good decisions. They become good street bureaucrats.

This "value-neutral" model of decisionmaking comes up short. The value-neutral model presumes (1) that police have wide discretion, and (2) the use of discretion is untrained or uncoordinated decisionmaking that can be corrected with proper training and thoughtful policy. The model, however, doesn't adequately consider the values that motivate police officers. It utterly fails to recognize that officers are making morally important, value-based decisions on the use of discretion. If the values that underwrite the decisions are known, then the "unpredictable" nature of police discretion disappears. The administrative problem is consequently framed as follows:

Figure 5.3

Decisionmaking in a Moral Environment

The proper question facing administrators is not how to coordinate uncontrolled decisionmaking, but how to bring value-based decision-making under the umbrella of administrative and lawful influence.

Mike argues that if someone's values are known, their behavior can be predicted, and the issue of discretion disappears. He compares the police to the military.

In order to get people to do something you want them to do, especially if it's risky, you have to underpin their behavior with a value system. If you can do that, you can predict what their behavior's going to be.

You can't get people to fight wars if they don't believe in the reasons for fighting. If you understand that, you have already explained away most decisions that are called discretionary.

Think about the "war on crime" mentality. We underpin anti-drug police tactics with a simple morality. Good, bad. Good cop. Bad drug user. One value system against another. We hire for this. When an officer starts work, he's already thinking this way. It's not discretion he doesn't understand. He's making moral decisions, and his morally good ends determine his means. He has to learn how to avoid getting caught.

This is why all this literature about discretion is nonsense. We can assert that police officers have little or no discretion. They are selected from a narrow value set. You hire them from this value set, you train them to focus on officer safety, thus even further removing them from the policed. You train them for quick, "in your face" decisions. Make a decision, move on to the next. Instant solution-makers.

You arm them, give them a car. You've aimed the weapon and cocked the trigger. You know how they think and what they're going to do. Where's the discretion? How can you NOT know what they're going to do?

The police task is often described by outside observers as highly flexible and vulnerable to many discretionary outcomes and cannot be brought under the control of administration or the law. That means that outsiders, examining what police do, would conclude that a wide range of outcomes are possible, even reasonable for the kinds of encounters in which police find themselves.

Police officers, however, don't use discretion from a value-neutral perspective. They are hired with a sense of "noble-cause" morality already fully in place. As soon as they begin patrol work, their values influence and are refined by the decisions they make about suspects, assholes, and victims, about when and where to intervene, about who is a good guy and a bad guy, and about loyalty to their colleagues. Their decisions about appropriate means are based on terminal or ends values, and knowledge of those ends values enable an insightful observer to predict police behavior in any given police-citizen encounter. And the central end value is the noble cause – getting the bad guys off the streets.

Values and the Training Officer

One of the ethical dilemmas noted by many observers of the police is the powerful influence the training officer has on new recruits. The training officer introduces recruits to the craft of policing. However, training officers sometimes undercut all administrative efforts to control line-level behavior.

Training Officers (TOs) are one of Mike's favorite topics. *What person has the most influence on your new recruits?*

The answer, of course, is the training officer.

Your recruits are going to be with the officer for maybe six months. They're going to role model that young recruit down to the last doughnut. If that TO you've got out there that is taking him to the doughnut shop is not the individual you want them to emulate, then it's your screw-up, not theirs.

Let's think about this for a minute. Mike is talking to command-level police managers. They've heard all this ethics talk before. They know that some officers are not molded from the "right stuff." They believe that a few bad apples always slip through the screening process. But they haven't been told that it's their fault. How can this be?

From their earliest training in POST, officers have been taught to avoid any illegal conduct. They are taught to avoid such activities even if other officers around them don't. They are expected to resist the activity **and** to report it. Even the appearance of unprofessional behavior is unacceptable. They've been drilled in ethical conduct. They've been scolded for looking cross-eyed at a free hot meal. They may have studied the Law Enforcement Code of Ethics, the California Highway Patrol Statement of Professional Values, and all 51 standards of the eight canons of ethics of the Code of Professional Conduct and Responsibility for Peace Officers (see Miller, 1995). Then they're turned loose to their TO, who wants to know if they're loyal and will back up other officers. And they know that the TO can make or break their careers.

Mixed signals? What recruits are being told in their "formal" ethical training or education is to ignore or report any inappropriate or illegal behavior. They're provided an elaborate, complicated set of written standards to guide their behavior. When those written standards conflict with the behavior of their fellow officers or their TO, what is the message to recruits? "Our organization won't change, and we want you to be a member of our organization, so we'll have a TO train you, but you better not do anything wrong like your TO or fellow officers. And if they do something wrong, stop it, and report it to their superiors." Mike mimics a Sergeant cynically telling an officer what will happen to him if he turns on his TO or fellow officers. *Yea, that'll work. How are you going to explain that to the orals board on your next job interview?*

Van Maanen and Early Organizational Experiences

How influential is the TO? Van Maanen's (1978) research provides us with an understanding of the influence of the TO in training new recruits. New recruits, he suggested, are the most vulnerable to organization pressures. During the probationary period, an officer has no job protection and can be terminated for failing to satisfy the expectations of his or her TO. Van Maanen put it this way:

> It is during the breaking-in period that the organization may be thought to be the most persuasive, for the person has few guidelines to direct his behavior and has little, if any, organizational support for his "vulnerable selves" which may be the object of influence. (Van Maanen, 1978:293-294)

The most important influence on a recruit, Van Maanen observed, was the Field Training Officer.

> It is commonplace for the rookie to never make a move without first checking with his TO. By watching, listening, and mimicking, the neophyte policeman learns how to deal with the objects of his occupation – the traffic violator, the hippie, the drunk, the brass, and the criminal justice complex itself. . . . A whole folklore of tales, myths, and legends surrounding the department is communicated to the recruit by his fellow officers – conspicuously by his TO. Through these anecdotes – dealing largely with mistakes or "flubs" made by policemen – the recruit begins to adopt the perspectives of his more experienced officers . . . he learns to be protected from his own mistakes, he must protect others. (Van Maanen, 1978:301)

And we think that we can provide ethics training in college or in training, and recruits can overcome this kind of organizational influence?

Mike describes to his audience a program in a department in California. *This department has a program in their academy. It is acted out. A cadet is riding along. A routine stop is made. Of course, it's a minority person. They tell him to get out of the car. And sure enough, they get into a fight. Another car shows up. And then there are five cops fighting. Mob mentality has taken over. They're beating him into the ground. The cadet is expected to push everybody away and turn right around, get all of their names, and report the incident. Can you imagine that happening in your favorite city?*

Every officer out on the street knows that, if they turn on another cop, their life is going to take an unpleasant turn. This is not unique to cops. Our research on whistle-blowing shows that whistle blowers – a person who seeks recourse to organizational problems by reporting those problems outside the chain-of-command or to authorities outside the organization, the media for example, suffer a variety of professional indignities (see Figure 5.3). Moreover, they rarely recover their jobs or their professional reputations. In police work, a whistle-blower will be ostracized by his or her fellow officers, and if the whistle-blower is a recruit, is unlikely to receive regular employment. As one observer of the training film described by Mike above observed, "He's (the recruit expected to report the wrongdoing) got a sidearm. He might as well take it out and pull the trigger, because he's just committed suicide on the job." Now let's see that training film again. . . .

Figure 5.3

> **Retaliation**
>
> Consider the following description of a retaliation, reported by Pollock (1998).
>
> A typical example of retaliation is reported in a San Diego newspaper concerning an officer in the San Diego police department who arrested a sergeant for driving while intoxicated. Even though the officer previously averaged fewer than two complaints a year during his eleven years at the police department, after he arrested the sergeant, he received nine complaints resulting in a total of 68 days of suspension.
>
> He also experienced the following: he encountered hang-up calls on his unlisted home telephone, his belongings were stolen, his car was towed away from the police parking lot twice, officers refused to sit next to him, and officers did not respond to his calls for back-up . . . The sergeant who was arrested for drunken driving was released before being taken to a magistrate, contrary to departmental policy, and received no disciplinary actions.

Source: Casey, 1966, in Pollock, 1998:196-197.

Managers understand line officer morality, even if they no longer have a practical sense of the "street." They were selected from the same moral cloth. TOs fine-tune recruits so that they don't embarrass the department, and managers guard against blunders that threaten departmental legitimacy or create liability problems. Managers, nevertheless, can't resist trying to control line personnel. They are patriarchal, like those they hire, and take a view of their line officers as untrained children who need discipline to act right. Of course, failure is inevitable. Characteristics of police organizations mitigate against effective oversight of discretion. These characteristics are discussed in the next section.

Police Departments Are Upside-Down Bureaucracies

Who, Mike asks, are the guys who make the discretionary decisions that reflect the nature of your police organization? Who are they?

Line officers are the public representation of departmental activities and policies. They carry out the purposes of the department in view of the public. When the press writes about the police organization, they are usually writing about what some line officer did, not what the chief did. Yet this answer to Mike's question, seemingly clear as it is, reveals profound differences between business organizations and police work.

Consider large businesses. The role of the Chief Executive Officer (CEO) is as the top decisionmaker. The CEO makes decisions about the future of the organization. Delegates responsibilities. Decides about product sales and distributions. Hires and fires at will. Makes big dollars. Retires with a "parachute" of valuable stocks and bonds. A CEO exerts almost unlimited power over the conduct of the organization and can make or destroy it. His or her power is limited primarily by the organization's board of stockholders.

Police organizations reverse the distribution of organizational authority in important ways. Chiefs have limited influence over the day-to-day affairs of street officers, even in today's bottom-line oriented business-mimicking world of public services. A chief certainly cannot hire and fire at will.

In a business, discretionary decisions that reflect the organization's values are the province of the CEO, at the top of the organization. In a municipal police organization, discretion that reflects the organization's values is acted out at the bottom of the organizational chart and is vested in the decisions made by line officers. It is the line officer, not the chief, that makes the decisions that reveal to the public the nature of the police organization. Police organizations reverse the organizational location of discretionary decisionmaking, and in this sense are upside down when compared to businesses. Why are police organizations like this? There are two kinds of reasons, one logical and the other historical.

The three logical reasons have to do with the nature of the work that police officers do. It is unrealistic to think that variability and unpredictable situations can be removed from the line officer's task (Wilson, 1968), for three reasons. First, the uncertainties of the task environment preclude tight administrative management. By task environment is meant the physical space in which a police officer does his or her work, usually an assigned beat. Police work is characterized by dealing with unpredictability in citizen encounters and by having to make decisions based on anticipated behavior of other people (Crank, 1998; see also Harmon, 1995).[12] Uncertainty is particularly important in police work because police officers occasionally deal with individuals who have something to hide and who will resist providing incriminating information. Much of the uncertainty that police encounter is intentionally produced by citizens and sometimes gives a dangerous edge to police efforts to uncover truth.

Secondly, the occupation of policing, unlike business, has few clear or "bottom-line" outputs that provide a measure of work activity. Some departments use informal quotas for arrests and traffic stops, but there is little beyond this for which officers are held accountable. As in other public sector organizations, police work is mostly about the well-being of citizens, not the marketability of an economic good. Third, police work is **low-visibility decisionmaking**. This means that officers do their work mostly out of sight of supervisors, and usually involving only a few citizens. Consequently, it is difficult to bring line-level activity under administrative control.

There are also historical reasons for the limited control chiefs have over lower-ranking officers. Limits on the power of police chiefs over line personnel can be traced to the early days of the International Association of Chiefs of Police (IACP). The position of the IACP paralleled the views of political progressives in that era (Walker, 1977). A component of the progressive platform was to further the political independence of municipal police organizations. Its platform, however, held two goals that worked at cross-purposes. These goals were (1) hiring independent-minded executives for the position of chief, and (2) protecting line-officers from arbitrary personnel policies.

Central to the platform of the IACP at the end of the nineteenth century was acquiring independence of the chief from local party machines. The IACP advocated the selection of chiefs from the ranks of the military and business. The position of chief under machine politics was largely ceremonial, with little real influence over the day-to-day activities of the organization.

The IACP believed that, by hiring business and military professionals rather than political cronies as chiefs, the powerful influence of local politics would be weakened and chiefs could assert control over their organizations. In retrospect, we see that this goal was partially achieved. Today, about one-half of all chiefs in municipal departments in the United States are selected from outside the organization, and large urban departments are more likely to hire outside chiefs.

Another important goal of the IACP was the implementation of hiring standards for line officers. During the late 1800s, police officers were selected primarily for their loyalty to local political machinery. Their positions were what we call **patronage**, meaning that hiring and continued employment depended on their loyalty to the political party holding office.

Reformers thought that the powerful influence of political machinery over the police could be broken if officers were protected from arbitrary hiring and firing, that is, by ending the patronage system (Fogelson, 1977). The idea that police personnel should have employment protections was, however, controversial. Should line officers, reformers wondered, be provided with civil service protections? *Civil service* was a new governmental form in that era: it protected governmental employees from arbitrary hiring and firing, and established job standards for work performance. Reformers saw it as a double-edged sword. If officers received civil-service protections, they would be protected from arbitrary firing when an election swept in a new mayor. On the other hand, civil service protections would limit the ability of chiefs to hire, reward, or punish its officers.

Ultimately, the idea that officers should have civil service protections carried the day. However, a price was to be paid. Chiefs, though gaining a limited degree of independence of their organization from municipal politics, nevertheless had scant authority over their own officers. Their influence within their own organization was severely constrained by a powerful and protective personnel system. Even to the current era, many observers argue that civil service protections are so deeply entrenched in contemporary law that changing them is like "bending granite" (Guyot, 1979). For police commanders, this means that personnel decisions made during hiring will be around for a long time. If a mistake is made at hiring, it will be very difficult to undo.

> Mike continues. *This guy got out of the academy yesterday. He's out there making decisions, writing traffic tickets, making arrests, risking his life and limb. Where's the chief? When the public looks at the organization, they see this guy. They don't see the chief.*
>
> *Where's the chief? The chief's probably out having lunch with the mayor somewhere. Worrying about his heart.* Mike points to the chief attending the meeting and chuckles. *How ya doin' chief?*

Chiefs tend to participate in their department's early retirement program. The average tenure of a police chief in the United States is about four years. Unless a chief voluntarily retires from office, an infrequent occurrence, they are fired. When a new one is hired, they are hired with a mandate to fix whatever went wrong and caused the previous chief to get fired (Crank & Langworthy, 1992). Often they are hired to fix problems over which they have no control. They have to overcome resistance in the organization while implementing changes in a timely way. This is often impossible. As Ahern (1972) observed, a chief may spend the remainder of his or her career in an agency fixing the problems seen on the first day of employment. In most instances, the remainder of the career is brief.

A new chief is hired. The chief has a new broom to sweep, out with the old, in with the new. Maybe he or she is going to convert a department to community policing. Will his or her officers follow?

> Mike continues. *You can put a set of rules out there, but if I don't believe in them (he pats his heart) they're not doing you any good. Who governs policing? If I'm one of your officers I do. What really governs policing? I'm making a case for morality, not law, which has a lot to say about an organization you call law enforcement.*

The Chief and Traditional Leadership

Chiefs are not as influential in the affairs of street officer activity as we would like them to be, and indeed as they themselves would like. A chief, concerned that he or she has control problems, may take a harsh, "no-nonsense" approach to line indiscretions. Yet this approach may backfire, intensifying resistance and further weakening control. Consequently, we do not believe that chiefs have much of an effect on the early organizational experiences of line officers.

Mike: *Beware of chiefs who say "thou shalt change."*

By "thou shalt change," Mike is describing how crime control chiefs tend to approach their work. They believe in crime control, in the military style of command, and in the importance of discipline. Chief executives have sometimes viewed their responsibilities from a tough, no-nonsense perspective. This perspective is well-received by the public and street officers alike when it focuses on crime. However, the traditional, rigid leadership style creates control and management problems and is particularly inefficient for dealing with noble-cause dilemmas. Bordua and Reiss (1986) have discussed problems associated with traditional leadership:

Figure 5.4

Bordua and Reiss: Problems of Traditional Leadership

1. ***Corruption.*** A traditional, top-down style is viewed by traditional crime-control chiefs as a primary way to control corruption in the department. However, it is reactive, which means that it reacts to corruption after wrongdoing is uncovered. It can't deal very well with entrenched corruption, where practices are hidden by the rank and file. It is especially difficult to control vice. Bordua and Reiss (1986:33) noted that:

   > it is precisely in those operations where corruption is most likely to occur, namely, the control of vice, that a centralized command is least effective. . . . Vice requires an essentially proactive strategy of policing in the modern metropolis. . . .

   Police departments are upside-down organizations. One of the consequences of this is that bad news passes up the chain of command only when lower-ranking managers can't contain the problem or when they are afraid that the chief will hear about it from someone else. This means that, in their efforts to deal with problems among line officers, chiefs are likely to be one step behind.

2. ***Professional Development.*** A rigid, traditional management style undercuts professional development. Line officers' willingness to make professional decisions based on their expertise is repressed by an autocratic managerial style that seeks to control what line personnel do. Chiefs can be obsessive in their fear that line officers will make a mistake. Over the long-term, this kind of leadership will alienate lower-ranking personnel.

3. ***Intensifying Resistance.*** Traditional chiefs want to control line-officer behavior. They believe in the rigid, military chain of command. But police organizations are inverted pyramids; this means that the chief is technically the boss, but actually has limited power. The kinds of decisions that directly affect the public increase in frequency as you move down the chain of command. Executive efforts to control the behavior of line officers too closely are ultimately futile. Officers will resist the executive and become more secretive. The chief will ultimately bring about precisely those problems he or she is trying to control.

In other words, if a police department has a noble-cause corruption problem at the line level, the traditional strategies that chiefs use – reliance on chain of command controls – are unlikely to have much of an impact. Indeed, they're likely to cause more problems than they will solve. Their impact is likely to generate resistance on the part of line officers, create increased tensions between line personnel and supervisors, and intensify the darker aspects of the police culture, those aspects that hide line behavior from external accountability.

You want to hold your officers accountable for their behavior, Mike concludes. *When your chief says "thou shalt change," you've just lost control.*

Figure 5.5

Rank-and-File Resistance to Stern Chief in Los Angeles

Chief Bernard C. Parks, the Chief of the Los Angeles Police Department, is incurring a great deal of hostility from the rank-and-file in his police organization. As reported in the *New York Times* (1999:10), Parks is a department veteran and a disciplinarian. He was hired as chief in August, 1997, replacing Chief Willie L. Williams. However, the paper noted that "the hardness that served him so well on the mean streets and the treacherous world of office politics at police headquarters is now apparently a source of growing dissatisfaction within the ranks of the 9,730-officer department." In a highly visible sign of discontent, several officers have requested that their emergency information cards include a no-Parks last wish. They do not want him to attend their funerals if they are killed in the line of duty.

Parks has initiated numerous efforts at reform in the department. In 1998, 54 officers were fired for infractions and seven others resigned before they could be removed. This is a dramatic increase from previous years: 11 were fired in 1997 and 13 in 1996. Some of those fired were removed for excessive force. Yet this does not mean that the department is becoming more friendly to civilian input: critics have accused Parks of being unfriendly and hostile to meaningful civilian input into departmental activities. Discussions of his leadership style frequently include the word "autocratic." Yet he has many supporters as well. A representative of the Police Commission described Park's leadership as "outstanding."

Clear is that his tough, no-nonsense style is alienating line-level personnel. His style of leadership, as described by his critics and supporters alike, is intensifying resistance among the rank-and-file. Will the outcome of this be an erosion of line-level control, as Mike suggests typically happens to commanders whose style is described by the aphorism "thou shalt change?" And to what extent can a chief confront his or her line-officers with harsh, discipline-oriented reform and achieve reform goals? In the case discussed here, the verdict is not yet known. Parks may be able to achieve what few other chiefs have – the control of the unwieldy Los Angeles Police department. Yet the case reveals how harsh discipline can escalate and bring into public view conflicts that exist between traditional chiefs and the line ranks.

Source: Adapted from the New York Times National Edition, Sunday January 17, 1999, p. 10.

Values and the Limits of Ethics Reform

This chapter has developed three closely related themes. The first is that police recruits undergo a recruitment process designed to winnow out those who fail to carry appropriate values. Second, early socialization experiences reinforce those values. Third, historical and logical features of the police organization, and "upside down" bureaucracy, enables police to enact their values in discretionary encounters and creates substantial difficulties for chief executives to control their officers. This has implications for ethics training.

Most contemporary ethics education and training occurs either in universities and colleges, or in POST academy training. Ethics instruction ceases after pre-service training. Organizational accountability shifts to oversight vis-à-vis the enforcement of standard operating procedures (SOP) and internal affairs. The organization backs up SOP with threats of punishment for violators, and may have undercover officers in the field testing the corruptibility of traffic officers and detectives.

When officers are introduced to local police culture, they learn practical rules-of-thumb for maintaining harmony with other cops and for dealing with routine police problems. They learn to trust only other officers, to take charge of their assigned territories, to keep a low profile and avoid making waves, to always back up another officer, and how to use force. (Van Maanen, 1978; Reuss-Ianni, 1983; Shearing & Erickson, 1991; Manning, 1997; Crank, 1998). Their commitment to the noble cause is enclosed in a culture that will protect them from accountability, particularly by organizational management.

Recruits are hired because they satisfy minimum criteria of intelligence and physical health, and because they carry particular values about society and the role of police in it. They are then introduced to a working environment that encourages value-based decisionmaking. These values are reinforced during the training process. Ethics training that is counter-productive to those values is ineffective, is considered to be silly and a waste of time.

Ethics, to be taken seriously, has to be consistent with local cultural values, not run counter to them. The temptations of police work, the "seductions" of the unknown, the desire to be a prince of the street, of being tougher than the tough guys, must be acknowledged in efforts to deal with police ethics. These things link closely to police activity and morality – they are not inconsistent with it. Telling a cop not to accept a "free cup of coffee" just doesn't capture the wild, self-affirming energy of smashing a scumbag that just stole an old lady's purse. Besides, what cop's going to turn on another cop for "street-cleaning?" If ethics training doesn't recognize noble-cause corruption and how closely it's tied with values carried by line officers, then it's doomed to irrelevance.

Ethics should help an officer be a good cop. By good, we mean that ethics has to be consistent with other moral elements of the police craft, particularly the use of coercive force. Ethics cannot exist as a vaporous, universal set of beliefs taught at training and subsequently abandoned. If it is expressed as an abstract set of beliefs about rightness and wrongness, then it is useless. However, if it is a way to think about policing that actually makes police work more effective, and it is believed in and carried by commanders and trainers alike, it can infuse the organization with vitality and strength. Part 4 in this book will present a way to think about police ethics that we believe can achieve this goal.

Stress, Accountability, and the Noble Cause

6

In this chapter we look at some of the implications of value-based decisionmaking for managers and police organizations. We begin by considering the relationship between stress and value-based decisionmaking. This is followed by a discussion of the community environment in which police decisionmaking occurs, how the "system" protects itself, and implications for liability suits against police officers.

Stress and the Noble Cause

You're in a room full of police commanders. Ask them where their primary sources of stress come from – you might be surprised.

Mike did this. Looking across the room after a short break, he asked the commanders, *What is your primary source of stress?*

Before we get to what they said, some background is in order. Several years earlier, we collaborated in a paper about police stress. The paper was from research conducted among medium-sized departments in Illinois, but it could have been done anywhere and the findings probably wouldn't have changed much. At the back of the survey, there was what some researchers call a "throw-away" question, added without hope that there would be significant or even interesting findings, but inserted to involve the respondent in the survey. In this survey, the question was simply "What is your primary source of stress?" The question was asked without fanfare, just put out there bald-faced, as it were.

Findings were surprising – for non-cops. Some reviewers looked at our findings and thought that they represented a bunch of line officers grousing about their work. How would police executives respond?

Back to the room full of police executives. At first no one answered. But this is itself typical of cops. They don't tend to answer questions quickly. They'll sit back and look the question over, carefully, warily.

Mike repeated himself. *What is your primary source of stress? Where does it come from?*

One officer finally speaks, shrugging his shoulders at the same time "Well, the department."

You're exactly right. That, Mike observed, *is always the first choice that police make.*

Other officers murmured agreement.

What's another source?

The room was quiet for a minute. Another officer looked at the board, thought for a minute, and said "The department?"

Mike gave him a long look. *Exactly. The department, the department, the department. It's always the department. Why are you all killing yourselves?* It took a moment to digest that and move on. To use an old slang phrase, cops don't like being "put in the trick bag."[13]

Another officer responded "rules and regulations" a third, "policy." And so it went. Added to the list were the courts and the media. That was the list. What was missing?

Mike looked over his audience. *Do you realize that not one of you mentioned the dangers of police work?*

An officer in front responded "that's stress reduction." The commanders chuckled at this comment. Danger releases built-up police stress. To get a hot call – a crime in progress – and then show up and discover it's a bogus call, now that's stressful. How do many officers release the pent-up anxiety? They get off work, get a six-pack and toss it down.

Why isn't danger one of the commanders' sources of stress? It is because danger happens when a police officer is acting on behalf of the noble cause. Burning calories. Pumping adrenaline. Getting bad guys. Complaining about danger is too much like admitting weakness. Danger is not permitted to be a source of stress.

The perspective of these commanders was astonishingly similar to the perspective of the respondents to the survey we conducted in Illinois, although they were separated by a thousand miles and although one group was mostly line officers and the other police commanders (Crank & Caldero, 1991).

What source of stress is hard on the commanders in this session? The department. They aren't stressed out about the dangers of police work. One might respond that since they're managers, they aren't exposed to as much danger as line officers. But their answer was the same as the Illinois line officers. Go into any department and ask the officers there. Are you an officer? What stress is hard on you? When you feel those chest pains in your mid-forties, will it be from the danger of police work, or from putting up with all the organizational hassles?

Mike continued. *Look at stress. I think it's like this in every department. And what's number two on the stress list? The public. These are supposed to be the good guys, the guys you protect.*

The third source of stress identified by the group was the courts. Mike responded, *Oh, I really love this, especially from cops with bachelor's degrees.* "I just busted him and he's already back out on the streets." Mike pretends to be knocking someone in the forehead. *Hello in there. These are a series of procedurally regular steps. These steps apply to all citizens. It's the law. You had it in school. Innocent till proven guilty. Released on recognizance.*[14] *ROR . . . It's how things work. Don't these guys know that? There is a real lack of understanding.*

Let's review this. The organization is the principle source of stress. Second is the public. Third are the courts. Anyone who's read *Alice in Wonderland* can make perfect sense out of this. All the things that are supposed to be the most important, the most valued things in the professional life of a police officer are the things that they state are the most stressful.

Research on Police Stress

Stress is broadly defined as any condition that has adverse consequences for an individual's well-being. Adverse consequences include psychological characteristics such as depression, and physical characteristics might be suicide or divorce. An area of stress often studied is **role stress**, which refers to characteristics of a person's organizational role that produces adverse consequences for the individual. Role stress has been of particular concern to police researchers, who have been interested in the unique ways the occupation of policing affects the psychological and physical well-being of police officers.

Stress has been the subject of a great deal of research on the police (Goolkasian, Geddes & DeJong, 1989; Terry, 1985). Police stress research has historically focused on dangers of police work. This research followed the seemingly common-sense view that police work was dangerous, therefore danger was a principal source of stress. However, the relationship between danger and stress did not hold up under close scientific scrutiny, though fear of danger did (Cullen, Link, Wolfe & Frank, 1989).

The authors of this book conducted an investigation into perceptions of stress among eight Illinois Police Departments in the early 1990s. Findings were clear – stress was produced by the organization or factors related closely to the organization. Our findings have been supported by other related research (Launay & Fielding, 1989; Thomas, 1988). When stress, police officer burnout, and resignation was studied, the police organization played a prominent causal role.

The organization is also a source of stress for chief executives. Crank, Regoli, Hewitt, and Culbertson in 1993 found that police chiefs' stress was affected by both organizational and institutional features in their working environment. By institutional stressors, the authors referred to characteristics of their working environment over which they had little control. Together, the body of these findings suggest that, across the ranks in an organization, police are affected by organizational sources of stress, and these sources of stress are endemic to police organizations. Mike believes that this stress is closely tied to the noble cause.

Do you see what's going on here? I mean where your stress comes from? Your organization and the courts cause you stress. Why? It's because the way you think about the world is value-based.

You are committed to the noble cause, and these organizations have principles of procedure that interfere with your ability to seek noble-cause ends. That's stressful. And you blame rules of procedure. This us why you need to understand the values that motivate your officers. And this is why you need to understand yourselves.

Officers will resolve their role conflicts in a way consistent with their moral predispositions, by seeking noble ends. Hiring procedures and early departmental socialization guarantee this. But the value-based decisions made by officers carry consequences for managers and for the police organization. Mike describes these consequences as legitimacy and liability, and they are discussed in the next section.

Organizational Accountability Issues: Legitimacy and Liability

This section looks at police departments' efforts to maintain legitimacy in the municipal arena and what happens when legitimacy is undermined by the improper behavior of street officers. Liability will undercut organizational efforts aimed at legitimacy. This section discusses the overlapping issues of legitimacy and liability, and explains how the municipal system will protect itself when the credibility of the organization is undermined.

Mike continues. *Here are two reasons why you might begin to think about the value-based decisions your officers are making. Legitimacy and liability. L and L. If your officers are making the wrong decisions, you're going to have legitimacy problems, and you're going to have liability problems.*

Legitimacy and the Noble Cause

Do your officers understand about legitimacy? Chiefs do. Assistant chiefs do. Sheriffs do. It's when someone tells you that "you no longer represent the public."

This is a statement that riles police officers. Who says that the police don't represent the public? Well, sometimes the press says it. Sometimes a city council member will say it. They will accuse the police of being particularly brutal to some minority group member, or of corruption, or of excessive use of force during a routine encounter. Mothers Against Drunk Driving may accuse the department of not stopping and arresting enough drunks on the highway.

Legitimacy is whether influential constituents, who can be groups or individuals, agree with the way police do their work. Police organizations are embedded in police organizations in municipal and county politics, and departments are tied to other community groups who can make police work exceedingly unpleasant at both the executive and line levels. The close ties between police agencies and other municipal and county organizations need to be considered in conjunction with the behavior of street officers. Officers are value-based decisionmakers, and their decisions have enormous potential to create problems in the municipal arena of organizational interrelationships. Legitimacy affects police differently, depending on their rank. In the following section, we're going to consider the legitimacy issue at each rank level.

Legitimacy and Chiefs

For a police chief, maintaining legitimacy requires that they balance their expectations with those of municipal and departmental constituencies. Constituencies that they must work with include the mayor, city council, mid-level executives in the department, the public, media, business groups, the courts, the prosecutor's office, school boards and school administrators, police union and non-union labor representation, and sometimes other police organizations and the FBI.

Legitimacy is challenged when one of these constituents questions whether the police are doing their job. A department cannot simply ignore the opinions of people whose views affect the public or important voting constituencies. Chiefs and Sheriffs know. They will be fired or voted out of office if they don't address the concerns of powerful constituencies (Crank & Langworthy, 1992).

The chief's role is oriented toward the building of external liaisons with community groups. Chiefs are frequently involved in boundary-spanning activities – a great deal of their activity is in community-relations work with civic and political groups. **Boundary spanners** are individuals who represent the interests of the organization to other organizations and agencies in its environment. As Geller (1985:3-4) observed, chiefs confront the dilemma of balancing their professional autonomy with a need to be responsive to political constituencies, particularly the mayor. This is a large and compelling task.

Chiefs must also have legitimacy within their own departments. The chief may be hired as an outsider, but has to demonstrate to the rank and file as well that he or she is a *cop's cop* (Bordua & Reiss, 1986). Command control is achieved by acquiring personal loyalties, not in demonstrations of skill. The chief, more than any other actor in the organization, must convincingly demonstrate that he or she too is committed to the *noble cause* and to the loyalty that accompanies its moral territory. If the chief cannot gain the loyalty of the troops, even the most reasoned of organizational plans will quickly shatter against the shoals of internal department conflicts and cliques.

Legitimacy, Commanders, and Mid-Level Executives

Legitimacy issues have a direct bearing on the responsibilities of commanders and mid-level executives in police organizations. Police commanders and executives don't work the street unless they are in a small department. They do other kinds of work. Executives have responsibility for planning, management, and budget. Resource allocation is central to their work. The higher the rank of a police officer, the more they are involved in long-range budget forecasting. On a day-to-day basis, they are extensively involved in meetings with other executives in their organizations.

Geller and Swanger (1995:7-10) provide an excellent discussion of the responsibilities of middle managers in police organizations. They observed that, most of the time, middle managers are involved in keeping the promises made by higher-ups. These higher-ups are the chief, a city council member, and the mayor. Police managers consequently become involved in carrying out some of the concerns of people with political clout in the municipal arena. They may act on behalf of the chief to trans-

form those concerns into department policy, strategy, and concrete tactics that can be carried out by lower ranking officers in large organizations. Here is an example described by Geller and Swanger (1995:7).

Figure 6.1

> **Geller and Swanger:**
> **Administrators and Political Needs of Chiefs**
>
> Suppose that the chief or a city council member promises to develop
> the conflict management skills of first-line officers and sergeants to
> help reverse an escalating pattern of violent street conflict between
> Latino young men and young Anglo officers during field interroga-
> tions. Then the training manager and perhaps a special projects man-
> ager from the chief's office will need to explore ways to adjust the in-
> service and pre-service training curricula to accommodate the new
> topic without slighting other crucial aspects of education for effective
> training.

Recall the television series "Star Trek?" Each program began with a
vast expanse of space seen through the view-screen of the Starship Enterprise. The view is astonishing. Bells and buzzers suddenly go off, and
some sort of problem rapidly unfolds. The second-in-command quickly
briefs the Captain about what they have encountered. He suggests a way
to identify and correct the problem. The Captain responds *Make it so,
number 1*.

Managers adapt to a task environment fundamentally different than
street officers. Street officers adapt to a task environment made up of
unfriendly motorists, assholes, and petty criminals. Managers adapt to a
task environment made up of other managers, politicos, civic leaders and
community organizations. Put differently, while the work of line officers
are full of community non-respectables, the work of managers are full of
community respectables. These respectables want the police to do something about the kinds of problems that are meaningful to them. This
means that the nature of the noble cause shifts. Managers learn about
crime from the community itself, or from its elected or chosen leadership. Mothers Against Drunk Driving (MADD) wants to do something
about drivers that are drunk. A city councilman wants to make sure some
group is treated fairly. Another city councilman wants to find out why
police are so rude (his daughter was just arrested for DUI). The city manager wants police to stop stealth patrolling inside a downtown park
because some passed-out drunk was run over by a prowl car with its
lights out. The mayor's office wants a written report from the chief justifying the proposed budget. Or the prosecutor is miffed because a detective blew a crime scene investigation and ruined the evidence.

What do managers do? They are expected to respond to these respectables, to take into consideration their concerns while holding down their own particular responsibilities. So their commitment to the noble cause expands to encompass the views of these audiences. They have to demonstrate their loyalties to police values in the context of community respectables. In essence, they are constantly trying to "make it so," that is, make the organization legitimate in the eyes of powerful people whose opinions *count*. They are committed to tasks to satisfy political influentials, the mayor or the city council – or to help the chief make good his or her promises to those individuals – even when they think those tasks conflict with their work. They seek to carry out the chief's directives while protecting their small slice of the budget pie.

Although managers often complain about line officers, one can detect the noble-cause theme in their complaints. If one listens to ranking officers talk about line personnel, one might get the impression that they don't think too highly of them. That there's no bond across the ranks. That managers and line personnel are fundamentally different kinds of personalities. Without a doubt, there are rifts and clicks in all police organizations. But managers and line personnel are not different kinds of people, and one needs to read between the lines to understand this.

What are manager's principal grouses? They talk about how line officers are not committed to their work. Line officers won't follow procedures. They're just there for an 8 to 5 job. They can't deal with simple problems. What is the common theme in these complaints? They are saying that line officers today are not committed to the noble cause. Once you understand this, you realize the extent to which managers are themselves still committed to the noble cause. The moral commitment doesn't disappear when an officer moves into the ranks of bureaucracy. For many managers it's keener than ever.

Legitimacy and Patrol Officers

To understand legitimacy and patrol officers, we need to recognize that they respond to an altogether different constituency than chiefs. Their constituency is primarily the population that inhabits the street or that has been victimized: they deal with victims mostly, because they respond to calls about crime that have already taken place. They also deal with disinterested citizens, troublemakers, motorists, small-time criminals, and street people. These groups make up a street officer's social territory, the boundaries of which are determined by their assigned beats. The most important concerns officers have on these beats are maintaining control and preventing problems from getting out of hand. A great deal of their work consists of responding to calls, report taking and looking for criminal activity. Opportunities for "real police work," which means dealing with dangerous felons, are rare. Legitimacy in this environment is acted out in terms of loyalty to other officers and in commitment to the noble cause.

Line officers also deal with the courts. When they are called to testify, they find that the noble-cause standards of the street conflict with court expectations. As Crank (1998:34) observed, legitimacy in the courtroom involves "issues of the quality of the evidence and demeanor in front of the judge . . ." The courts are concerned with the technical quality of the evidence and behavior that conforms with the requirements of due process. Police are primarily interested in the factual guilt of suspects – virtually all of whom are presumed guilty (Klockars, 1983) – and consequently view the courts as being soft on crime. Police typically view the courts as untrustworthy; only they (police officers) can make the best determination about factual guilt or innocence. Crank (1998:256) captures the distinction between police and the court's standard of guilt:

> What is the standard? To get bad guys off the street. To use the law if it will work for them, but to use whatever tools cops have if the law won't. The ideal cop is trickier than the law. Cops know who is bad. When the courts disagree, it is a sorry day for the courts, a sad day for the public. That's the standard.

This quote captures the imagery evoked by the noble cause, and the way in which the noble cause has a different standard for justice than the courts. Legitimacy for police thus can put them squarely in conflict with the courts.

Legitimacy, Mike observes, has three operative principles. First, the department is part of a system, the municipal system of government. The second is that the system will protect itself. The third is that the toilet backs up.

Principle 1: The Department Is Part of a Municipal System

For line officers, the business of the police is dealing with bad guys. For commanders and executives, the business of the police is not so simple. Chiefs are not, and I can't emphasize this strongly enough, politically independent. They are in power at the pleasure of a mayor and city council, and if their organization is involved in scandal, they may be replaced (see Figure 6.2).

By **municipal system**, Mike is referring to the mutual interdependencies and obligations shared by the various members of the city and county business and public governance. A municipal system is made up of actors and groups who can directly or indirectly influence governance.[15] Consider, for example, chiefs and mayors. What do mayors want from chiefs? Consider the words of William Hudnut III, mayor of Indianapolis, Indiana. He stated simply "I have replaced two chiefs during my 10 years in office, and I would not hesitate to do so again to insure a responsive police department" (1985:26). But what does "responsiveness" mean? It is a term with an exceedingly vague meaning.

Figure 6.2

Mayors and Chiefs

The fate of mayors and chiefs are often closely aligned. Consider the following comments of Donald Frazer, former mayor of Minneapolis:

> In that decade alone (the 1970s) the department changes police chiefs seven times, with an equal number of turnovers at the command level. My own first campaign for mayor in 1979 was dominated by the issue of who should run the police and how best to professionalize the department. The conflict within the department began in 1969, when the head of the police union was elected mayor of Minneapolis on a strong law-and-order platform. He was re-elected two years later, but lost his third election to a democrat. His fourth try found him back in office, but on his fifth attempt, the public returned the democratic mayor, whom he defeated.
>
> This seemingly endless round of musical chairs in the mayor's office kept the department in a high pitch of political ferment. Each new shift in administration brought new shifts in departmental fortunes. Those who had pounded political signs for a losing candidate found themselves pounding remote pavements on graveyard shifts. Choice assignments were regarded strictly as political plums. (Frazer, 1985:42)

And Patrick Murphy (1985:38) notes darkly that "It may be tempting, especially for a new mayor, to place an informer or two inside the department to keep tabs on the chief's loyalty to city hall." These quotes reveal how tightly the fate of police chiefs is tied to municipal leadership in the mayor's office.

Former Chief Patrick Murphy observed that many issues should be negotiated between a mayor and a chief. **Negotiable issues** include the handling of media relations, issues incidentally related to crime control such as zoning matters and the management of school integration, and the mayor's role in personnel and organization of the agency. Although, Murphy noted, the chief should draw the line on the negotiability of some issues, he or she should tactfully take the mayor's counsel on those issues. **Non-negotiable issues** include some personnel decisions such as salaries and promotions. Even with non-negotiable issues, however, Murphy advises that the mayor's counsel should be taken. He observed, for example, that "the mayor should not be making decisions about appointments, promotions, transfers, or assignments, this is not to suggest that he should be deprived of a right to input" (1985:34).

Mayoral input into promotions? Assignments? Undoubtedly the provision of mayoral input into such areas requires political tact by a chief. The potential to alienate the troops with ill-advised promotional decisions is substantial. What is clear is the extent to which the police chief is more than a "cop's cop." The police chief is also a citywide policymaker whose decisions are influenced and acted out in the municipal political arena, and whose success, and longevity on the job, rises or falls on his or her political acumen. The legitimacy of the police organization is worked out in this arena.

Principle 2: The Municipal System Will Protect Itself

Departments will endeavor to resolve problems before they threaten the working relationships in the municipal system. What kinds of problems can do this? Sometimes only a single incident can create legitimacy problems, for example, a line officer who used too much coercion on a suspect, or departmental corruption uncovered by the newspapers. In the case of Rodney King in Los Angeles, a case in which officers were ultimately prosecuted for criminal conduct, the precipitating incident was an instance of brutality captured on camera, released to the Cable News Network (CNN), and broadcast on national television. The loss of legitimacy means that the municipal audience no longer accepts the way in which the police organization does its business.

The process of legitimacy lost and regained can be ugly. When legitimacy is lost, a ceremonial process occurs (Crank & Langworthy, 1991). The newspapers and media publicly degrade the police department in front-page exposés. Previous political friends of the chief will no longer talk to him or her. Various groups begin to create pressures for the removal of the chief. Ultimately, the department will be publicly humiliated and the chief likely fired and replaced by a new chief who promises to clean up the department. It is an ugly process carried out in public, providing rich carrion for the newspapers and their readership. Departments will avoid a loss of legitimacy at all cost. This is where the third principle is activated.

Principle 3: The Toilet Backs Up

Meyer and Rowan (1992) observed that public sector organizations operate by a **logic of good faith**. They act out powerful values carried by society, and their members believe in what they do. Members have good faith that the organization will do the right thing, and it is difficult for them to understand how their organization can be responsible when problems occur.

Figure 6.3

> **Good Faith and the Logic of Confidence**
>
> The logic of confidence is what Goffman (1967) calls "face work" – the process of maintaining the other's face or identity and thus of maintaining the plausibility and legitimacy of the organization itself. Face work avoids embarrassing incidents and preserves the organization from the disruption of an implausible performance by any actor. (Meyer & Rowan, 1992:90). In a police organization, an "implausible performance by an actor" would be an incident in which a street officer acted in a way inconsistent with the official purposes of the organization, such as using brutality or violating a suspect's due process rights.

It is like this with police organizations as well. It is almost impossible for police officers to think that their department, which in the public mind refers to line officers, is itself morally at fault in some way. The notion rings of disloyalty. So when a legitimacy problem occurs, a police department will not look at what it's doing wrong. It will try to protect itself, absolutely believing in the rightness of its purposes. It will blame "rotten apples" rather than look at what the organization might be doing wrong. What line officers don't understand is that the department will sacrifice them in order to maintain legitimacy.

How do police organizations respond to problems that might result in a loss of legitimacy? The Knapp Commission (1972), an investigatory body in New York City in the early 1970s noted that departments tend to respond with the "individual officer explanation."

The Knapp commission was investigating widespread corruption in the New York Police Department and issued its report in 1972. They noted that, even in the face of pervasive corruption, higher-ranking personnel did not accept the notion that the organization itself was fundamentally at fault. Managers, they observed, were unable to acknowledge the depth of the problem. In Meyer and Rowan's (1992) terms, they were operating on a logic of good faith. They believed that the problem could be explained by the presence of "bad apples," individual officers who were themselves bad.

So, to use the colorful phrase, the toilet begins to back up, as it did during the Knapp Commission investigation. First, individual officers, so-called rotten apples, were blamed. They were prosecuted. But the toilet was still backing up. The department blamed "rotten pockets:" groups of officers working together. If the toilet is still backing up after rotten pockets are corrected, the mayor will fire the chief. If the department cannot maintain its legitimacy, the system will act to protect itself.

The Liability Issue, or "What Did I Just See on CNN?"

The chief picks up the phone. It's 6 a.m. "Who's this?"

"Chief, I'm sorry to call you at home."

"Yea, well, what's up?"

"Chief, I think you ought to turn on CNN. The one where they play the same news every half hour. Call me back later on a secured line. We'll talk then."

Outsiders have a mythical idea about the control police chiefs have over police departments. They think that a directive from the police chief can immediately change the behavior of street officers. They think that if a city councilman tells the chief to quit being so tough on Latinos, well, the chief can go down and harangue the troops, and everything will change. Indeed, many chiefs have been fired because city leaders believed that chiefs had more power over the day-to-day operations of their department than they actually did.

Line officers know better. They know that the chief doesn't come down and talk to them, and that chiefs have very little effect on what they do. The person that they respond to is the sergeant. And the sergeant is easy to satisfy. Sergeants have their activity that they want line officers to do, and that's about it.

Line officers know what the chief expects of them primarily because they hear new policies being read during roll call. Officers are getting their leads primarily from other officers in the field, and their behavior is motivated by the values of noble cause and loyalty.

If your officers are taking their leads from other officers in the field, they're making value-based decisions, not law-based ones. How can you know if you have a problem? You'll have a lot of litigation against the department. It's a sure indicator of that your officers are using the law to carry out a moral standard.

An Overview of Law Regarding Litigation Against the Police

Let's review the law regarding litigation against the police. The following discussion on litigation is adapted from Meadows (1996).

Police can be held liable for inappropriate or wrongful behavior, regardless of intent. The most common action that citizens can take against the police is called a Title 42 of the United States Code, Section 1983. It is printed in Figure 6.4.

Figure 6.4

Title 42 of U.S. Code, Section 1983

Every person who, under color of any statute, ordinance, regulation, custom, or usage, of any State or Territory or the District of Columbia, subjects, or causes to be subjected, any citizen of the United States or other person within the jurisdiction thereof to the deprivation of any rights, privileges, or immunities secured by the Constitution and laws, shall be liable to the party injured in any action at law, suit in equity, or other proper proceeding for redress, except that in any action brought against a judicial officer for an act or omission taken in such officer's judicial capacity, injunctive relief shall not be granted unless a declaratory decree was violated or declaratory relief was unavailable. For the purposes of this section, any Act of Congress applicable exclusively to the District of Columbia shall be considered to be a statute of the District of Columbia.

Title 42, Section 1983 was written originally to protect American citizens against the Ku Klux Klan. It is currently the most popular tool to use against the police, for the following reasons:

1. Civil lawsuits are filed in federal court, where discovery is relatively liberal. It is easier to acquire documents and records from the defendant.

2. Cases filed in the federal courts do not have to first exhaust state court remedies.

3. The prevailing plaintiff can recover attorney's fees under the Attorney's Fee Act of 1976. Attorneys consequently may be more inclined to accept these cases. (Meadows, 1996:105)

Under what circumstances can a "Section 1983," as these cases are commonly called, be filed against a police officer? First, the police officer has to be acting under the color of law, which means that an individual is acting in an official capacity as a police officer. This includes illegal acts performed while on duty. Second, there has to be a constitutional violation of some federally protected right. Third, the courts will accept both intentional acts by a police officer and acts in which an officer acted negligently. **Intentional torts** refer to a wanton disregard for a person's rights. **Negligent torts** refer to a failure to protect the public from harm. For an incident to be negligent, the following conditions apply:

1. The officer must have a duty.

2. The duty wasn't performed.

3. There must be a relationship between the duty and the failure to perform.

4. There must be damage or injury. (Meadows, 1996:106)

Use of force is a common type of suit brought against the police. The police are permitted to use non-deadly and deadly force, but the use of force must be reasonable and appropriate. Moreover, an acquittal in a state court does not necessarily mean that a federal case will end the same. As Meadows observed, two Los Angeles police officers acquitted in the Rodney King case, a case involving the use of less than lethal violence, were later convicted in a federal court.

Use of force is not the only kind of incident that can prompt litigation. The other principle causes for litigations are auto pursuits, arrests and searches, employee drug tests, hiring and promotion, discrimination, recordkeeping and privacy, and jail management (McCoy, 1987, in Meadows, 1996:107).

One of the officers responds to Mike's statements on liability. "We take liability pretty seriously in this department." Mike does a double-take. *Oh, you do? I'm glad to hear it. I'm really glad. Because most departments don't. Did you know that officers who are sued are twice as likely to be promoted as to be punished?* (see Figure 6.5) *I'm glad to hear that this department doesn't promote officers who are sued.*

Mike concludes. *If you are being sued and are paying large liability payments, you need to ask yourself why. What kind of case generates liability? Officer incompetence? Sure. Look at the newspapers. Are the big liability settlements from incompetence? Or are they from noble-cause corruption? If you look at them closely, can you see how value-based decisionmaking is costing you a bundle? This is why you need to know the value-basis of the decisions your officers are making on behalf of your department.*

Figure 6.5

Litigation, Brutality, and Promotion

Current research suggests that liability is infrequently punished. Consider the following report from the Human Rights Watch (1998):

Gannett News Service published a series of investigative articles in March 1992 examining the fate of police officers named in 100 civil lawsuits in 22 states in which juries ordered $100,000 or more to be paid to plaintiffs between 1986 and 1991. The awards from the lawsuits totaled nearly $92 million. Of 185 officers involved in these cases, only eight were disciplined. No action was taken against 160, and 17 were promoted. The reporter concluded that taxpayers are penalized more for brutality than the officers responsible for the beatings.

Stress and Ignoble Consequences

Do you see why these things bother you? The department, the courts? The public? Mike asks. *You believe in the noble cause. So do I. But you're facing legitimacy problems, and you're being sued. Whose fault is it?*

"The organization again?" offers a captain. The other participants laugh.

It's always the organization. Mike responds, smiling. *Always. But you're the organization.*

The room is silent.

The principal sources of stress are not from the organization. Nor are they from the courts, or from the public. These groups are the manifestations of the problem. The problem lies in the commitment to the noble cause, a logic of good faith that all will work out if only officers are committed enough to good ends, and an almost blind failure to recognize how the noble cause is implicated in legitimacy and liability problems. Officers don't recognize that they resent the courts, the organization and the public when these groups interfere with the noble cause, the good end.

Remember that officer I mentioned at the beginning of the chapter? The one who, with his college education, didn't understand how bad guys were back out on the street the day after they were arrested? He was stressed over the courts. And he knew better. That officer's going to get you in trouble. There's your problem. Not the courts.

This, Mike concludes, *is why we need to recognize how value-based decisionmaking can bring many problems to you and to your department. We'll talk about some other ways of thinking about values after lunch.*

The Means-Ends Dilemma

Part 3

Noble-cause corruption is a particular kind of ethical dilemma. But what kind of dilemma is it, and how can we think about it ethically? How does it manifest itself on the job? Part 3 looks at both the theoretical or ethical aspects of noble-cause corruption and its practical applications. Chapter 7 locates noble-cause corruption as a kind of ethical problem widely described as a means-ends dilemma. By looking at different ethical systems, we see how noble cause is consistent with some ethical systems and violates ethical principles in others. Packer's due process and crime control model is used to illustrate ethical viewpoints and show some of the problems associated with noble-cause corruption. We conclude this chapter with the argument that police officers acquire their working sense of ethics from other important actors in their working environment who are committed to court efficiency and noble-cause outcomes. Various actors in the criminal justice system, including prosecutors and judges, directly or indirectly encourage noble-cause corruption.

Chapter 8 looks at the relationship between police culture and noble-cause corruption. We argue that police culture is a powerful shielding force that protects officers from external inspection and accountability. When noble cause is systematically corrupted in an organization, police culture becomes a principle force for its perpetuation. The chapter closes with a discussion of the types of noble-cause corruption, and how police culture perpetuates them.

Ethics and the Means-Ends Dilemma

7

Key Terms

code of silence	justice efficiency
crime control model	means-ends continuum
dilemma of ends- oriented-ethics	station-house sergeants
due process model	street sergeants
deontological	teleological
golden apples	value-based decisionmaking
	wall of silence

Ethical Systems

Commanders return from lunch. Mike begins the afternoon's presentation with a discussion of ethical systems. The purpose of this discussion is to distinguish between the types of systems, and then to identify the ethical perspective that the police tend to use.

Mike: *Ethics is an expression of a person's values. You hire cops that have a common perspective. That's what you hired them for. And that common perspective is underpinned by a common set of values. If we can identify those values, we can predict how they're going to make decisions. If we apply that knowledge, we can lower their stress, save lives, cut down on liability, improve the legitimacy of the organization, make policy more effective.*

To do ethics, go to the old philosophy books. I did this. You can read in that field for 10 years and not know what you've read. You have to pare it down. I'm going to throw two terms at you. Deontological and teleological.

Deontological and teleological are long-winded terms that describe the way a person thinks through ethical problems. **Deontological**, in its simplest form, means that a person is means oriented. The Christian maxim "do unto others as you would have them do unto you" is deontological – it provides a basis for behavior regardless of consequences. In a democracy, a belief that due process outweighs considerations of factual guilt is a form of deontology. Both Christianity and democracy are grounded in the idea that means – specifically, the way we act – are more important than the ends sought by actors.

Teleological ethics, simply put, means that a person is goal- or end-oriented. Utilitarianism is teleological.[16] It is grounded in the notion that what is good is determined by what produces the greatest good for the greatest number, *regardless of how that end is achieved*. To be ethically teleological is to be focused on "the bottom line." For example, a business manager might decide that he or she must focus on profit above all other considerations. If the manager concludes that employee layoffs are necessary in order to maintain a satisfactory profit margin, the manager is making a teleological, or ends-oriented, decision. In Figure 7.1, Joycelyn Pollock provides the following summary definition of these two ethical principles:

Figure 7.1

Deontological and Teleological Ethical Systems

A deontological ethical system is one that is concerned solely with the inherent nature of the act being judged. If an act is inherently good, then even if it results in bad consequences, it is still a good act. Teleological systems are interested in the consequences of an act. An act may look "bad," but if it results in good consequences, then it can be defined as good under a teleological system.

Source: Joycelyn M. Pollock, *Ethics in Crime and Justice*, 1998:27-28.

The interested reader is referred to Pollock (1998) for an excellent review of these and other ethical concepts and their applications across the criminal justice system.

The Dilemma of Ends-Oriented Ethics: You Can Never Know

Mike presents four scenarios to commanders. *Think of the difference between teleological and deontological ethics like this. If I do a dirty car stop, and I find drugs as a consequence, conduct an illegal search, and I'm ends oriented or teleological, then I've done something good. If I'm deontological, concerned about the ethical means of my behavior, then regardless of the outcome, I have committed an immoral act.*

I'm going to give four scenarios that show that the outcome is always unmanageable. Mike describes the following four scenarios, and they are discussed by the commanders.

Scenario 1 has a great deal of meaning for police officers. It will boil the blood of many officers, and fear of this kind of event will justify corruption of the noble cause.

Figure 7.2

Scenario 1

Two officers observe a vehicle containing a suspected drug dealer driving down the street in a high-crime area at 2 a.m. Although the vehicle is exceeding the maximum posted speed limit, the officers only have the legal right to stop the vehicle, issue a traffic citation, and question the driver. Upon stopping the vehicle, the officers' suspicions are confirmed, the driver has been previously arrested several times for drug dealing. However, he has no outstanding warrants, appears to be perfectly sober, and produces a valid driver's license. The officers issue the citation and allow the driver to proceed on his way.

Later that evening it is learned that the same suspect sold one-quarter ounce of contaminated heroin to two high school students who both suffered fatal overdoses. The suspect was not apprehended.

Scenario 2 is a different outcome for the same event, what we call an "over the rainbow" scenario. The officers acted out of a commitment to the noble cause: the bad guy was put away because they cared enough. The law didn't stop them. It is the way noble-cause corruption is supposed to end – a bad guy is off the street and officers are rewarded. However, it does not always end this way. Consider Scenario 2.

Figure 7.3

Scenario 2

Two officers observe the same vehicle under the exact circumstances. On this occasion, feeling a strong sense of moral outrage over the death of young victims, they proceed as follows. One officer orders the suspect out of the car and to the rear of the patrol car, where he is legally patted down for weapons and questioned in detail concerning his activities in the area, a perfectly legal procedure. However, the second officer proceeds to search the interior of the vehicle and locates under the front seat a brown paper sack containing numerous plastic bags each holding approximately one-quarter ounce of a white powdery substance resembling heroin. The officer then removes two of the plastic bags and drops them in plain sight on the passenger side floorboard. Of course, these actions are entirely illegal.

The second officer then walks back to the rear of the patrol vehicle and begins his own questioning of the driver. The first officer proceeds to the suspect vehicle and looks through the passenger-side window and from the outside observes the suspicious plastic bags. He quite legally retrieves them and extends the search to the rest of the vehicle where he discovers the brown paper sack with the remaining plastic bags. The first officer promptly places the suspect under arrest for possession of a controlled substance with intent to deliver.

The suspect is convicted. In order to secure a lesser sentence, he reveals information about his drug source. The operators of an illegal lab are quickly arrested and convicted through quite legal procedures. Both officers are officially commended by the mayor.

In Scenario 3, the officers pay a heavy price in terms of their careers. As Mike noted, they had failed to consider the police version of Pascal's wager (see Chapter 1).

Figure 7.4

Scenario 3

All of the facts of this case are identical with Scenario 2, except that during a subsequent trial a witness surfaces with a videotape of the entire stop and arrest of the suspected drug dealer. Pointing to the illegal search of the vehicle, the suspect's attorney quickly obtains the release of his client. Both officers are severely reprimanded for their conduct and denied the possibility of promotion for several years.

Scenario 4, with unanticipated outcomes like the previous one, also reveals one of the darker aspects of police culture. Officers who will not back up another officer, even when the issue concerns the illegal conduct of a police officer rather than danger on the job, will suffer an unkind fate. Fellow officers are likely to unite against him or her.

Figure 7.5

Scenario 4

The facts of the case are identical to Scenario 2 except that during the trial, the second officer is called to testify concerning the actions of his/her partner. Under unrelenting pressure from the client's lawyer and believing in the oath, the officer gets cold feet and testifies that officer number 1 illegally searched the suspect's vehicle just prior to the discovery of the illegal drugs. The case is subsequently dropped, and the offending officer is fired.

The second officer is subsequently shunned for failing to back up his/her partner and cannot find a compatible partner for several years. Subsequent difficulties force the officer to seek employment in another profession.

These scenarios describe a central moral dilemma confronting ends-oriented ethics. You can never be certain beforehand that the outcome will be what you think it will be. You can never know.

Let's consider a slightly different kind of scenario. This is a "thought experiment." Imagine that you're a patrol officer. Suppose you pull in behind a speeding motorist, and instead of pulling over he takes off and tries to outrun you. Many departments in the country have an unwritten rule that runners get thumped. It's a question of territorial control. When someone runs, it's disrespect, and they get thumped. You are able to force the driver into a stop. You know your partner expects you to thump this guy. What are you going to do? If you don't, your partner might not think that you're trustworthy. If you do, you're acting with brutal force.

Can you say to yourself "I thought that beating the crap out of this jerk would make the city safer?" Sure you could, if you were ends-oriented. You made a decision that you thought was good for society. The greatest good for the greatest number. All done by thumping one "jerk." That is an example of a teleological ethical judgment.

Let's imagine that you are videotaped and what you did is broadcast on national news, and the cameras show you beating this troublemaker. Now the world sees you as the bad guy, the problem cop that has to be fixed. The chief may hang you out to twist in the wind. Where can you hide?

This example again reveals the uncertainty in ends-oriented thinking. A police officer can never be certain that the outcome will be what they want it to be. In the "thought experiment" above, the outcome could have become a multi-million dollar lawsuit against the city, civil litigation, and possibly, criminal litigation. But it could as easily have been a non-event – the officer might have gone home, feeling good about himself or herself.

Efforts to bring about "noble-cause" good ends can sometimes go catastrophically wrong. Such an incident is described by Barker and Carter (1999) in Figure 7.6 below.

Figure 7.6

The Death of a Boston Detective

Consider the efforts of a Boston detective to bring an accused cop killer to justice:

> Recently, charges were dropped against an accused cop killer and three Boston police officers were suspended with pay pending a perjury investigation. The perjury involved a Boston detective who "invented" an informant. The detective maintained that the informant gave critical information which was cited in the affidavit for a search warrant (*New York Times*, 1989:K9). The "no knock" search warrant's execution led to the death of a Boston detective. (Barker & Carter, 1999:347-348)

The officers, subsequently charged with perjury, had "fluffed up the evidence." They illegally invented an informant in order to conduct a search. In this instance, a detective's life was sacrificed in the name of the noble cause.

Ends Control and the Wall of Silence

Many observers of the police have described what they call a code of silence. By **wall of silence**, we mean the inability of outsiders, including managers, to find out information about incidents involving line officers. The wall of silence is marked by officers who refuse to talk about what other officers do, even when it involves illegal behavior. It is viewed by managers as a principal source of resistance to police reform.

The wall of silence, we think, is closely linked to efforts to control "ends." It represents an effort on the part of officers to control the outcomes of events. By erecting a "wall of silence" around street happenings involving officers, a principal threat to ends-oriented behavior is removed – managers and the public will not know about questionable police behavior that might result in review or negative publicity.

The wall of silence, in other words, is a mechanism to control information. Yet even the wall of silence may sometimes fail. Figure 7.7, an example of a crack in the wall of silence, is an example of how ends cannot be controlled.

Figure 7.7

The Wall of Silence and Perjury

Sometimes the wall of silence cracks. Under enough pressure, it can crumble. In the following incident, officers tried to cover up the beating of a suspect who was actually an undercover officer.

The incident began when a large number of officers rushed to the scene of a shooting, having mistakenly heard that a police officer had been injured. The suspects led the police officers on a 10-mile chase, and eventually were cornered in a cul-de-sac. In the ensuing melee, some of the officers confused an undercover officer for one of the suspects and attacked him. He was treated for a concussion, kidney damage, and multiple cuts to his face.

The official report did not report the attack by police. Instead, the official report stated that the undercover officer had lost his footing and cracked his head. None of the officers on the scene came forward to tell the truth at a subsequent hearing, in spite of the fact that several of them were in the vicinity and were involved in the pursuit. Two dozen officers reported that they saw no beating. One of the officers on the scene, however, testified that he had not seen the undercover officer pursue the suspects. He was subsequently convicted of perjury and obstruction of justice in a federal court.

The event has all the indications of noble-cause revenge – emotionally charged officers, acting on erroneous information that another officer was injured, attack a suspect. Two mistakes were made, however. No officer was injured, and the suspect was another officer. The wall of silence descended to protect the officers in the case. Yet it was not enough to protect all the officers; one was convicted of serious federal charges. This example shows that, even when the "wall of silence" is invoked to control outcomes, outcome control is not always possible.

Source: Adapted from The New York Times Online, "Officer Convicted of Perjury," http://www/nytimes.com/aponline/a/AP-Police-Beating.Html

Golden Apples and the Noble Cause

Chiefs will explain away corruption problems as individual-level corruption. They will find fault with what they call "rotten apples," officers who are morally corrupt but somehow slipped through pre-employment screening. What's a rotten apple? A rotten apple is someone who's bad to the core, who is acting alone out of his or her own badness, who, left unchecked, will spread the rot to the rest of the department. It is a favorite explanation for departments deeply in denial (Knapp Commission, 1972).

However, in the case of moral-cause corruption, officers who violate the law or department policy aren't rotten apples. To the contrary, they're dealing with crime in an efficient and effective way. Mike explains the dilemma as follows: *If you believe in the moral rightness of good ends, that the noble cause is incorruptible – and remember, that's what you hired your officers for – these are your golden apples and you're one of them.*

What is a golden apple? A **golden apple** is an officer, intelligent, committed to the noble cause, and highly focused on efficiency and effectiveness. These officers may represent the "best" police officers in a graduating police academy, that is, those who score the highest on tests and who morally exhort their fellow officers. They are morally committed to their work, dedicated, and energetic. Golden apples view crime from a teleological ethical perspective. They believe in the morally right ends of police work. Yet, sometimes the golden apples will be the officers that corrupt the noble cause, that break the laws and violate policy in order to "do something about crime and criminals." In some cases, they believe in their work too much, and sacrifice all for the "good end."

Mike addresses the chief, also present at the conference. *Chief, how well do you know your troops?* This is an unexpected question to ask a chief. The chief attends out of courtesy, to show he's supporting the conference. Mike continues.

Look at how it would force us to address the problem differently if we faced it squarely. If you acknowledged that you had people working for you who were making moral decisions, acting in the name of the noble cause.

Instead of blaming a rotten apple, we begin to see how the department's policies and practices are implicated in the problems police departments face. The rotten-apple argument is a form of denial.

Mike decides to push the point. He turns to the commanders. *Is there a moral justification for thumping an asshole? It happens all the time. You should look for another explanation. Have you ever done an asshole?*

The commanders don't respond.

Have you seen someone do an asshole? I know I have. Now, if I'm means-oriented, then thumping a jerk is morally wrong. If I'm means-oriented, what am I not doing anymore? No free coffee. No thumping. No free meals. No bending the law to do the right thing.

He looks at his audience. *No one's reacting. Someone react.*

A supervisor responds. "I think that there are a lot of us who believe in doing the right thing. Our cases would be thrown out if we weren't. Prosecutors have to review cases. A lot would be thrown out."

I hear both sides. What you said is what supervisors say. They don't see it very often. They've forgotten about the magic pencil. You show me any rules and I can write around them. The report will be fantastic. You won't know. If the decisions are made at the bottom of the organizational pyramid then how can you check? Have you checked? Do you really understand what's going on? It's nice to think that there isn't much, but do you really know?

For the first time, the supervisor begins to understand. Mike has brought the point home. They supervise, they take and file reports, but they don't know what's going on in their department. Not for sure.

Due Process and Crime Control –
Where's Your Department?

In this section we're going to think about value-based decisionmaking. Some simple ethical exercises will show how values influence decisionmaking. We'll then develop a means-ends continuum and overlay it with Packer's crime control model to describe police values.

Value-Based Decisionmaking

Value-based decisionmaking means that police officers make judgments about the likely predispositions, behaviors, and social worth of citizens, suspects, citizens, street people, and troublemakers they talk to, and their behavior follows from these judgments. Central to police values are a commitment to the noble cause and the departmental loyalties that reinforce that commitment.

The following imaginary cases are fanciful, but they help to clarify the kind of judgments that involve value-based decisionmaking. These imaginary cases initially focus the good of the many versus the few, but gradually introduce noble-cause kinds of decisions.

Case #1. You're a switchman. An out-of-control train is barreling down the tracks. If you don't throw the switch, the train is going to run over a drunk collapsed on the tracks. If you do, the train is going to run into a schoolbus full of children. Are you going to throw the switch?

Case #2. You're a switchman. An out-of-control train is barreling down the tracks and is going to run into a schoolbus full of children. If you throw the switch, it will change tracks and run over an unconscious drunk instead. Are you going to throw the switch?

These cases are similar in that both involve a decision that seems as if it will end in a loss of life. Case #2 has a more complicated morality for individuals who want to save the bus of children – they must make an active move to save the bus, a move that will kill the drunk. They do not need to do anything in the first case.

A teleological (ends-oriented) ethic will direct most readers to save the schoolbus full of kids. The good of the many are placed ahead of an individual. The decision is fortified by a moral sympathy about the kinds of people they are saving and opinions about the social worth of the characters in the example. What could go wrong in a decision to save the busload of kids? In fact, several things could go wrong.

1. The decisionmaker misunderstands the design of the switch and throws it the wrong way, sending the train into the busload of kids.

2. The train doesn't change tracks after the decisionmaker throws the switch, but gets caught on a track spur, derails, and kills everyone.

3. The decisionmaker changes the switch to kill the drunk, and the bus starts up, and pulls off the track in time to save the students.

4. The drunk is not killed but loses both legs, sues the decisionmaker and her department. The decisionmaker is also charged with involuntary manslaughter. Convicted, the decisionmaker spends a year on probation and the police department settles out of court for $800,000.

5. All of the students in the bus have exited, but they're on the other side of the bus and the decisionmaker can't see them. The "real" choice, though the decisionmaker didn't recognize it at the time, was between killing a drunk and killing no one. The decisionmaker is subsequently charged with involuntary manslaughter. Though found not guilty, she becomes despondent and commits suicide.

You Can Never Know That the Outcome Will Be What You Want It to Be

How about the following case?

Case #3. You're a surgeon in a small hospital. There was a bus accident. Three injured passengers need transplants immediately to survive. A climber is brought in who has been knocked out from a short fall. What will you do? Will you sacrifice the climber to save the three injured passengers?

A teleological ethic will lead a decisionmaker to respond "yes," and a deontological, means-oriented logic will lead to a "no" response. I suspect that if the reader is a doctor he or she won't violate the Hippocratic oath and sacrifice the climber. Let's change the case a little.

Case #4. You've just arrived at a hospital. You're a trained doctor and one of the few unhurt victims of a bus accident that killed 14 youngsters. The driver of the vehicle that caused the accident is brought in. His breath smells of alcohol. He has a head wound and you think he might die without immediate medical attention. Three children need transplants immediately to survive. What would you do?

In this instance we can see how ethical judgments are complicated by the values we carry. To fail to try to save the drunken driver is a violation of the Hippocratic oath. If a person can make a decision in the fourth case unaffected by the feelings and values in which they're immersed at the hospital, they probably aren't human and certainly will never be a cop. Cops identify with victims, particularly children. And they have bad attitudes about drunken drivers that kill people. For many police officers, the decision is not morally difficult. The driver of the vehicle causing the wreck would be proudly volunteered to mend his ways (if not his body) and take the honorable route to immortality.

A Continuum of Value-Based Decisions

Mike: *Ethical orientations can be put on a continuum.*

He sketches a continuum on the blackboard, with means orientation on one side and ends orientation on the other. The continuum is reproduced below.

In this section, we're going to create a continuum that enables us to think about value-based decisionmaking. It is a means-ends continuum, and criminal justice values will be placed on it. By looking about the way in which individuals locate themselves on the scale, we can assess the values that undergird their decisionmaking.

The means-ends continuum is presented below.

Figure 7.8

The Means-Ends Continuum									
Ethical Orientation									
1	2	3	4	5	6	7	8	9	10
	Means-Oriented or Deontological or Due Process			Value Balance			Ends-Oriented or Teleological or Crime Control		

On this continuum, a score of 1 means that a person is deontological in their decision-making ethic. They are concerned about the way they act, independent of the consequences of their actions. A score of 10 indicates that a person is teleological. How things come out outweigh the behavior we choose to get there. In Cases 1 and 2 discussed earlier in this chapter, decisionmakers tended to be ends-oriented, with scores at the 8 or 9 level. Examples 3 and 4 were more complicated, but they showed that decisionmakers still tended to be ends-oriented. An ends orientation is characteristic of the way police think about their work, as we'll see in the next section.

Means-Ends as Crime Control Versus Due Process

Teleological (ends) and deontological (means) ethics can be observed in Herbert Packer's (1968) models of criminal justice. Herbert Packer described two models of criminal justice, models that matched widely shared views of how the justice system should operate. The **crime control model** focuses on the ends of justice – obtaining conviction and treating felons harshly. Punishment of the guilty is a primary concern. The **due process model** looks at how the justice system treats suspects and offenders. Protection of the innocent is a primary concern. These assumptions reflect the central values embodying crime control and due process in the United States. They fit a means-ends model as well. Mike uses Packer's models to demonstrate the ends orientation that characterizes most police officers as well as criminal justice organizations generally. Figure 7.9 presents the seven elements of Packer's two models.

Mike addresses the audience of commanders. *Now we're going to examine the values that characterize your department. We're going to superimpose a model of Herbert Packer's two models of criminal justice over the ends-means continuum.*

What I want you to do is to think a minute, and then tell me where your department falls on this continuum. Consider each of the seven items. Are you on the left? In the middle? On the right? Chances are that, unless you have had a major shake-up in your agency recently, you will have higher scores and be over on the crime-control side. We have seen managers rate their departments up around 9 and 10.

If your department is 8 or above, there is a pretty strong likelihood that you are either having problems you know about or problems you don't yet know about. Let's think about the officers you have in the department. You will have very few if any officers that are means-oriented. If they believe due process is more important than crime control, they have probably self-selected themselves out of the occupation of policing. Or they're in internal affairs.

Figure 7.9

Herbert Packer's Two Models of the Criminal Justice Process

Crime Control Model

1. Repression of criminal conduct is the most important function performed by the criminal justice process.
2. A failure of law enforcement means a breakdown of order, necessary for freedom.
3. Criminal process is the positive guarantor of social freedom.
4. **Efficiency** is the top priority of the model. By efficiency is meant the ability to apprehend, try, and convict high numbers of criminals whose offenses become known.
5. There is an emphasis on speed and finality. Facts can be provided more quickly through interrogation than through courtroom examination and cross-examination.
6. The conveyor belt is the model for the system. This is a steady stream of cases from arrest through conviction.
7. A presumption of guilt makes it possible for the system to deal efficiently with large numbers of felons.

Due Process Model

1. The reliability of the criminal justice process is closely examined. The model focuses on the possibility of error. It is particularly concerned with the third degree and coercive tactics.
2. The outcome is in question as long as there is a factual challenge. Finality is not a priority.
3. There is an insistence on prevention and elimination of mistakes in factual assessments of culpability.
4. If efficiency demands shortcuts around reliability, then efficiency is to be rejected as a system goal. The aim of the process is as much the protection of innocents as punishment of the guilty.
5. The combination of stigma and deprivation that government inflicts is the end goal.
6. The coercive power of the state is always subject to abuse. Maximum efficiency means maximum tyranny.
7. A person is to be found guilty if and only if a factual finding of guilt is accompanied with procedural rigor in the criminal justice process.

Recall the nature of the hiring and training process and how the noble cause is at the center of it. The question is not the extent to which your officers are committed to doing something about bad guys. Oh, they're committed, all right. The question is what they're willing to do to get bad guys off the street.

If your officers are overfocused on the crime control end, you're in an organization that may have some problems. In high-scoring orga-

nizations, there is a strong likelihood that there are many complaints against officers. It is also likely that cliques are dominating line-admin-istrative relations. You are getting a lot of litigation. Are you? Mike scans the room, making brief eye contact with various commanders. Their faces are expressionless, giving nothing away. Mike lets the moment linger, then continues.

You're probably being trashed by the newspapers. If you're an administrator, this means that you know you're getting a lot of bullshit from your rank and file.

When problems emerge, police managers are often in denial about what is going on, either from the logic of good faith or because they are out of the information loop. If commanders are intensely focused on crime control, they may not want to admit that too much crime control may have a negative impact on their department. They will not want to think that their golden apples are causing problems, or how the depart-ment itself unintentionally encourages noble-cause corruption.

Mike looks over his audience. This group of commanders did not show a strong preference for a crime-control perspective. On the crime-control continuum, they were only slightly on the crime-control side, scoring between a 6 and a 7 on a scale of 1 to 10. *You're only scaling around 6? That's pretty good. That's real good. I've been to other depart-ments, and they all are around 9 or 10.*

One of the higher-ranking officers responds. "If you look back 5 years, there are differences. We've had changes in direction, we have a different orientation." Another officer adds "We've had changes in leadership in our organization."

A third: "The previous chief was pretty far to the right on your con-tinuum. Really crime control. The things he wanted to force on people weren't acceptable. The current chief has improved a lot of problems from that administration."

Mike responds. *That's good. It's a tough transition. But I also see commanders scoring further away from the crime-control side than their line officers. If I measure your street officers tomorrow, how will they score? I'll bet that they're more crime-control oriented, around 7 or 8 on the continuum. Don't be lulled into complacency by the logic of good faith. It's up to you to make sure that your organization isn't sur-prised.*

Where Do Your Officers Get Their Leads?

Mike discusses the tendency of street officers to display a strong crime-control orientation. *Where do your officers get their street ethics from? I've made the case that they are hired because they have a par-ticular ethical point of view, and that their ethics are reinforced during training. But why do so few officers ever return to the middle of the continuum? What keeps them over there* (he taps the crime-control side) *so completely? The answer is that their principal referents all push them toward crime control. They don't do it in the same way. But it has the same result. It encourages noble-case corruption. I'm going to tell you about three of them that might surprise you. They are their sergeants, the courts, and – are you ready for this? – college education.*

Police officers' crime-control values are embedded in a justice environment that reinforces those values. Officers' predispositions toward crime control are fine-tuned by people on whom officers come into contact in their daily routines and some of whom they admire and respect. Only by understanding how elements in their working environment encourage the corruption of noble cause can we recognize how difficult it is to change police values.

Police officers are predictably on the crime-control side of the continuum. They were, after all, hired with a commitment to the noble cause already in place, and training reinforces their commitment to the noble cause. Powerful groups in their environment, however, unintentionally or intentionally encourage the corruption of noble cause. We'll discuss three of these groups: The courts, college teachers, and sergeants.

Courts and the Prosecutor

Mike begins this part of the presentation with a discussion about one of Packer's crime control elements – efficiency. He contends that prosecutors who emphasize efficiency undercut due process.

I want to talk about where your officers take their leads from. How about the courts? What do the courts stress? What happens to most of the cases that go before the courts?

One of the commanders responds "Acquitted." Others nod in agreement.

Mike expected this. It is the usual answer. Police everywhere believe that the courts are exceptionally lenient on defendants. They are convinced that bad people are frequently released on legal technicalities. Yet the evidence is compelling: the courts in the United States are harsh by most standards. Less than one percent of all individuals charged with violent and property crimes are successfully challenged for due process reasons (Maguire & Pastore, 1995). Moreover, courts are routinely hard on arrestees: If an arrest is made, more than 70 percent of the defendants will ultimately be found guilty (Walker, 1994). This is precisely as it should be, given that the legal standard for conviction of a crime – guilty beyond a reasonable doubt – is more stringent than the probable cause standard for arrest.

The vast majority of defendants plea to a guilty charge prior to a trial, thereby providing prosecutors with the best of all worlds – a high conviction rate and a small investment of time and precious tax dollars in the prosecution process. When prosecutors don't sustain cases, what reasons do they give? The predictable – lack of evidence, lack of witnesses. How does our criminal justice system stack up when compared to others around the world? There is compelling if not conclusive evidence that, in terms of the proportion of citizens incarcerated, the United States has the most punitive criminal justice system in the world.

Given the practical, common sense nature of police, how can they believe something that is wrong? The answer lies in part in the way the mass media portrays the courts and criminal defendants. The myth of the lenient court system is daily fare on most television news shows. It's great for selling TV and movies, but it's all malarkey.

It is unclear why there is so much misinformation about justice system processes from legislators who should know better and should inform citizens in a responsible manner. In most cases, they may simply not know. Like the rest of us, legislators may form their opinions by the exceptional, celebrated cases (Walker, 1994). They see headlines about a *Miranda*-type case, a person whose conviction is reviewed because of illegal police behavior. They have no knowledge of the tens of thousands of cases that typify the criminal justice system, nor are they familiar with the circumstances of the approximately 1.2 million people behind bars. They rarely let their views get complicated by messy facts.

The answer also lies in the feelings that police have about due process protections for defendants. It is not important that such protections are rarely used or that they are ineffective. What matters to many police officers is that they exist. There are many officers who feel betrayed by the courts every time they read a suspect their rights. It is a powerful sense of treachery, motivated by their commitment to the noble cause and the corresponding belief that they alone can stem the tide of crime. For some officers, it justifies noble-cause corruption. Consider Barker's conversation with a police officer regarding efforts to gain consent for a search:

> Barker: That sure sounds like telling a lot of lies.

> Officer: It is not police lying: It is an art. After all, the criminal has constitutional protection. He can lie through his teeth. Why not us? What is fair is fair. (Barker & Carter, 1994:145)

Mike continues. *Acquitted? Really? They're not plea-bargained? They don't plea-bargain cases here? Sure they do. They do everywhere.*

One of the commanders considers this for a moment. "They have to get filed first."

OK, I'll take that. You're not getting them filed, unless they're really, really good. Unless they're solid. What's the prosecutor telling you? That he's worried about someone's constitutional rights? Or that he wants to make damn sure that he gets 'em convicted?

I'll bet you that the prosecutor in this county tells you that "I have a 95 or a 99 percent conviction rate." Ever hear them say that? Sure you have. They're politicians. It's a political statement. They have to back it up.

You have to make sure that you write up the report just right to get the conviction. None of this "But Sarge, that's not exactly what happened." Sarge'll look at that. "I don't give a shit," he'll say. "You've got to do this, and this, and this."

You're putting pressure on your people to be efficient and effective. No messy complicating factors. Suppose an officer writes it up like it really happened. You pat 'im on the back when he goes out and tries real hard, and the case gets dropped. And the Sergeant says to him "Dumbshit. If you'd done what I'd told you to do, you'd have a conviction." So the case is dropped, the Sergeant's pissed, the prosecutor's pissed. What's this good officer going to do the next time?

With the widespread use of plea bargaining and the scant resources available to indigent defendant offices, there are few checks on the validity and reliability of evidence. It is easy for considerations of prosecutorial efficiency and effectiveness to dominate in such an environment. If due process considerations were taken seriously at all stages, and if full-blown adversarial trials were required for all felony defendants, it would be like adding sand to a Corvette crankcase. The courtroom workgroup would grind to a halt.

You see? Plea bargaining is about efficiency and effectiveness. It guarantees conviction. It guarantees minimal municipal investment. Do you think it's about this? Mike points to the due process side of the means-ends continuum. *Or about this?* Mike points to the crime-control side of the continuum. No one answers the question. Mike concludes. *You see. This is the lead your officers are getting from the courts.*

Prosecutors provide one of the primary leads for the police. But prosecutors themselves are often committed to the noble cause, and in their zeal to convict, step across the line in order to prove guilt in courtroom proceedings. Unfortunately, they all too many times strike "foul blows" as well as hard ones. Consider the research conducted by the *Chicago Tribune* on prosecutorial misconduct in murder cases, presented in Figure 7.10.

The Strange Morality of College Education

Police officers increasingly acquire college education. Their education ranges from a few courses at a junior college to advanced degrees in university programs and departments. These programs influence how recruits think about police work. They have become one of the places where officers get their leads.

Figure 7.10

Prosecutors – An Example for the Police?

Do prosecutors engage in misconduct? An investigation carried out by the *Chicago Tribune* found that, since the passage of a 1963 ruling designed to suppress misconduct by prosecutors, at least 381 defendants nationally have had homicide convictions thrown out. These convictions were discarded for the most egregious of prosecutorial misbehaviors: either prosecutors concealed evidence suggesting innocence, or because they presented evidence they knew to be false. Of the 381 defendants, 67 had been sentenced to death. And nearly 30 of the 67 death row inmates were subsequently freed.

The *Tribune* articles observed that prosecutors can engage in this sort of conduct with virtual impunity. They cite the convictions of two African-Americans in upstate New York. The lead prosecutor withheld information in an eyewitness statement from the victim's brother, who stated that the murderers were white. In Indiana, South Carolina, Colorado, Illinois, and Arizona, prosecutors received weapons used in self-defense and later hid the weapons, arguing in court that no weapons were used in self-defense.

Why do prosecutors engage in these unethical behaviors? Part of the answer is because they can. Prosecutors have rarely been punished for their conduct. In the 381 cases cited in the *Tribune*, not one of the prosecutors was convicted of a crime. As the *Tribune* observed, many saw their careers advance, becoming judges or district attorneys. One became a congressman. Two were indicted, but charges were dismissed before a trial. Moreover, a wrongly charged defendant cannot file suit against a prosecutor. In the game of checks and balances, there is no reasonable check on prosecutors who misbehave, even in the most serious of cases.

Prosecutors have responded that the public can vote them out of office if their conduct is deemed unacceptable. Yet it is rare that the pubic finds out about prosecutorial misconduct. When cases are reversed for prosecutorial misconduct, the names of the prosecutors are rarely noted in the decision. Thus, aside from the public statements of defense counsel or released defendants, there is no way for the public to find out about decisions that have been reversed.

These 381 cases may well be the tip of the iceberg. They represent only those cases where misconduct has come to the court's attention and been reversed. It is likely that many cases of misconduct have gone unnoticed.

Most troubling is that these cases represent the worst kinds of prosecutorial conduct for the most serious kinds of cases – cases in which an individual's life hangs in the balance. It appears that the outcomes of capital cases are much more vulnerable to error than is widely thought. Common wisdom is that, because murder cases are so

Figure 7.10, *continued*

important and protections for defendants so strong, these are the kinds of cases where an error is the least likely to occur. Yet the opposite may be true. One of the *Tribune*'s sources observed that:

> "We generally condone a great deal of misconduct when we think it serves the ultimate ends of justice. There's a feeling that is how it works, that it's legitimate to bend the truth sometimes when you are doing it with – quote the greater good, end quote – in mind." (Possley & Armstrong, 1999:15)

In other words, prosecutors justify their behavior in terms of the ends produced. And the ends are the most important in murder cases, where the public is often outraged and a prosecutor's reputation hangs in the balance. The noble cause thus also provides a basis for corruption among prosecutors as it does for the police, and is strongest in the most serious cases. Hence, murder cases, thought commonly of as that area of court activity with the strongest defendant protections, may actually be the source of the most serious mistakes by the system, doubly egregious because they are intentional.

Source: Adapted from Armstrong and Possley, "Break Rules, Be Promoted," January 14; 1999; Possley and Armstrong, "Prosecution on Trial in DuPage," January 12, 1999, Chicagotribune.com/news.

A widely shared vision of the universities and colleges in the United States is that they are centers for the transmission of liberal and radical ideology. This idea is exaggerated. Are there liberal instructors? Of course. There are conservative instructors as well. Most college instructors aren't particularly interested in politics. A few politicians, such as the former Speaker of the House of Representatives Newt Gingrich (a conservative), have emerged from the ranks of academia, but this happens infrequently.

Liberal instructors complain about conservative politicians. Conservative instructors complain about liberal politicians. Yet the underlying dynamic in a university environment is intellectual freedom, loosely translated as "leave me alone!" Teachers zealously guard their right to express their views, whether they are liberal or conservative in their political philosophies. Politics don't mobilize faculty. Issues like tenure denial and merit pay mobilize faculty. Like the rest of the working public, university and college faculty are motivated primarily by bread-and-butter issues – salary, job benefits, and working conditions.

A variety of forces in higher education today emphasize the noble cause, and in some instances can justify the corruption of the noble cause. There are four forces: teaching materials that encourage noble-cause corruption, the moral predispositions of criminal justice students, the use of part-time instructors, and funded research in local agencies.

Teaching Materials That Appear to Encourage Noble-Cause Corruption

One of Mike's concerns is that university faculty use teaching materials, yet they don't fully understand the way those materials affect students. *I want you to listen to something*, Mike says to the commanders. *I heard this in classes when I was in college.*

The quote below is from an article called "The Dirty Harry Problem," by Carl Klockars, that we discussed at length in Chapter 2. Recall that Harry used dirty means – torture – to achieve what he thought would be a good end, saving the life of a buried kidnapping victim. In the end the kidnapping victim died anyway. The author of the article observed that:

> I suspect that there are very few people who would not want Harry to do what he did, and what is more, I would want anyone who policed for me to be prepared to do so as well. Put differently, I would want as police officers men and women of moral courage and sensitivity. (Klockars, 1991a:415)

Holy mackerel! Does that sound like he's leading someone down the garden path? An academic speaks to his students, or to a group of law enforcement officers, and says this? I hear this and I think "uh-oh."

In the Dirty Harry example, violence in the name of the noble cause is championed *even though* it had no impact on the outcome. The Dirty Harry ethic separates noble-cause corruption from its outcome. Corruption becomes acceptable for its own sake, simply for inflicting pain in the wrongdoer. If you are a commander, do you want your college-educated recruits thinking like this?

This article is representative of a growing literature that encourages a commitment to the noble cause, and can justify the corruption of noble cause as well. Klockar's perspective is not atypical: We also discussed in Chapter 2 how Muir's (1977) discussion of police styles was frequently interpreted by students as encouraging the use of violence if the case was sufficiently just.

The Use of Local Agency Instructors

Most criminal justice departments make extensive use of part-time instructors. These instructors are typically drawn from local agencies. Their perspective of criminal justice tends to focus on effectiveness and efficiency in doing something about crime, and rarely encompasses a critical review of the criminal justice system. These instructors have a powerful impact on departments for two reasons: (1) they tend to teach large introductory classes and their views can influence many students, and (2) they are often admired by students. They represent role models for many students who themselves are seeking a locally based career in criminal justice. Their impact can consequently have an impact on departments out of proportion with their seemingly low status in academia.

The Moral Predispositions of Criminal Justice Students

Criminal justice departments are frequently presented with an anomalous instructional environment. The full-time faculty have often been drawn from educational fields that provided a critical overview of criminal justice institutions and agencies. Yet many of their students are seeking careers in criminal justice, and they are already morally predisposed to the noble cause. Faculty who are openly critical of criminal justice risk alienating their students – and more practically, receiving negative student evaluations. One of the authors recalls a critically oriented instructor whose student evaluation simply stated "This man is dangerous!"

Faculty critical of criminal justice agencies consequently risk negative student evaluations. And poor student evaluations can have a negative impact on young faculty who are not yet tenured and who need to show that they are competent teachers in order to acquire tenure. Instructors find themselves ceding moral ground, emphasizing areas of the noble cause that they find compatible with their beliefs, or sometimes becoming cheerleaders for local agencies, in order to protect their academic careers.

Research and Service in Local Agencies

Criminal justice faculty are responsible for research and service as well as for teaching. When undergoing review for promotion and tenure, full-time faculty's portfolios will be scrutinized closely for the quantity and quality of their research, and for service to a lesser but nevertheless important degree. One of the primary paths for the development of research and service goes through local agencies.

Faculty will frequently contact an agency about conducting research. The research will be funded by a major funding source such as the National Institute of Justice if they are fortunate, though the grant-writing skills for funded research typically come later in one's career.

The opportunity to conduct research in an agency is a sobering experience for younger faculty. It is a "hands-on" experience with real-world criminal justice, and in order to be effective they must interact with and understand the justice professionals with whom they work. For seasoned faculty, it is sometimes an opportunity to renew old acquaintances. For all faculty who must conduct research to gain academic recognition and rank, research conducted in criminal justice agencies will sensitize them to the noble cause and practical agency concerns.

Sergeants

What kind of lead do officers get from their supervisors? Not from brass, but their sergeants? Don't they get efficiency and effectiveness too? What do supervisors want from officers?

Sergeants are line supervisors. They straddle two worlds, the world of administration and the world of the street. Their loyalties may reflect one or the other of these domains, but typically they don't reflect both. **Station-house sergeants** tend to see their work in terms of controlling the conduct of their officers on the beat. They are interested in the production of reports, quotas, rules and regulations (Van Maanen, 1997). **Street sergeants**, on the other hand, take a more active role in their officers' assignments. Station-house sergeants are also more likely to be promoted. Once promoted, they focus on the production of statistics rather than craft excellence.

> Selection procedures favor administratively inclined candidates, and those candidates, when bestowed with the sergeant rank, tend to take a relatively remote supervisory stance toward the supervised. Matters of subordinate craft and competence in the field are not of great interest to station house sergeants. More often than not, these sergeants direct and evaluate the performance of their men on the basis of official, albeit indirect, productivity measures (e.g., calls answered, tardiness, tickets amassed, arrests logged, citizen complaints filed, street stops, miles logged, sick or vacation days taken, etc.). (Van Maanen, 1997:180-181)

Station-house sergeants are not responsible for quality in the production of police work. This is not because sergeants don't like good work – like other officers, they appreciate a good bust and a difficult case solved. But sergeants need to accumulate the kinds of numbers and the reputation for toughness that will get them promoted. Officers everywhere know that they have to produce activity for their sergeants. It is a characteristic of the authority and promotional structure of American police organizations. In Figure 7.11, Skolnick and Fyfe capture the implications of the way authority is number-driven:

Figure 7.11

The Numerology of Authority

[The] objectification and quantification of police work – how many arrests? how many field interrogations? how many tickets? how many minutes and seconds responding to calls? how many pounds and ounces of drugs seized? how many dollars was it worth? how many outstanding robbery cases did this shooting solve? – trickles down to the department's lowest level, its patrol cars and foot beats. When that occurs, everybody up and down the line becomes driven by what the New York cops used to call "big numbers," without regard to whether they accomplish any desirable end. When that happens, street cops, who know from every source that they have been assigned to their department's dirtiest job, also learn that their supervisors are interested only in the figures on their activity reports, not in what the police may have done to put them there.

Those are bad messages to give repeatedly to people who are expected to serve professionally as first responders to some of society's most pressing and sensitive crises. It tells them that the cardinal sin is not to break the rules but to be caught breaking the rules.

Source: Jerome Skolnick and James Fyfe, *Above the Law*, 1993:189-190.

Mike concludes this section of ethics training. *You have academia leading people to believe that all they have to do is unfurl their moral flag and everything will be fine. You have the courts and prosecutors telling them that all they have to do is be efficient and effective. Then everything will be fine. Their Sergeant is telling them to do the paperwork right, make the arrests, be efficient, and everything will be all right. They're getting their leads from these groups. How can they NOT* – Mike taps the crime-control side of the curve all the way over on the crime-control side – *be way over here? How can they be any other way?*

Consider the continuum. When officers are hired, they are already on the crime-control side. Important references in their environment encourage behavior that is focused on the ends of crime control. Prosecutors, sergeants, and college educators – all people that in different ways represent authority for line officers – emphasize work that is passionate and effective. It all reinforces corruption of noble cause. Consequently, from an organizational point of view, something has to go wrong for line officers to move back to the middle, toward a balanced perspective. There's not a way for them to get there in the natural scheme of things.

Police Culture, Ends Orientation, and Noble-Cause Corruption

8

Key Terms

act utilitarianism	police brutality
avenging angel syndrome	police culture
boomerang effect	rule utilitarianism
the code	sixth-sense suspicion
crevasse	street cop culture
edge control	street environment
excessive force	type II drug corruption
legal suspicion	victim-centered
management cop culture	warping effect

Part I: The Crevasse and Police Culture

The Crevasse

Mike thinks for a minute. This is always a difficult topic. *Do your officers understand the crevasse in your department?*

Note that Mike does not ask commanders if a crevasse exists in their department. There always is. He has noted that outsiders like himself are often brought in to talk about ethics when managers are having problems with line officers and they don't know how to deal with them. Nor, when he gives the same talk to line officers that he does to commanders, does

Mike ask if they know about the crevasse. They live it. Do they understand it? Usually they do not – they think it is unique to them.

Every department that we know about has some sort of a crevasse in it. Call it a chasm, a barrier, a conflict, management versus street culture, it describes the same thing. Line officers are on one side of the crevasse. Managers and commanders are on the other side. New sergeants fall into it, and they often don't understand what happened. They don't yet comprehend the distrust their lower-ranking officers feel in their presence, the silence with which sometimes they are now greeted, or how their former friends are off talking to each other when he walks down the hall. They can't believe that they are no longer one of the guys. They will learn in time.

Managers don't know about their agency problems because these problems are on the other side of the crevasse. What's the crevasse? By **crevasse**, we mean two things: the "official" rank-determined boundary between line officers and everyone with a rank of Lieutenant and above, and the antagonisms and conflicts that occur across that boundary. We use the word "crevasse" instead of a more neutral term like "space" or "distance" because a crevasse is a wide, treacherous rift whose dimensions can't be seen by outsiders and because its glacial connotations are an apt description of management-line relations in many police departments.

The crevasse can be almost undetectable. Managers often do not hear about problems at the line level. But it can be present nevertheless. However, it is not always a silent barrier. In its strongest manifestations, line personnel will openly challenge commanders in the organization.

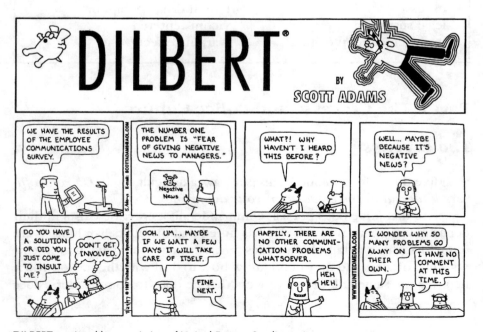

DILBERT reprinted by permission of United Feature Syndicate, Inc.

Unfortunately, crevasses are present in varying degrees in most municipal police agencies in the United States. A recruit's first exposure to the crevasse is when he or she is told by a TO to "forget everything you learned in Peace Officer Standards and Training (POST): I'm gonna show you how we really do it on the street." Crevasses exist where commanders are having significant problems finding out about problems at the line level. For managers, an indication of the crevasse is when particular objectives aren't carried out in spite of support from sergeants. This chapter of the book is an introduction to the crevasse and its street side – the secretive side of police culture.

Elizabeth Reuss-Ianni captured the idea of the crevasse in her book the *Two Cultures of Policing*. Her idea of the informal organization of policing is presented below.

Figure 8.1

The Two Cultures of Policing

The organization of policing is "best described and understood in terms of the interactions of two distinct cultures: a street cop culture and a management cop culture. These two cultures are increasingly characterized by competing and often conflicting perspectives on procedure and practice in policing. (Reuss-Ianni, 1983:1)

These two cultures, she argued, are marked by conflicting value systems. The **management cop culture** is characterized by a belief in principles of scientific management. *Scientific management* means that the department should be organized hierarchically, and that employment and advancement should be based on merit. An individual's formal role on the organizational chart should have in writing what the individual actually does on the job. Managers are concerned with crime but have a different perspective on it than do line officers, who have to deal with its immediate impact. Managers have a citywide focus. They have to allocate resources throughout the system based upon a system of priority. They must "weigh and establish those priorities within political, social, and economic constraints and justify them within each of these contexts as well as within the police context" (Reuss-Ianni, 1983:7). Law enforcement is a carefully planned, well-designed, and efficiently implemented program in which individual officers' patrol units are impersonal resources to be used for the advancement of interrelated organizational goals.

Street cop culture, on the other hand, finds its meanings in the traditions of the department. The organizing ethos of street police is the idea of the "good old days" of policing when police were respected by the public, officers could count on each other, and managers were part of the police family. Relationships are familial rather than bureaucratic, and officers count on informal friendships and alliances to do their work. Officers believe that they must protect each other from administrative oversight. A central organizing principle of line officer behavior is called CYA (cover your ass.)

Mike discusses Reuss-Ianni's concept of culture. *Your officers have rules. You used to play by these rules. A lot of times commanders forget these rules. An observer of the police once wrote them down. Let's go over them.*

Reuss-Ianni identified 21 precepts of police work. The first 12 define relationships with other cops. The second nine describe relations to superior officers. Her precepts are presented in Figure 8.2.

Figure 8.2

The Cops Code: Reuss-Ianni

Rules defining relationships with other cops:
1. Watch out for your partner first and then the rest of the guys working that tour.
2. Don't give up another cop.
3. Show balls.
4. Be aggressive when you have to, but don't be too eager.
5. Don't get involved in anything in another guy's sector.
6. Hold up your end of the work.
7. If you get caught off base, don't implicate anybody else.
8. Make sure the other guys know if another cop is dangerous or "crazy."
9. Don't trust a new guy until you have checked him out.
10. Don't tell anybody else more than they have to know, it could be bad for you and it could be bad for them.
11. Don't talk too much or too little. Both are suspicious.
12. Don't leave work for the next tour.

Rules relating street cops to bosses:
1. Protect your ass. (If the system wants to get you, it will.)
2. Don't make waves. Supervisors pay attention to troublemakers.
3. Don't give them too much activity. Don't be too eager.
4. Keep out of the way of any boss from outside your precinct.
5. Don't look for favors just for yourself.
6. Don't take on the patrol sergeant by yourself.
7. Know your bosses. Who's working and who has the desk?
8. Don't do the bosses' work for them.
9. Don't trust bosses to look out for your interests.

Source: Elizabeth Reuss-Ianni, *Two Cultures of Policing*, 1983:13-16.

Mike continued. *Do you remember these? You may no longer be line officers, but your line officers still think this way. And they're applying these rules to you. Just like you did 10 years ago to your supervisors.*

The crevasse is a barrier created and sustained by line officers to protect themselves from managers. It is maintained by their practical code of departmental conduct, a code that provides rules of thumb regarding who to talk to, who to avoid, how much work to do, how to treat other officers. It limits the ability to influence them.

Mike continues. *I'm making the case that your officers make value-based decisions. You don't hear about it because the code keeps you from hearing about it. So if you aren't hearing about problems, don't think that everything is OK.*

When Mike says **the code**, he's referring to the code of secrecy stated by Reuss-Ianni above. The code, in its most general sense, means that the activities of line officers (and their closest friends) on a particular shift are not to be discussed with others.

The crevasse is in place in large part so that line officers can protect themselves from managers. What are they protecting themselves from? To answer this question, we will spend some time discussing police culture.

Police Work and Police Culture

Many writers have described police culture (Manning, 1997, 1989; Reuss-Ianni, 1983; Crank, 1998). Manning (1989:360) defines **police culture** occupationally as the "accepted practices, rules, and principles of conduct that are situationally applied, and generalized rationales and beliefs." Culture emphasizes particular "contours" of its environment, that is, particular aspects of daily work activities are more important for defining police culture. Police culture particularly emphasizes uncertainty in police-citizen encounters. Police concerns over personal autonomy and authority reflect how they adapt to uncertainty in their working environments.

Culture may be different in different parts of the organization. As we noted above, Reuss-Ianni distinguished between street cop and management cop culture. Manning (1989) suggested that police organizations contain three distinct but overlapping cultures, a command or executive level culture, a middle-management culture, and a line-level culture. In this book, by culture we refer specifically to line officers within a particular police organization. Culture, though referring to a specific organization, is similar across police departments, because the type of individuals recruited to police work and the kinds of problems and groups the police encounter are similar everywhere.

Some writers have presented an image of culture that is dark and forbidding. They focus on how culture contributes to corruption, to deviance, and to resistance to change. This view is held also by many administrators within police organizations. The best of this "dark" perspective of police culture has contributed substantially to our knowledge about problems facing the police and how they respond (see, for example, Kappeler, Sluder & Alpert, 1994). However, if someone were to limit his or her understanding of police culture to these readings, they would have a stark and unpleasant idea of how the police feel about their work. Police work is not all dark and foreboding. Police work is entertaining, celebratory, bitter and sad at times, with bright, as well as bleak, moments. It is a human creation, carrying in it all those things that identify us and give meaning to our lives.

Police culture is in many ways similar to other contemporary human cultures. It is made up of interdependent actors, arising and existing in a broader social environment of social values and personal meanings. Beliefs and values that characterize police culture are in part imported from particular groups, what we called previously the culture of policing. Pre-existing values and beliefs are molded and refined in response to the particular groups that police officers have to deal with on a day-to-day basis. These groups, which include the courts, prosecutors and the legal environment, criminals, newspapers and television, city government, and other criminal justice organizations, are similar across the United States. Consequently, the local cultures of individual police organizations have developed along similar lines everywhere, and a person can speak of police culture generally.

Police culture, as Manning (1989) observed, tends to isolate its members. Officers are isolated from the friends they grew up with, mostly because rotating and late shifts segregate the police from the 8 to 5 work-a-day world that most of the working world inhabits. In the conduct of their daily routines, however, they are profoundly separated from the public they serve: they believe that it is their moral responsibility to control their assigned territories, including all the people and places in it. Cops consequently inhabit a world of their own, from the day that they enter the police academy until the day they retire. Their primary identity is a shared sense of copness (Ahern, 1972). They look in a mirror, adjust their belt and their hat, and they see a cop looking back. They are the police, and they protect and serve.[17]

Layers of Culture

Think of police culture as an onion. It has a heart that animates every police officer and gives meaning to police work. The heart is how police officers feel and think about their work, how they celebrate their victories and mourn their losses. It is how they do their work and how it is meaningful to them. Mostly, it is about their commitment to the noble cause and how that commitment is animated in training, in daily police work and in conversations with other police officers.

The "heart" of officers' values, particularly their commitment to the noble cause and the belief that they can make a contribution to society, are imported from broader society. These values are the subcultural traits that we discussed in Chapter 2. The layers over the heart of the onion, however, are cultural creations, which means that they come about from the daily experiences of police work and how the experiences are shared by officers.

The first layer, the layer that encloses the heart and animates its pulse, is their assigned beat, romantically called the **street environment.** This is where patrol officers and detectives carry out their daily work and refers to the various kinds of people line officers come into contact with. Meaningful street work is about suspects and troublemakers. It is doing something about bad guys – responding to calls, being involved in the chase, making an arrest, the "huff and puff of the chase" as some have called it. Police territories – their assigned spaces – are accepted in a profoundly moral sense. They are responsible for their assigned geography. All of its problems are their problems. Their reputations and self-esteem rise and fall on how well they control their territories.

Suspects are bad guys, and troublemakers are frequently called "assholes" (Van Maanen, 1978). Cops don't see a lot of differences between criminal suspects and troublemakers, who are often believed to be criminal wanna-be's or whose crimes aren't yet known to police. "Assholes" are troublemakers who openly criticize the police, who are deliberately rude, or who do not show adequate respect. Sometimes, in racially divided communities, police use ethnicity or skin color to identify who they think is an asshole.

For a few officers, all citizens are assholes and potential criminals. These officers have what is called a "siege mentality." For them, there are no friends, but brother and sister officers. The world contains no joy, only dark threats everywhere. For "siege mentality" officers, police culture has ceased to be a source of celebration and growth and has become a psychological prison.

The second layer around the heart of the onion is uncertainty. Manning (1989) recognized the central role uncertainty played in police culture. A psychological sense of uncertainty was intimately tied to the external world of disorder and risk. An officer's external focus on order protected him or her from the unpredictable. Crank (1998) identified five different aspects of uncertainty that he called "themes of the unknown." They are presented in Figure 8.3.

Figure 8.3

Themes of the Unknown

Suspicion. Police work carries two different, opposing kinds of suspicion. **Legal suspicion** is based on a legal standard of reasonableness, and is determined by a officer's ability to articulate reasons why he or she thinks that a suspect might be a danger to a police officer or might have committed or is about to be involved in a crime. On the other hand, **sixth-sense suspicion** is the ability to identify wrongdoing from the most trivial of clues. It is based on intuition, not fact, though when it is highly honed it will produce solid evidence. This latter type is the special craft of police work, and officers who construct cases from the most seemingly innocent of clues gain a great deal of status in their organization.

Danger and its anticipation. Thinking about and preparing for danger are central features of police work. Police officers confront not only real dangers, but operate in a working environment where danger can occur unpredictably. The threat of danger, Crank noted, mobilizes much of what the police are about, and danger realized unifies the police.

Unpredictability and situational uncertainty. Situational uncertainty refers to the ambiguity police face both with regard to their daily work routines and with regard to the organization itself. The unpredictability inherent in all police work underscores the need for apprenticeship-type training. Common sense among the police lies in their abilities to negotiate their way through uncertain settings to a successful, injury-free conclusion.

Turbulence and edge control. Turbulence means two things. First, in a police-citizen interaction, a great deal of activity can happen in a short period of time – in bursts of energy. Second, activity unfolds unpredictably. Turbulence can be fun, up to a point, and make police work exciting. However, activities can become so turbulent that they are physically dangerous. By the "edge" is meant the point at which turbulence turns into physical danger. Police do not like to go beyond the edge, because events can escalate up to the point where someone is killed. **Edge control** refers to the skills police officers have to contain turbulence below the edge of significant danger. It is a central skill to police work, and important to understanding the way police officers view danger. A great deal of police work is about edge control.

Seduction. The theme seduction conveys the idea that police work, especially danger and the thrill of the chase, is attractive to police officers. It's more than excitement. Crank (136) describes a retiring officer looking back over his career "It is a view that still triggers in him a brief surge of adrenaline, a sense of being in special places, dark corners, dealing with wild things, and riding the wind."

Source: Adapted from John Crank (1998). *Understanding Police Culture*. Cincinnati, OH: Anderson Publishing Co.

The third layer around the onion's heart is the strong sense of solidarity that police officers feel. Their sense of solidarity, what we call the "mask of a thousand faces," is often attributed to camaraderie, the sense of coming together in the face of danger. Certainly, individuals who share dangerous work have high levels of camaraderie (Lyng, 1990). The perceptions of real and potential danger are a shared bond among police officers. Solidarity is also reinforced by the perceptions of many officers that they are isolated from and in conflict with many elements of the public. Both the isolation felt by officers and the conflict and resentment they feel toward many outside groups is a powerful stimulus to a shared sense of identity (Coser, 1956). Constant daily contact with such groups as the courts, criminals, media, and unfriendly motorists contribute to police solidarity.

The fourth layer is described by themes (strategies and tactics) used by line officers to protect themselves from external oversight. These themes represent ways, widely observed in many police organizations, that line officers avoid observation and control. These themes emerge when line personnel think that particular groups interfere with their ability to do their day-to-day work. One such group is the court system. Police everywhere tend to believe that the legal system is soft on crime, and some of them develop a repertoire of "street justice" skills and techniques so that they can both punish offenders and avoid the courts. Police officers also develop strategies to get around due process constraints on their behavior.

The most important group that line officers protect themselves from are their own administrators and commanders, sometimes simply called brass. Officers tend to have a powerful distrust of their departmental managers (Crank & Caldero, 1991). The influence of influential outside groups, the mayor for example, or the press, is translated into policy through the department's chain of command. Consequently, many of the frustrations line officers have toward outside groups are also focused on the department itself.

By recognizing layers of culture, an observer can understand how the working world of the street officer is insulated from and resistant to control by police supervisors. The values most central to line officers, the "noble cause" heart of the onion, are encased by the first layer, which is their daily work, dealing with bad guys, and the moral sense of responsibility they feel over their territories. The middle layers create a special identity, a sense of solidarity in the "outsider" status felt by many officers and from the unpredictable danger that characterizes their work. The outermost layers of the onion enable police to protect themselves from external influences, particularly the upper management levels of the organization itself, so that they can maintain their moral control over their territories.

Culture and Secrecy

When we look at police from a cultural vantage, the difficulties that reformers have encountered in their efforts to change the police become apparent. The outermost layers of police culture protect line officers from oversight so that they can continue to focus their day-to-day energies on that which is closest to their heart – the noble cause. Efforts to change the police, vis-à-vis the courts, departmental policy, chain-of-command, or due process procedures will tend to have either a *boomerang* or *warping* effect. The **boomerang** effect is that efforts to change the police increase the resistance of line officers, who develop strategies that makes change more difficult in the long term. Many observers, for example, have noted that the effect of the "due process" revolution of the Warren Court in the 1960s was an increase in police strategies designed to circumvent the Court's decisions.

The **warping** effect is that police culture adapts to and assimilates proposed and intended changes into its own values, thus shifting the effects of changes in unplanned ways. For example, states increasingly require due process to be taught as a component of POST training. Due process instruction is typically taught in two-hour or four-hour blocks of classes. Sometimes an instructor will make a derogatory comment about rights for criminals, or tell a story about how Joe Bum was released on a technicality, only to commit a more serious crime. These stories subvert the purpose of training by emphasizing that, while it is important to follow the letter of the law – at least on paper, it is more important to believe in the noble cause. POST training thus can become a tool for the subversion of the law through noble-cause corruption. It's not an optimistic vision for people who want to reform the police by changing the training they receive.

Let's put this discussion in perspective. The hiring process recruits a particular kind of officer and a training process that reinforces it. It is an officer committed to an end, not a means. The end is the noble cause. Police culture nurtures noble cause and protects officers from efforts to control it. When the "means" of policing – due process, civil rights, and department policy – interfere with the noble cause, then the culture shrouds police behavior in protective secrecy. Reform efforts, whether through POST or through department policy, tend to boomerang or warp.

We can see from this discussion that the rifts between police managers and line personnel are an important aspect of police culture. The onion's heart, how officers think and feel about their work, are socially imported values that are reinforced by the hiring process and fine tuned by local police cultures. If managers want to change policing, if they want to do something about the crevasse, they must work with, not against, police culture.

Mike describes police culture, its relationship to hiring, and the role of commanders in the hiring process. *If you understand police culture, if you really, really understand it, you see how it is constructed around the noble cause. Police officers are hired so that they can protect the weak and hurt the mean and the bad. In a whole lot of ways, commanders encourage that view.*

For a police officer, local police culture can be a wonderful thing. It is how police celebrate their work. It carries all the stories, the successes, the tricks and gambits, the history and habits of a department. But it also can be a dark master. When culture is in the service of noble-cause corruption, police departments have a problem with line behavior that they can't control.

For commanders in departments where police culture hides corruption, it's almost impossible to find out. Commanders find themselves operating on the logic of good faith, hope against hope that they aren't hearing about problems at the street level because there aren't any.

Mike provides the following warning for commanders. *Here's a sign that problems are emerging: a few officers begin quietly requesting changes of assignments. Has this ever happened? You may hear a request for assignment change and ignore it. Yet this may well be the only sign of internal problems you get.*

The noble cause corrupted is the source of a great deal of secrecy that is associated with the "dark" side of police culture (Kappeler, Sluder & Alpert, 1994), which is why commanders don't hear about problems.

Let me ask you a question, Mike says to the commanders. *Do you have patrol officers wolf-packing routine stops?*[18]

One of the commanders responds. "We have some dangerous stops sometimes. We went off two-person vehicles a few years ago."

Mike pauses for a moment. A thin, dark smile creases his lips. *I get that a lot. If your officers are wolf-packing, you've got a problem. And none of them are going to tell you.*

Part II: What Happens on the Other Side of the Crevasse

Managers, though having worked their way up through the rank and file, adapt to the needs and philosophies appropriate to their current rank. They sometimes forget what happens on the other side of the crevasse. They know that line culture can be a powerfully insulating force, shielding line officers from the scrutiny of commanders, but they tend to forget why. This section examines what it is that is being shielded.

The Conflict Between Noble Cause and Legal Cause

The noble cause is rooted in a gritty, utilitarian ethic. According to utilitarianism, behavior is justified in terms of the good that it will produce. It is consequently a teleological, ends-oriented system. Pollock (1998) distinguished between act utilitarianism and rule utilitarianism. **Act utilitarianism** means that we "look at the consequences of any action for all involved and weigh the units of utility accordingly." **Rule utilitarianism**, on the other hand, suggests that "one judges the action in reference to the precedent it sets and the long term utility of the rule set by the action" (Pollock, 1998:34). Utilitarianism as practiced by the police is more similar to act utilitarianism than rule utilitarianism. Police tend to focus on the immediate consequences of their behavior and the good that their behavior will produce.

In police work, there is seldom a measure of some "good" that is produced or increased. Police utilitarianism consequently is about the reduction of some "bad," for example, by arresting a suspect or by ticketing traffic offenders. Police utilitarianism, in the form of the reduction of some "bad," is thus carried by individual officers as a belief that they, acting alone or with other officers, can deter the moral and criminal badness of society. By doing something about bad people, police act out a utilitarian ethic.

Patrol officers, however, operate in an accountability environment that is means oriented. The courts expect officers to operate within the constraints of both the criminal law, civil law, and constitutional due process guidelines. Their agency expects them to operate within the confines of administrative procedure and departmental ethical standards. Officers are not supposed to intervene into the activities of citizens unless the law has been broken or they think that the law is about to be broken.[19] They are expected to follow both agency and legal guidelines when they decide to intervene, particularly if they are carrying out an arrest or they are using force. Citizens can sue if police act inappropriately. The federal government can bring criminal and civil charges if the police violate a suspect's civil rights, and police administrators expect officers to follow department guidelines – and will punish them when they do not and are caught.

Procedural "means-oriented" guidelines concerning what police can and cannot do sometimes conflict with "ends-oriented" noble-cause actions. Although police can talk with anyone they wish in the conduct of their official duties, their authority to do more than approach someone and talk to them is circumscribed by law. Only the law provides a legal basis for police intervention, and intervention must conform to democratic protections afforded to American citizens. The ends-means conflict is typically resolved by efforts to have the best of both worlds – a moral commitment in the service of noble ends in the conduct of daily police work, and a legal commitment to means later, to the prosecutor and the courts – with the assistance, of course, of the magic pencil and support-ive fellow officers.

We hire an officer with a particular kind of morality and reinforce that morality through training, education, and the expectations of the courts, the public, and their TOs. Police involvement in citizen affairs is mobi-lized by the noble cause and justified by their sixth-sense suspicion, often operating on an intuitive level well below the legal threshold for reason-able suspicion or probable cause. At a later date, they must put pen to paper to explain their decisions to intervene or to provide critical docu-mentation for the prosecutor. Their explanation must be in terms of a legal standard, not noble cause (see Klockars, 1991b).

When police officers intervene in the name of the noble cause, they must justify their actions in terms of correct – departmental or legal – pro-cedures. The following axiom describes the incongruity between the decision to act and its subsequent justification.

Figure 8.4

Axiom: Action and Justification

When noble cause is corrupted, the after-the-fact justification for the actions will be different than the actions that were originally carried out.

This axiom is about the magic pencil. Police will act to reduce the "bad," and will sometimes use dirty means in order to do so. When legal and administrative procedural "means" are in conflict with noble ends, it is usually the means that are sacrificed. But an officer can never tell this to a judge.

Suppose an officer encounters an individual in a park where drugs are known to be sold, and the officer wants to know if this individual is car-rying drugs. Her sixth-sense suspicion tells her so. Can the officer search the individual? Not legally. But the officer can approach him and pat him down for concealed weapons. Police sometimes use this ruse in order to find out if an individual is carrying drugs. An additional ruse can be used to justify an arrest and search. The axiom above explains this kind of encounter.

Mike explains this as follows: *Can you imagine a police officer say-ing to a judge "But your honor, this guy was a certifiable asshole. What do you want me to do? Let him keep selling drugs to kids? Do you want me to say 'gee fella, I won't put my hand into your pocket to pull out that small bag containing a powdery substance I felt when I patted you down?' Do you have kids, your honor?"*

What will the officer say to the judge? "Your honor, as I approached the suspect I observed a small bag containing a white powdery substance on the ground next to him. Suspecting that the bag contained an illegal substance, I searched the suspect, wherein I found two additional bags also containing a white powdery substance." This is why officers have a magic pencil, and why as authorized representatives of a moral order, they use it to do something about crime.

When noble-cause corruption occurs, behavior is made to conform to the law and department policy after the fact, in order to justify an ends-oriented ethics. Skolnick (1994) describes this as the "post-hoc construction of legal compliance," and his definition is in the box below.

Figure 8.5

> **Post-Hoc Construction of Legal Compliance**
>
> The policeman respected the necessity of complying with the arrest laws. His "compliance," however, may take the form of "post hoc" manipulation of the facts rather than before-the-fact behavior. . . . when he sees the law as a hindrance to his primary task of apprehending criminals, he usually attempts to construct the appearance of compliance, rather than allow the offender to escape apprehension. (Skolnick, 1994:214-215)

Types of Noble-Cause Corruption

In this section, we discuss various types of noble-cause corruption. Though the kinds of corruption discussed are diverse, we believe that they all represent efforts to circumvent the law in order to achieve good ends. They consequently qualify as types of noble cause corruption.

Illicit Force

The topic of police use of force is large and its use by the police is commonplace. Many have argued that it is the defining element of police work (see Bittner, 1970; Westley, 1970; Klockars, 1991a). Police use of force varies widely in intensity, from the relatively mild use of "command voice" where officers speak directly to citizens as "adults to adults" in order to steer their behavior, to deadly force where suspects may be seriously injured or killed.

Officers sometimes use too much force. **Excessive force** occurs when officers use a greater degree of force than is necessary to counter a suspect's resistance. Excessive force occurs when force is justified but an officer uses a greater degree than is necessary. If an officer were to use forceful grips, for example, to restrain a suspect when the officer could have accomplished the task with command voice, the officer is using excessive force. **Police brutality** is more severe and represents a gross imbalance between citizen noncompliance and level of police force. The use of a baton to strike a compliant handcuffed suspect, for example, is an example of police brutality.

Rotten Apples and Police Violence

Police executives tend to use the "rotten apple" theory to explain excessive force and police brutality. If circumstances are compelling, the department will blame the misuse of force on some sort of psychological or moral weakness of the offending officer. Recall the principles of legitimacy stated in Chapter 6: the system will survive, and the toilet backs up. Newspapers always want to dig deeper, find the dirt, embarrass the department, sell copy. Reporters and the media whom they represent also tend to think simply about problems, and succumb to the rotten apple theory. They know that the best way to sell a story is to emphasize the "personal element." So they will try to find out about the personal background, family life, and the psychology of the offending officer. Reporters will publicly wonder what there was about the officer that led to such an explosion of violence. They will question the officer's motives.

Noble Cause and Police Violence

Noble-cause violence, however, is not so easily explained. John Van Maanen (1978) described what we consider to be noble-cause violence in his article "The Asshole." Police violence, he observed, emerged in concrete street encounters and was about asserting moral authority over individuals that, simply put, gave the police a difficult time. Van Maanen noted that police officers identified some individuals as "assholes." Those so labeled were vulnerable to rough street justice. When police roughed up assholes, they were acting out a *moral* judgment. Moral?

The asshole, according to Van Maanen, represented an individual whose behavior was viewed as a challenge to the authority of the police. It might have been a motorist that rudely questioned why a police officer is not out chasing dangerous criminals.[20] Assholes, Van Maanen concluded, to a great extent represented what the police were about. The physical violence carried out against an asshole re-affirmed on the body of the victim the rightness of the police to control their territories.

Barker (1996:19) characterized moral violence acted out against certain individuals or groups as the **avenging angel syndrome.** The avenging angel syndrome is the idea that officers exact their sense of street justice on individuals or groups they personally dislike. When citizens acted rudely or disrespectfully, they sharply increased the likelihood that they would go to jail or get citations for "contempt of cop – COC" Barker, 1996:19). Street justice communicated the message that an officer was above the law.

Noble-cause violence, however, occurs in situations that do not always fit well into Van Maanen's model. Some police officers initiate police-citizen interactions with the assumption that a citizen is an asshole, and under some circumstances will allow a citizen to prove that he or she is not (Crank, 1998). Sometimes racial stereotypes are enough for police to label someone as an asshole, and to act violently against them.

Secondly, the argument put forth by Van Maanen underestimated the extent to which police violence can be explosive, sometimes well beyond any possible need to rectify some "out-of-kilter" situation. Consider Figure 8.6, a description of the case involving Manuel Villa:

Figure 8.6

Noble-Cause Violence: A Case Example

When police officers took Manuel Villa to St. John's hospital in Queens on Nov. 10, 1994, his face was so bruised that doctors thought he had been in a car wreck.

Villa, a mechanic with no criminal record, said he had been pummeled by dozens of blows from two detectives questioning him about his brother's role in a shooting.

The police officers who brought Villa to the hospital after he was beaten told doctors that he had slipped and hit his head on a desk. But once the officers had left the room, Villa told a nurse that he had been pummeled by two doctors and two detectives, who handcuffed him, pinned him to the floor of the 106th Precinct detective squad room and took turns punching him in the face, hitting him with more than 50 blows.

Source: David Kocieniewski, *New York Times*, April 23, 1988. Internet.

Was Villa an "asshole" as described by Van Maanen? He was certainly treated violently. However, as the author of the article cited above notes, Villa was a volunteer auxiliary police officer, had passed the Transit Police Department's examination, and was scheduled to take the city exam. Villa was hardly a likely candidate for an "asshole" list.

Perhaps the most disturbing part of the incident involved the circumstances that sparked the beating. Villa had been asked to come to the 106th precinct station house to pick up his brother's belongings. An angry interrogation began when he arrived. He was hit in the face with a ruler. After several bows, Villa threatened to file a brutality complaint. It was at that point that he was cuffed and beaten.

In what way did Villa bring into question the police detective's notion of moral order? The answer is clear. He suggested that they were responsible to the law. By threatening to file a brutality complaint, Villa was suggesting that they weren't above the law, but indeed had a responsibility to it. The beating quickly followed, a demonstration acted out on Villa's body that he was factually wrong.

Testimonial Deception or Perjury

Rarely will police administrators admit, and indeed few believe, that perjury is routine when officers give sworn testimony in the courts. However, it may be that perjury is commonplace, a widely shared characteristic of many local police cultures. In a survey of drug cases in the late 1960s, Skolnick (1988) was able to provide a glimpse into the pervasiveness of police perjury. He noted a dramatic increase in "dropsy" testimony, where individuals apprehended for drug possession after the *Mapp*[21] decision were dropping drugs on the ground rather than being caught holding them. Findings were striking; looking at the Narcotics Bureau in New York, Skolnick observed that prior to the *Mapp* decision (concerning the exclusionary rule), the narcotics bureau claimed that 92 percent of the narcotics found were hidden on the person, eight percent on the ground. After the *Mapp* decision, only 28 percent were found on the suspect's body, with 72 percent found on the ground. As one of the authors of this book observed elsewhere:

> If, as some argue, criminals rationally adapt their behavior in order to take advantage of the criminal law, why then would criminals, as suggested by these numbers, modify their behavior in such a way to dramatically increase their likelihood of arrest? (Crank, 1998:244)

Some readers might consider Skolnick's data to be outdated. Not by a stretch! Our fear is that testimonial deception is a widespread contemporary problem. Thomas Barker conducted a questionnaire survey of police behavior in a city he called South City, his findings published in 1994. The survey was conducted in a small city with a population of about 25,000. The questionnaire he used was designed to measure the pervasiveness and support for various aspects of police deviance.

One of the topics presented on the questionnaire was testimonial deception. Police officers reported that they thought that about 23 percent of their fellow officers had lied in court. When asked about how often an officer would report another officer for perjury, 28 percent, slightly more than one in four, stated "always." Sixty-four percent of the officers stated that they would report another officer for perjury either rarely or never.

Keep in mind that the findings on this survey were reported by the police themselves, not an outside group who might have motives different from the interests of the police. Perjury was defined as those who have "lied in court." The clear conclusion, at least in this small city, was widespread tolerance – nearly three-fourths of the officers in the survey – for police perjury.

Mike discussed this research with the commanders. It is always uncomfortable. Mike lightly laughed. *You may think that you know your officers. But do you? You know the song and dance that you put on for reporters? Where did you learn it?*

Barker's research, some observers might contend, represents an isolated and atypical example. Consider another assessment of police lying by Barker, Friery, and Carter (1994). The findings of this research reveal how central the noble cause is for young recruits, and how willing they are to set legal means aside in order to achieve noble causes.

Barker, Friery, and Carter conducted their research among rookie officers in five academy training sessions. The majority of these officers had field experience, with a few having up to five years. The authors found that "58% of the respondents gave moderate acceptance to deviant lies that were told for legitimate purposes" (1994:161). What were legitimate purposes? Barker and his colleagues (1994:161) cited "frustration with the criminal justice process," and "get the bad guys off the street." In other words, lying was an acceptable strategy if it contributed to the noble cause.

Officers in Barker and his colleagues' study were in training. The majority had limited exposure to their organization's local cultures, though most had been in their departments for a year or more. Yet they were prepared to lie if it would put bad guys behind bars – the noble cause was firmly instilled in them. These officers were in POST academy. *What were they learning?*

Drugs

The use and sale of illicit drugs is one of the most grave violations of ethical conduct that a police officer can commit. As we noted in Chapter 4, Sherman (1985:259), presented drug corruption as the final stage in an officer's moral decline. An officer that used drugs had slid all the way down the slippery slope, had lost all personal dignity.

Some officers may be morally vulnerable to illicit influences in their agency or on the "street," as Sherman's model suggested. However, we believe that drug corruption is more ethically complex than suggested by his model. Some officers find that narcotics use and sales are part and parcel of police work. Indeed, their effectiveness as police officers requires that they be intimately involved with illicit narcotics.

In other words, in order to understand the way in which officers can become "bent" in the use and sale of narcotics, we recommend that the reader not start by trying to figure out what's wrong with individual officers corrupted by greed. One should begin by taking a look at the organizational and personal pressures on narcotics agents.

Consider the investigations of Manning and Redlinger (1977). These authors found that there are departmental pressures on agents that compel them to commit noble-cause corruption associated with drug use and sales. Pressures to corrupt officers, they observed, were of two types: Pressures to violate laws to enforce narcotics laws, and pressures to obstruct justice. These pressures are listed below.

Figure 8.7

Pressures to Enforce Narcotics Laws and Obstruct Justice

Departmental pressures to violate laws to enforce narcotics laws:

1. Aspirations for promotion and salary. Officers need a good track record of busts.
2. Implicit quotas for arrests.
3. Directives from administrators.
4. Self-esteem maintenance. It feels good to be good at your work.
5. Moral-ideological commitments. You're "protecting the kids" in winning "the war against drugs."

Pressures to obstruct justice include:

1. Protect informants.
2. Create informants through threats of prosecution and its abeyance if they cooperate.
3. Suppress information on cases pursued by other officers. (Manning & Redlinger, 1977:155-156)

A casual inspection of this list might lead one to conclude that there's nothing particularly wrong with organizational pressures that encourage the suppression of illicit drug activity – after all, don't these pressures simply reflect how the organization encourages good police work? However, let's think about these pressures in the context of narcotic suppression.

Pressures to carry out narcotics enforcement occur in a crime control environment in which agents have to find ways of obtaining information that aren't **victim centered**. This means that information about drug-related crime is not obtained from "victims" who report crimes to the police. Police consequently have to resort to other techniques – usually informants or undercover activity – in order to unmask illegal activity. They have to have informants that are willing – or can be coerced – into giving information. To make cases, they have to be able to buy or sell. They have to know what marijuana smells like. They have to be willing to taste it and know what it should taste like. If they want to be effective, they have to move up in the criminal organization. They have to be prepared to "turn on" individuals, introducing outsiders or non-users to techniques of narcotics use. In short, they have to be better at being bad than the bad guys. And they will be. They believe in their work. They are "morally ideologically" committed, to use Manning and Redlinger's (1977) phrase. The noble cause is in their hearts. An inspection of departmental and obstruction of justice pressures listed above shows that they focus on the "good end." In a word, the police organization itself encourages "noble-cause" corruption. How can officers, already committed to the noble cause, resist these pressures?

Figure 8.8

> ### Simulation
>
> Trainers will emphasize to their officers that it is never, never appropriate for them to taste drugs. They will insist that good undercover work can be done without using drugs. That you can simulate drug use, you don't actually have to do it. Poppycock! Consider the words of one of Carter's (1999) confidants:
>
> > Simulation is crap – any user knows if you're smoking or faking, and you can bet they're watching the new guys to see if you're taking a real hit. If I'm at a [drug] deal and I try to simulate, I might as well be wearing a sign that says COP . . . so you've got to take a real hit of marijuana – it's got less bite than tequila. (Carter, 1999:320)

Agents corrupt themselves in order to be good agents. To be *golden apples*. What are the patterns of agent corruption that Manning and Redlinger identify? They are listed in Figure 8.9. The reader will not find them comforting.

Figure 8.9

Patterns of Corruption

1. *Taking bribes*. This can be in the form of payoffs from dealers to officers. If an arrest is already made, an officer can "make the case badly." This kind of corruption was reported to be widespread by the Knapp Commission (1972) in New York.

2. *Using drugs.* Undercover agents, to show their loyalties to those on whom they are doing surveillance, have to "turn on" with them.

3. *Buying/Selling narcotics.* Narcotics can be used to pay off informants. Potential customers can be introduced to dealers.

4. *Arrogation of seized property.* This is a complicated way of describing the disappearance of narcotics, and sometimes cash, in police lockers.

5. *Illegal searches and seizures.* Smoke can be smelled. Drugs can be seen in "plain sight," later planted in plain sight to prove the point. Drugs can be flaked, that is, planting illicit drugs on someone. Padding is where drugs are added to an already confiscated seizure.

6. *The protection of informants.* All major agencies provide money for informants. This has a number of negative consequences. Informants can be protected from other charges while they are working. Manning and Redlinger cited one case in which:

> the confidential informant was caught breaking and entering a home, but the agents "fixed" the charge with the Prosecuting Attorney's office on the basis that the informant was "one of the best." The prosecutor then added five cases to the informant's caseload." (Manning & Redlinger, 1977:162)

The message in Manning and Redlinger's research is clear. To understand how officers become corrupted by narcotics, we should not look for flaws in their character. To understand narcotics corruption, one should consider their commitment to the noble cause, and how the organization reinforces that commitment with pressures to put bad guys away through the circumvention of legal due process. Some officers become corrupt, not because they have character flaws, but because they are carrying out organizational purposes efficiently and effectively.

Carter (1999) described noble-cause drug corruption as **Type 2 drug corruption**, or corruption in the pursuit of legitimate goals. It is consistent with our definition of noble-cause corruption. Figure 8.10 presents Carter's definition of Type 2 drug corruption.

Figure 8.10

> ### Type 2 Drug Corruption
>
> There are persons whom officers "know" are involved in drug traf-
> ficking, however, the police are consistently unable to obtain suffi-
> cient evidence for arrest. Similarly, there are "known" criminals which
> have been found not guilty in court because the government has not
> been able to prove its case – frequently because evidence has been
> excluded on "technicalities." The officers see these recurring circum-
> stances and become frustrated because the trafficker is "beating the
> system."
>
> It is argued that in the case of Type 2 corruption, the acts are com-
> mitted not only for the personal psychological gain of the officer but
> in support of organizational goals through which the officer may be
> rewarded by commendations, promotions, and/or recognition.
>
> Type 2 corruption is further compounded because this behavior
> is not traditionally perceived as being corrupt. There is a degree of
> informal organizational tolerance for behavior which gets "known"
> traffickers off the streets or seizes the trafficker's cache of drugs.

Source: David Carter, "Drug Use and Drug-Related Corruption of Police Officers," 1999.

A Warning to Commanders

If you are a commander, you may resent the suggestion that this could
happen in your agency. It is difficult for commanders to believe that their
officers will be involved in drug-related corruption. For many commanders, it is unthinkable. You may think that this research discussed above
is outdated, that this kind of thing doesn't happen today. Consider a
recent case in Chicago described in Figure 8.11, the case of the Austin 7.

If the reader is firmly in denial, you will argue that this is an isolated
case. Let's see. In Miami, 100 officers have been or are currently being
investigated on corruption-related problems, and up to 200 may face
investigation (Dombrink, 1994). Most visible among these were the
Miami River Cops, indicted for major drug rip-offs. In the 1980s,
Philadelphia convicted 30 police officers for gambling-related misconduct – a crime similar to drugs in enforcement strategy – that reached to
the second in command in the police department. In New York, 644 nar-
cotics-related official complaints were brought against the police. As
Dombrink (1994:73) observed, "even the many advances made by the
NYPD, as far as instituting mechanisms for corruption control, were
being questioned."

Figure 8.11

The Austin 7

Seven officers were arrested in December, 1996, on federal charges of conspiracy to commit robbery and extortion for shaking down undercover agents they thought were drug dealers. In their lockers were found crack cocaine, powder cocaine, marijuana, and possibly heroin. The indictment included the following charges:

1. robbing an apartment used as a safe house by drug dealers.
2. revealing the identity of an informant to an undercover agent thought to be a drug dealer.
3. Payments for escorting a cocaine shipment.

This case also produced some new language into the argot of drug interdiction. Planting drugs on defendants, stated by one of the officers to be common, was called a "blind date." Another practice was called "reintroduction." If someone dropped drugs during an encounter with a police officer. The officer would put it in his pocket until the next time they met. Then the officer would make an arrest and "reintroduce" the drugs.

Source: *The Chicago Tribune*, December 21, 1996, "7 Chicago Cops Indicted in Shakedowns." *The Chicago Tribune*, January 29, 1997, "1st Break in Austin Code of Silence."

Recent enough? Consider Cleveland. In January, 1998, 44 Cleveland police officers were charged with corruption. Charges included providing protection for shipments of cocaine. As of this date, 10 have pleaded guilty to the distribution charge.

These are big cities. You might feel relieved that you are from a smaller place. You shouldn't. Consider Cicero, Illinois, population 67,000. Nearly one-third of the officers have been suspended or forced to resign. The acting police chief was suspended because he had ties to a former Stone Park, Illinois, officer (Stone Park – population 4,383) convicted to helping run a large, mob-linked marijuana-growing operation.[22] Where was internal affairs? The captain of internal affairs was removed after he blocked the investigation of two officers who were involved in an attempted theft at an electronics store.

We are concerned that drug-related noble-cause corruption is becoming more frequent in the United States. Chuck Wexler, the executive director for the Police Executive Research Forum, stated that the drug trade was behind a "sea change" in the growth of corruption among the police (Johnson, 1998). He attributed the problem to the tremendous amounts of money available to tempt officers into corruption. We think that some of the growth in the corruption is associated with the noble cause. A commander should ask him or herself – What motivated officers who later faced corruption charges to become involved in anti-narcotics activity in the first place?

If the reader is a commander, he or she knows that narcotics vice is among the most poplar assignments for detectives. It is an elite unit. Why is that? The answer, we believe, is that an assignment in narcotics vice enables police officers to act out the noble cause against a clear moral wrong – drug use and sales. It also allows them to act without a great deal of messy bureaucratic oversight, and with easy opportunities for arrests. As Manning and Redlinger (1977) noted, the sense of moral fulfillment for successful undercover drug work is great.

Mike expands on this theme. *Commanders, do you understand how your officers think about undercover work? I know. I've done it. It's exciting. I'm out there doing something about bad guys and no one's watching me. Do I believe in getting the scum off the streets? Oh yeah. I believe.*

To understand the extent to which drug enforcement officers are committing this kind of noble-cause crime, one needs to recognize the compelling nature of the noble cause and how organizational pressures reinforce it in narcotics cases. One has to recognize how the organization's values can be used to compel officers to become involved in a wide variety of illegal drug activities.

Finally, if the reader is a commander and is absolutely convinced that this couldn't happen in their agency, consider the following words of another commander, from Carter (1999:319):

> The last problem I ever thought I'd face is my officers robbing drug dealers *for drugs*. I mean, the reports are here – but my mind just can't accept it. I don't know if I let [the officers] down or they let me down. Something definitely went wrong in the system.

Consider yourself warned.

The Treacherous Psychology of Deceptive Legal Practices

For those of you who are police officers, recruits, or students who want to become police officers, it is unreasonable to think that there could be problems with anything you do that is legal. After all, the law is what the legislature says it is, and the police carry society's responsibility to enforce it. We believe, however, that there are deceptive practices that the police use, that are themselves legal, but that create a working environment that both justifies noble-cause corruption and alienates the public.

Deceptive practices justify morally questionable behavior in terms of the ends that are gained. These practices contribute to an ethical environment that encourages a focus on policing's "good ends." If a police department uses deceptive practices without thinking about their ethical implications, its officers are working in an organizational climate fertile for the growth of noble-cause corruption. Deceptive practices are an invitation to ethical chaos.

Deceptive practices can take a variety of forms. Skolnick and Fyfe (1993:61) describe several types of deceptive legal practices commonplace in police organizations. Consider the following examples having to do with the fabrication of evidence:

1. Tell a suspect falsely that he has been identified by an accomplice.

2. Present a suspect with faked physical evidence, such as fingerprints, bloodstains, or hair samples, to confirm the suspect's guilt.

3. Tell the suspect that he or she has been identified by an eyewitness.

4. Stage a line-up where a pretend eyewitness identifies the suspect.

5. Have the suspect take a lie-detector test and then tell the suspect that the test proved that he or she was guilty.

How would the practices listed above be analyzed from an ethical perspective? They are clearly ends oriented. They seem to offer the best of all ethical worlds – they are legal and they are ends oriented. They are faithful to the noble cause, but are acted out in accordance with the legal requirements of police work.

So what's wrong with them? Let's conduct another thought experiment about suspected spousal infidelity. The thought experiment is presented in Figure 8.12.

What can we learn from this thought experiment? We have a jealous husband, consumed by his passion but with no real evidence of his wife's betrayal. He knows it, is certain of it. How can he uncover the truth? His options are limited. So he becomes deceptive in order to try to uncover the guilt of his wife.

JUMP START reprinted by permission of United Feature Syndicate, Inc.

How would you the reader react if your spouse treated you this way every time you worked late – when, ultimately, the act of working late itself became the proof your spouse needed to prove that you were guilty? We don't think you'd like it very much. But what is it about the husband's behavior that's troubling? We suggest that it begins with the certainty of guilt in the accuser's eye, and proceeds to use deception to verify the guilt. Indeed, if each of the husband's accusations are reviewed, the reader will note that they are examples of #1 through #5 of Skolnick and Fyfe's (1993) deceptive practices described on page 165 of this text. Not much of a way to value a relationship, is it? Yet it's how we conduct this business we call policing – we too often start with a presumption of guilt and proceed to "trick" or badger a suspect into confessing. It's no wonder that some officers get confused and act out the noble cause at home, destroying their relationships. They carry principles of distrust into their family life, acting them out on their wives or on their children. And it's no wonder that citizens subjected to these techniques, guilty and innocent alike, end up disliking the police.

Figure 8.12

A Thought Experiment: Jealousy and Uncertainty

Imagine that you are a married woman, a street cop, and you come home late, and your husband wants to know what you've been doing. He doesn't trust you and he is certain that you're cheating on him. He absolutely believes it. So he tells you that a friend called and said that he had seen you with another man. You deny it. He pulls out a pair of your panties that were supposed to be in the wash and tells you that they've got semen on them. WHO IS IT? You deny the accusation a second time. He says that a friend of his has seen you having lunch with this man. You deflect the comment, responding "So what? What's wrong with having lunch with someone?" This third response to his accusations only makes him angrier, convincing him he's right. By now you are in the midst of a raging fight. He continues "I followed you yesterday. I saw you and him together. I know his name. I want to see if you'll admit it." He's bluffing to see if you'll admit being with a man that a friend says you had lunch with. You deny it for the fourth time. He says "Look me squarely in the eyes and tell me that you aren't having an affair." In response to this fifth accusation you blow up and storm out of the house, your relationship severely damaged by his crude harassment.

In the thought experiment in Figure 8.12, what has the husband accomplished? He has created an environment where the most important consideration is the noble cause – in this instance finding guilt of which he is certain – but in his spouse, not a criminal suspect. Does the husband ever wonder that sometimes accused individuals are so overwhelmed with the deceptive accusational practices that they finally admit guilt just to get on with their lives? And reader, have you ever done this to anyone?

There are two ethical questions evoked by deceptive practices, and I will end this section with the recommendation that the reader consider them carefully.

1. When deceptive practices are used, do they uncover truth or create it?

2. Does the reader understand how deceptive practices, legal though they be, encourage street officers to *cross the line* to noble-cause corruption?

Ethics for the Twenty-First Century

Part 4

The previous eight chapters have presented a frustrating image of pressures for police to commit noble-cause corruption. Moral-ideological commitments, hiring procedures, organizational pressures to produce, prosecutorial pressures for efficiency, and an occupational culture that shields officers from oversight and control insure that the noble cause will be corrupted, and that corrupted officers will be protected. Given these pressures, it is unreasonable to think that officers committed to the noble cause can avoid corruption.

Yet it is necessary that our efforts are directed and re-doubled in intensity toward this important. Rarely in our history have Americans invested their internal security so completely to the trust of the police, and never before has so much been at stake. The legal authority of the police to intervene in citizens' affairs is increasingly relaxed by a congress and court system panic-stricken over media-amplified images of crime and social decay. Police expansion of legal and extralegal authority is supported by a crime-fearing public and academics who champion innovative police strategies.

Today, a broad change in the police is occurring. Reforms carried out under the rubric of community policing carry a promise to improve the quality of American life and reduce fear of victimization, particularly in inner cities that have been devastated by deteriorating social infrastructures and high levels of crime (Frank, Watkins & Brandl, 1997). Under the umbrella of community policing, the courts have supported aggressive and highly invasive tactics in efforts to control drug sales and trafficking. And in this movement, there is a dark potential: the subversion of democratic ideals in the quest for order over law (Bayley, 1988; Kappeler & Kraska, 1998).

The late twentieth century is a time in which the social fabric of the country is in the midst of dramatic change. The age of Anglo-Saxon demographic dominance is giving way to a polyglot society, for better or for worse. Urban and rural spaces are increasingly characterized by different kinds of groups sharing the same local geography. Ethnic, religious, cultural, and age-based conflicts are possible. These conflicts and their resolutions will define the "order" that the police must deal with in our emerging future.

The police, Mike has argued, are authorized representatives of a moral standard and use the law to advance that standard. The standard is the noble cause. How will this moral authority mix with community policing? It depends on how community policing is implemented. Poorly carried out, community policing can leave the police unprepared for the future. Asserting their own brand of noble cause morality, they may damage those same communities they try to protect.

We will describe a different way of thinking about public order, and suggest how community policing can contribute to that order. In a society marked by diversity and conflict, successful maintenance of public order will require powerful skills in negotiating order among contending groups. Police will be prepared for the future if they possess the skills, and morality, and the patience to weave threads of order together from differing racial, ethnic, and religious accounts. In other words, they must *negotiate* order rather than *assert* it.

The following two chapters look at community policing. Chapter 9 looks at community policing and discusses problems in maintaining public order under a community policing environment. Chapter 10 looks at anticipated demographic changes in the twenty-first century and discusses what we think will be the appropriate role of the police.

Ethics in the Age of Community Policing

9

Key Terms

coactive function	police-community reciprocity
cognitive dissonance	proactive function
informal norms	quality of life
iron fist	reactive function
middle-ground institutions	social distance
order maintenance	velvet glove

The commanders return from the 2:30 p.m. break and prepare for the final discussion. Participants had taken a long break, and only two hours of presentation remain. This is where Mike presents his pitch for community policing.

Traditional policing is about law enforcement. But community policing is about community order, making communities safe for kids to play in. Isn't that it? So I'm going to talk about order.

Below, we will try to provide a balanced perspective on community policing, what we consider to be its bright promise and its dangerous weaknesses. We will begin this chapter with an overview of community policing.

Overview of Community Policing

The United States is in the midst of a sea change in policing. Traditional policing is giving ground to a new way to do police work, a way called community policing. Professionals and scholars alike are engaged in a bracing, vigorous debate on the merits and problems of community policing philosophy and initiatives (Mastrofski, 1991; Skolnick & Bayley, 1986; Sykes, 1989; Klockars, 1991a). Our purpose here is not to debate the merits of community policing, but to consider its implications for noble-cause ethics.

What is community policing? A review of the literature reveals little consensus on just what community policing is. By many accounts, the notion is fuzzy. Indeed, a principle complaint of many police officers in departments undergoing the transition to community policing is: "it all sounds well and good – but what do I do that is different?" We will return to this question, because evaluational techniques are integral to successful implementation of community policing.

In its most general sense, community policing is a reorganization of police work and rethinking of elements of traditional police strategies, roles, and tactics. A central component of community policing reform is the involvement of the public in the practice of police work. The police need and should solicit the assistance of local communities in order to engage communities in their own self-defense, and in order to adapt crime control to the particular needs of local community settings.

Community Policing Themes

Observers have identified two separate and occasionally conflicting themes in the community policing movement. Kraska and Paulsen (1996) describe the themes of the velvet glove and the iron fist. The **velvet glove** refers to "soft" police strategies and tactics, such as door-to-door crime prevention initiatives, community watch groups, and block meetings. Velvet glove initiatives encourage public participation. The **iron fist**, on the other hand, represents the hard edge of law enforcement. Iron fist tactics, such as street sweeps and aggressive enforcement of public order statutes, are designed to assert police control over crime-ridden neighborhoods. In its most aggressive form, the iron fist refers to the militarization of police units and their use in routine police activities.

Crank and Langworthy (1992) note a similar division within the community policing movement. They argue that one can see within the community policing movement the competing influences of conservative and liberal crime control agendas. Conservative themes aim at expanding police authority to intervene in crime and public order problems that appear to be endemic in many cities. Liberal themes are concerned with providing broad police services for residents of poverty-stricken minority neighborhoods and insuring that the police fairly treat minority citizens.

Oettmeier and Wycoff (1997:2) identify differences, and they describe the differences as distinct functions of policing. These functions are described below.

Figure 9.1

> **Oettmeier and Wycoff: Functions of Policing**
>
> The **reactive function**, they observe, is characteristic of traditional policing, and is characterized by routine police responses to citizen calls for assistance. This means that the police involve themselves in the affairs of the citizenry primarily when the law has been broken, a citizen calls the police dispatcher, and a patrol car is sent to investigate the circumstances. Police are reacting to the occurrence of a criminal or suspicious event.
>
> The **proactive function** refers to activities initiated by the police. The essence of proactivity is that the police act before a law has been broken. Proactive policing innovations include directed patrols, police initiated investigations, and a variety of crime prevention activities. Proactive innovations were characteristic of policing in the 1970s and 1980s.
>
> The **coactive function** means that the police work with citizen groups for the purpose of reinforcing community "self-defense." The coactive function is described as follows:
>
> > effective policing is the result of coactive citizen and police partnerships. Either party can identify conditions that need to be addressed to increase the safety of a neighborhood, but citizens and police will work together to define and design the response to threatening conditions. (1977:2)

The proactive function is similar to the "iron fist" described above. The coactive function is more like the velvet glove and is similar to the liberal conception of community policing. However, departments frequently pick and choose between proactive and coactive functions in order to determine which works best for them. It is not unusual for a police organization to decide that some areas in its jurisdiction are better handled by proactive law enforcement, while others are more responsive to coactive law enforcement.

Cordner and the Community Policing Model

One of the more detailed definitions of community policing is offered by Cordner (1999:138-146). Cordner's model emphasizes citizen input, and is consequently more similar to the coactive model described above.

By reviewing each of the four dimensions of community policing presented in Cordner's model (see Figure 9.2), the reader can recognize the complex and far-reaching nature of the changes that community policing can bring to a police organization.

Figure 9.2

Cordner's Model of Community Policing

The Philosophical Dimension. Community policing seeks greater citizen input than traditional policing. It also gives greater official status to non-enforcement functions, particularly order maintenance and service activities. And it supports tailored policing, typically at the neighborhood level, based on local norms and individual needs.

The Strategic Dimension. Community policing places less reliance on the patrol car and more emphasis on face-to-face situations. These include foot patrol, directed patrol, door-to-door policing, and other non-traditional forms of patrol. Community policing also focuses on more intense geographic focus for patrol. Assignments are permanent to increase officers' familiarity with their areas. Community policing also emphasizes more of a crime-prevention orientation, particularly in the reallocation of officers' time to problem-solving.

The Tactical Dimension. Tactics focus on putting officers in positive interactions with citizens. This includes the forming of associations, which are what Skolnick and Bayley call the lifeblood of crime prevention. These also include youth-oriented recreational and educational programs. Tactics also include problem solving. This means that officers develop ways of identifying and correcting underlying problems and conditions that produce crime.

The Organizational Dimension. This dimension concerns how the police department re-orients itself to do community policing. A variety of organizational changes are associated with community policing. These are of three types.

Structure. Authority and responsibility are delegated down the chain of command and out into station houses in the community. Organizations are flattened – layers, particularly in the middle management ranks, are removed. Employees are assigned to work together in teams. And there is a wider and strategic use of civilians to accomplish the organizational mission.

Management. Mission statements are re-considered. Greater use is made of strategic planning. Mentoring is emphasized. Lower-level employees, particularly line officers, are encouraged to take risks to demonstrate creativity and imagination. Discipline for mistakes is relaxed.

Information. Performance appraisals are used to evaluate personnel. Program evaluations are conducted regularly to assess the quality and success of policing efforts. Information systems collect data on the whole range of the police function, not simply law enforcement. Crime analysis is more detailed and sophisticated. Particular emphasis is given to the use of Geographical Information Systems.

Source: Adapted from G. Cordner (1999). "Elements of Community Policing." Pp. 149 in L. Gaines and G. Cordner (eds.) *Policing Perspectives: An Anthology.* Los Angeles, CA: Roxbury.

Community Policing, Public Order, and the Quality of Urban Life

Community policing is a different way to think about police work. Whereas traditional policing placed the enforcement of the law ahead of service, order maintenance, and crime prevention, community policing emphasizes an integration of these roles. It *particularly* emphasizes the way police can maintain public order. **Order maintenance** is sometimes called peacekeeping. Regoli and Hewitt (1996) define order maintenance as follows:

> When order has been disrupted, it is the police officer's job to restore it. Police intervention is intended to stop whatever has disturbed the peace whether it is the peace between a citizen and a neighborhood or the peace between two people. (Regoli & Hewitt, 1996:265)

Order maintenance is fundamentally different from traditional, legalistic law enforcement. Under a legalistic model of law enforcement, the police are responsible for the enforcement of a legal code. The legal code applies to all citizens regardless of where and how they live. Maintaining public order, however, requires that the police make subjective judgments about the appropriate level of public order, and act to maintain this order when it has been disrupted. In law enforcement, the police act on behalf of the law, regardless of its effect on a community or an individual; under order maintenance, the police are expected to maintain community order, even if, technically, no law has been been broken.

Order-maintenance activity is closely associated with neighborhood quality of life. By **quality of life** is meant two things: citizen attitudes, such as fear of crime and fear of participating in outdoor activities, and declines in the physical quality of neighborhoods, the accumulation of trash and graffiti. Some departments act on the belief that aggressive enforcement of public order laws can protect neighborhoods and communities from future "quality of life" decline and the onset of more serious crime problems. Consequently, under a community policing mandate, police departments may aggressively suppress public order problems in order to improve community quality of life.

Some police experts have been concerned that too much focus on quality of life issues might undermine the democratic traditions of the United States. Bayley and Shearing (1998) take note of this conflict in the following quote:

Figure 9.3

> **Community Policing and the Expansion of State Power**
>
> Because government is deeply distrusted in Anglo-American tradition, the powers of the police are circumscribed; their activities closely monitored. . . . Seen in these terms, community policing, which is community-based crime prevention under governmental auspices, is a contradiction in terms. It requires the police, who are bound by law, to lead communities in informal surveillance, analysis, and treatment. Community policing is a license for police to intervene in the private lives of individuals. It harnesses the coercive power of the state to social amelioration. This represents an expansion of state power, and is much more in keeping with the continental European than with the Anglo-American traditions of policing. (Bayley & Shearing, 1998:158-159)

Many observers of the police are fearful that if the police are granted increased authority to intervene in the affairs of the citizenry on behalf of public order and the quality of life, United States democratic traditions will be seriously compromised. They may be right – we don't know. The United States is in many ways an innocent among world powers – unlike most countries in the world, we have never experienced a history of autocratic rule or military dictatorship.[23] We might not know how to recognize encroaching totalitarianism.

Mike describes his thoughts on community policing to the commanders. They've heard most of it before – many of the ideas aren't new. He then discusses how a value-based decisionmaker might look at community policing.

Think of a value-based decisionmaker – which, you'll recall, is who you hire when you recruit a police officer. She or he is a hero type, remember, the type that runs toward the tower. You remember the tower. He's got all the symbols of authority – the badge, helmet, the insulating sunglasses, Sam Brown, pepper spray, 9mm, PR24, shotgun in the trunk, running for cover, ready for war. Whose values do they represent? The public? Not exactly. They are value-based decisionmakers, committed to the noble cause, and they use the law to advance that cause.

Mike waits for an answer. No one answers. *Where do his values come from?*

"Their upbringing," one of the commanders responds.

Right. Mike smiles. *Their values. It always comes back to that.*

If we are doing community policing, we then ask this officer to enforce neighborhood order. Whatever that is. We recommend to them not to take a "what the hell" attitude just because the law hasn't been technically bro-

ken. We want them to get involved in the community. What're we really asking them? We're asking them to apply their moral standard to this whole new area. We have to be very, very careful about this.

Informal Community Norms and Police Values

Community policing assumes that police officers can know and through their actions help maintain a community's **informal norms**. By informal norms is meant that a community has its particular ideas of acceptable behavior, ideas that are not written down but taken for granted by community members. Informal norms are different from laws, which are written down and provide the basis for law enforcement. For example, a community may think that it is unacceptable for homeless individuals to sleep in a particular park, even though there is no law that technically forbids it. Police officers might consequently roust out the homeless, arguing that by doing so they diminish the sales of drugs in the park. Reformers worry that informal community norms might include racial norms as well. What if, for example, an African-American community wants police to stop and question all young Asian males in their neighborhood? What would then be the police role? We will return to this question at the end of the chapter.

By enforcing the "informal norms of the community" is carried the idea that police will, in the day-to-day practice of their work, carry and enforce the same values as the communities they police. Whatever predisposing values or ethics an officer has, he or she will set these aside and adopt the standards of the neighborhoods for which they are responsible. Yet, as we have argued, this is precisely what many police officers don't do. The values that motivate police officers tend to stem from moral predispositions.

Mike continues. *What if we increase the authority of the police to intervene in the affairs of the citizenry – and we don't change their values?* Under a community policing philosophy, are we simply providing them with an expanded authority to exercise their moral predispositions over citizens? The danger is that community policing carries in it the seeds for noble-cause corruption justified in terms of community protection. The noble-cause corruption problem for community policing, simply put, is: "If community protection is a higher moral principle than the lawful constitutional protections given to individual citizens, why should we pay attention to the law if we can do something to protect communities?"

Mike taps the continuum with his knuckles. *Remember the continuum? With police values way on the right and community values on the left? If we just power up line officers with more authority, what do you think is going to happen? Do you think that they'll get along better with citizens? Giving them more power is not enough. You've got to get the police and the public on the same side of the continuum.*

Let's replay this dilemma as an ethical question. How can we provide police with a wider mandate to intercede in the affairs of citizens, and at the same time instill ethical protections against noble-cause corruption? This is a difficult question, yet one that must be answered if we want to both preserve our democratic heritage and expand the police role.

Mike presents his vision of community policing. *I'm an advocate of community-based policing, but it's got to be done right. Let's think about it for a minute. When we do community policing, we have to make sure that all officers are doing it. Not a special squad within the department, there's no commitment there. And they all have to get out in the public and mix with citizens. That's got to be part of the package. If you do this you've done two things that separate community-based policing from all other attempts to reform the police. First, you reduce the social distance between the police and the policed. Second, you empower the police and the policed alike, together.* Below, we consider these two differences between community policing and other reforms.

Proposition 1: Community Policing Can Reduce Social Distance

The first proposition is that community policing can reduce the social distance between the police and the policed. **Social distance** refers to the degree of friendliness and sense of comfort between two people or two groups. Social distance is small between two families, for example, if they would permit their children to intermarry. Social distance is large when a family would not permit one of their members to talk to someone, or would not be willing to live in the same neighborhood with that person.

Consider the crime-control/due process continuum again. The police, as we noted earlier, tend to be on the right side of it, on the crime control side. The policed tend to be more toward the middle or on the left side, the due process side. This is what the Rokeach et al. (1971) data show us in Chapter 3. Members of ethnic and racial minority communities tend to be on the due process side, not because they are sympathetic to criminals – they tend, in fact, to be victimized more frequently than middle-class Anglo citizens. It's that abuse by the police is historically greater among minority group members than among white middle-class citizens, and minority group members are consequently more afraid of them (see Cao, Frank & Cullen, 1996; Williams & Murphy, 1995; Powers, 1995; Kappeler et al., 1994; Kerner Commission, 1968).

What is the social distance between the police and the population policed? It tends to be large, particularly in minority neighborhoods, for two reasons. First, the police and the policed don't share the same values. This is particularly the case when the policed are also minorities. Our data show that the areas most heavily policed are minority communities, particularly African-American communities. In such communities, the police sometimes develop their images of crime, criminals, and appropriate police response, according to prevailing racial stereotypes. Consider Bouza's observation in Figure 9.4:

Figure 9.4

> ### Racial Stereotyping and Police Practices
>
> In Los Angeles, the police were forced to abandon choke holds, not because they were ineffective but largely because of a stupid comment made by the chief following the death of a black man who'd been subdued by the grip, which temporarily cuts off the flow of the blood to the brain, causing the suspect to pass out. The chief created an uproar when he blurted out that blacks were somehow physiologically different from "normal people" in the flow of blood to the brain. The resulting clamor was so intense that an aggressive agency, and an aggressive chief, had to abandon the practice.

Source: Anthony Bouza (1990). *The Police Mystique,* p. 94.

Second, police act out their role in an authoritarian manner. Many police officers make peremptory decisions about the likely guilt or innocence of a suspect, and their subsequent actions stem from that decision. They may decide, for example, that the person they are dealing with is an "asshole" and needs special, physical "treatment" – a beating or rough search. Such decisions, when linked to racial stereotyping, will sharply increase the social distance between the police and the policed.

Community policing, Mike contends, has the potential to lower the social distance between the police and the policed. It can do this by building relationships between the police and the policed in ways that do not depend on police authority, but instead are constructed around a shared capacity to solve community problems. One of the best discussions of the idea of a shared problem-solving is presented by Skolnick and Bayley (1986). They used a phrase, **police-community reciprocity**, to describe this idea. By police-community reciprocity, they meant that the police and community members work together to solve crime problems and to develop crime prevention tactics. What does reciprocity contribute to the police mission? Skolnick and Bayley (1991) suggested that "police who are substantially involved in reciprocal community crime prevention programs will experience significantly less fear of those communities." With regard to community members, they observed that: "The general reaction to community contact seems to have been 'Where have you been all along?' or 'It's about time'." This also makes for good policing:

Like policemen themselves, the public is tired of police arriving after harm has been done, understanding all too well that little can be done then, particularly with respect to catching the criminal. (Skolnick & Bayley, 1991:501)

Community policing increases the number of non-enforcement contacts between police and the policed. Police, we believe, will cease being faceless uniforms to citizens and the public will cease being treated as potentially dangerous strangers by the police. In short, the police and the policed become humanized – they are received as individual citizens to each other, seeking acceptable solutions to common problems. Guyot (1991), discussing the diverse services police agencies perform, captured the way in which non-traditional policing humanizes the police by changing the social distance between the police and the policed.

Figure 9.5

Towards an Understanding of Common Humanity

. . . when officers repeatedly assist diverse individuals and receive heartfelt thanks, they come to see beyond the jumbled fragments of other's lives to recognize the common humanity they share with people who ask for their help and even with many of the people they arrest. In learning to care for the people they serve, officers develop a tragic perspective on life that makes them less susceptible to cynical views. They become strengthened by their personal commitment to helping people. By contrast, if officers narrow their responsibility to dealing with crime – to attacks that people make on each other and their property – and focus on lawbreakers, then they have fewer opportunities to feel kinship with their clients.

Source: Dorothy Guyot, *Policing as Though People Matter*, 1991:271.

Much good, Mike states, *can come from lowering the social distance between the police and the policed.*

Guyot also noted that early contacts with citizens can have an amplifying effect on officers' attitudes. Officers who initially felt sympathy for their clients tended to find satisfaction in their work and develop a wide repertoire of social skills. On the other hand, those who started with distrust tended to cause distrust in the public as well and become vindictive in their police work. The responsibility for a TO was clear: to insure that officers start in the right direction.

Cognitive Dissonance and Community Policing

At this point, Mike decides to develop one of his favorite themes. He pauses for a minute, rubbing his hands together, composing his thoughts. It's important, he believes, that the audience understand this aspect of the training seminar.

If I bring different groups together in a non-arrest circumstance, what do you think is going to happen? It's going to lower the social distance between them. There is a psychological term for the way social distance is affected when people interact. It is called cognitive dissonance.

Cognitive dissonance is a concept that has been around for 40 years. First described by Leon Festinger in 1957, and reaching a high in popularity in the late 1970s, the theory of cognitive dissonance has generated a great deal of discussion. Let's review the central ideas of cognitive dissonance.

Mike taps the board on the right side of the continuum with his knuckles. *If your street officers believe that they are morally superior, and I'm making that argument that police are value-based decision-makers, why should they want to pay attention to what citizens think? If there's a lot of cognitive dissonance, if your officers are over here –* he taps the right side of the continuum on the blackboard – *and the policed are over here –* he taps the left side of the continuum – *they aren't going to like each other. That's the point. It's up to you to see that they not only work together, but that they want to work together. Otherwise your community policing efforts are probably going to fail.*

Cognitions include beliefs about people. For the police, cognitions can include stereotypes about those policed. We have argued that many police officers believe themselves to be morally superior, on "the side of angels" as Bouza (1990:17) put it. Moral superiority transforms easily into racist stereotyping when the population policed is different in some ethnic, religious, or racial way (Crank, 1998). When a police officer views his or her responsibility through the lens of moral righteousness and believes that they have the authority of the state on their side, will they feel cognitive dissonance in thumping, arresting or otherwise mistreating someone who they have negatively stereotyped? No. They'll enjoy it.

Community policing programs that are designed to bring the police and the community together in non-traditional ways has the potential to change this relationship. Skolnick and Bayley (1986) maintain that the police must convey to the public that they have something to contribute, that the police must recognize that the public is an equal partner. But what kind of behaviors can change the traditional authority imbalance between citizens and police?

Figure 9.6

Elements of Cognitive Dissonance

Cognition refers to knowledge that we have. They can be specific bits of information or general concepts. Sometimes we have cognitions – pieces of knowledge – that seem to be inconsistent or "dissonant" with each other. When this happens, the person is in a state of **cognitive dissonance** (Wicklund & Brehm, 1976). They have two (or more) cognitions that conflict with each other.

Let's say that someone is eating a strange food. The food is a mash that tastes like potatoes, but more meaty. The eater thinks that it tastes good. Then the eater is told that she is eating mashed insect grubs. The eater might have a cognition of what bugs look like, and what they don't look like is good food. Consequently, at that moment, there are two cognitions, (1) one is eating bugs, and (2) bugs aren't food, that are dissonant to each other.

The more important the cognitions that are in disagreement, the greater the cognitive dissonance. Hence the greater the motivational pressure to resolve the dissonance. Most people are extremely uncomfortable with high levels of cognitive dissonance. Eating bugs is highly dissonant for many people. How can the dissonance be resolved?

There are three general principles that describe the resolution of dissonance. First, when dissonance is too great, the reduction in dissonance will occur toward the cognition least resistant to change and away from the one most important to the individual. For example, in the previous "eating bugs" example, it may be far easier to simply stop eating bugs than to convince yourself that bugs are good food. If, on the other hand, the only food available was bug mash, one might reconcile oneself to the notion that bugs are, after all, good food and resolve the dissonance by munching away.

Second, all things being equal, when a recent behavior and a more distant behavior are dissonant, the dissonance is more likely to be resolved in terms favorable to the more recent behavior.

Third, personal responsibility is central to the resolution of cognitive dissonance. If a person acts freely, without sense of external constraint, s/he has a sense of personal responsibility for the relationship between the dissonant elements. Without the element of personal responsibility, the dissonant elements are psychologically irrelevant to the individual (Wicklund & Brehm, 1976). In other words, if someone is forced into a situation where they have to endure dissonant cognitions, the sense of disagreement between them will not go away. For example, if I am forced to eat mashed bugs, and I already know I do not want to, I am likely to continue to dislike it. But if I eat them voluntarily, I am more likely to decide that I like eating them.

If I bring different groups together in non-arrest circumstances, what's going to happen? Mike taps the right side of the continuum. *If I bring these people, the police from here –* He taps the left side – *over to the people over here, and they spend time trying to fix the problems over here, what's going to happen?*

Bringing the two groups together will cause a state of cognitive dissonance for police and policed alike. The police must treat as problem-solving partners a group previously thought of as morally inferior. The police, as Skolnick and Bayley (1986) noted, must be prepared for constructive criticism from the public. How will the dissonance be resolved? Let us return to the three principles for the resolution of dissonance in Figure 9.6.

The first principle was that dissonance would be reduced in the least resistant direction. For a line officer, which of the following is least resistant – to work in a crime preventive capacity as equals with a formerly distrusted group or to refuse to work, request a shift and ignore the expectations of superior officers? The tendency, we argue, will be to conform to managerial expectations. Forcing people to work together does not in itself reduce dissonance, however. Experiences with minority hiring programs in some police departments has taught us that laws requiring occupational integration can backfire, intensifying hostilities between Anglo- and African-Americans. Recall the third principle of dissonance: forced relations do not reduce dissonance.

Commanders, in order to resolve dissonance in a non-forced way, must be practically involved in the day-to-day implementation and activity of community policing. Line officers have to understand that the community policing program carries the moral weight and commitment of its leaders. Active command level support is important for successful implementation of the kind of value changes that will enable community policing to prosper. Commanders must take the lead through the art of example and persuasion, not punitive policy.

Commanders have to take the lead in bridging the gap between the policed and the police. If they abandon this work to their sergeants, the program will collapse under the weight of line resistance. Commanders have to get out into the field, work with the troops, be highly visible, and sell the program with their own commitment. Commanders may be the single most important and undervalued link in the implementation of community policing programs (Geller & Swanger, 1995). Through the aggressive and supportive activity of executives, including the chief or sheriff, commanders can begin to change the leads followed by line officers.

The second principle is that dissonance tends to be resolved in terms of more recent behaviors. This principle suggests that, even for officers with a tradition of negative feelings for particular groups, more recent positive behaviors or "good works" can result in a change in sentiments toward the groups policed. Here, we again consider Mike's question "Where do your officers get their leads from?" If they're being shoveled from assignment to make-shift assignment, or aren't being provided clear responsibilities and receive no command support, they're likely to end up despising community policing and the populations being policed. If, on the other hand, commanders are out in the field with them, their TO is preparing them to work with other groups, their performance evaluations are linked to their relations and activities with the policed, they have a clear set of job expectations and they are learning specialized skills for their craft, then they are gaining a set of behaviors that will encourage positive relations with community groups.

The third principle is self-responsibility. If a person is arbitrarily assigned to work with others they don't like, their sense of personal responsibility for the policed is absent and there will be no reason to resolve the dissonance. Arbitrary assignment can have backfiring consequences, with officers increasing their disdain and moral distance for the policed. Police officers doing community policing must be involved in the decisions about the kinds of assignments that they have or the way the assignments are organized. Again, to use the words of Skolnick and Bayley (1986), officers need the opportunity to do "creative, customized police work."

Proposition 2: Community Policing Empowers the Police and the Policed Alike

Empowerment means that the police and citizens together can cooperatively alleviate the root causes of criminal behavior (Frank, Brandl, Worden & Bynum, 1996). Community policing focuses on what are sometimes called the **middle-ground institutions** of American life: local neighborhoods and neighborhood organizations that are midway between individuals and large-scale governmental enterprises. Citizen empowerment at the neighborhood level is different from both conservative and liberal solutions to crime and public order problems, though it contains features of both. Traditional strategies have sometimes used large-scale governmental intervention to change the social structure of equality or opportunity. The unanticipated consequences of these policies on central state growth or on middle-ground institutions has rarely been examined by their proponents. On the other hand, policies aimed at individuals have typically taken the form of crime suppression efforts. These efforts have been designed around deterrence and arrest production, without thought given to their impact on the neighborhoods where the crime occurred.

The middle-ground institutions – the social, geographical, and economic arenas where we act out our daily lives at home and at work – are the proper focus of community policing. Community policing empowers line officers to make decisions about how normal affairs in their assigned area are carried out, with an eye toward the contribution of their efforts to the well-being of those communities. A guiding premise of community policing is that, by granting line officers wider authority in the way in which they carry out their daily routines, they will develop imaginative solutions to the problems of crime and its prevention (Trojanowicz, Kappeler, Gaines & Bucqueroux, 1990; Greene & Mastrofski, 1991). Crime and public order are intricately tied to the social and economic well-being of local communities, particularly in quality of life issues. For this reason, community policing, by empowering officers to assist communities in quality of life issues, helps protect and preserve the middle ground.

Some observers of the police have been concerned that the language of community policing is little more than a veil for the expansion of the criminal justice system into areas of activity traditionally private (Kappeler & Kraska, 1998). This literature asks a question important to the perspective we develop here: is empowerment any more than the expansion of police authority in the lives of citizens? We believe that the answer to this question depends on how community policing is practically implemented. Our position, presented below, views empowerment as a community property shared by police and policed alike.

Skolnick and Bayley: The Empowering Effects of Community Policing

Skolnick and Bayley (1986) describe the empowering effects of community policing for both the police and their communities. The following discussion summarizes some of their observations about line officer empowerment.

When officers are permanently assigned to neighborhoods and are provided wider latitude to develop crime prevention protocols, their identification with those neighborhoods increase. Efforts aimed at organizing meetings and activities among neighborhood residents place them in the social flow of their neighborhoods. Community police officers become sensitized to the particular character of crime, disorder, and quality of life concerns of residents in their neighborhoods. In short, they are more tuned into the life of their neighborhoods.

Line officer empowerment has many implications for the traditional relationship between line personnel and the police organization. Officers sometimes become popular spokespersons for their neighborhoods. They have the capacity to reverse the traditional chain-of-command authority in the department, arguing for resources on behalf of their neighborhoods while carrying the political support of their resident communities, instead of simply following orders from superiors. They are involved in making strategic decisions for their neighborhoods, a responsibility traditionally reserved for middle managers. They become neighborhood advocates, a position with political power. If they disagree with the department, they can take their cause elsewhere, possibly into the political life of the city. They are empowered by the political support of the communities they represent.

Mike always chuckles when he discusses empowerment. *Can you even visualize this? A line officer goes to the chief and says "You know, the problem here isn't crime. The problem is economic. That's what we have to work on. We need more jobs here." How many chiefs are ready for that?*

Skolnick and Bayley (1986) recognized that line-officer empowerment is facilitated by community policing. One of the innovative strategies in Detroit was a mini-station command, where officers were provided the opportunity to structure their work. Skolnick and Bayley described the work of one of the officers, Dagmar Lane, as follows:

> Approximately 30 years old, white, and 8 years on the force, Officer Lane loves her assignment, because it allows her to do what she calls "creative customized police work." She digs deep into the community in ways that could not have been done from a patrol car. She organizes a business watch and a CB patrol. When several incidents of child molestation occur at a nearby school, she immediately develops a lecture for children on avoiding pedophiles. She is able to pin-point drug dealing in neighborhood buildings, triggering raids by precinct personnel. She says that many problems are brought now to her before they became criminal incidents. (Skolnick & Bayley, 1986:65)

For police officers, empowerment is the ability to act in concert with the community and with other officers in order to achieve what cannot be done alone. It is the cooperative dimension of human interaction which seeks to engage our imaginations, to enable us as collective actors to participate in the shaping and enrichment of our lives (Ferguson, 1987). Citizens can also be empowered through an effective community policing problem. Through the organization of community groups – the lifeblood of community policing, as Skolnick and Bayley (1986) described them – citizens can reassert their control over the spaces in which they live. For the police and citizens alike, empowerment is the enabling process that reaches beyond traditional reactive policing in order to address larger social and environmental problems that create the conditions for disorder and crime. Empowerment affirms the middle ground institutions that, as deTocqueville noted 200 years ago, are the foundations of democratic participation in American social and political life.

de Tocqueville and Associational Life

Alexis de Tocqueville, (1969) was a French social philosopher who was also an observer of social and political processes in the United States. One of his most famous writings, *Democracy in America* (1835) was a chronicle of his vision the conditions and future of political democracy in the United States. He noted the wide prevalence of voluntary civic associations in the United States, and observed that they played a critical role for North American political life (see Kelling, 1985). Bellah and his colleagues describe de Tocqueville's views on the role of middle-ground institutions and his concerns over the future in Figure 9.7.

Figure 9.7

Bellah et al. on de Tocqueville

Bellah and his colleagues provide a clear description of de Tocqueville's idea of nineteenth-century agrarian America and his fears for its future.

de Tocqueville argues that a variety of active civic organizations are the key to American democracy. Through active involvement in common concerns, the citizen can overcome the sense of relative isolation and powerlessness that results from the insecurity of life in an increasingly commercial life.

The local community was for de Tocqueville the source of human dignity and participation in wider social life.

Through active involvement in common concerns, the citizen can overcome the sense of relative isolation and powerlessness that results from the insecurity of life in an increasingly commercial society. (Bellah et al., 1985:38)

Bellah and his colleagues conclude:

Associations, along with decentralized, local administration, mediate between the individual and the centralized state, providing forums in which opinion can be publicly and intelligently shaped . . . and responsibility can be learned and passed on. Associational life, in de Tocqueville's thinking, was the best bulwark against the condition he feared most: the mass society of mutually competing interests, easy prey to despotism.

Source: From Bellah, Robert N., Richard Madsen, William M. Sullivan, Ann Swidler, and Steven M. Tipton (1985). *Habits of the Heart: Individualism and Commitment in American Life*. Berkeley, CA: University of California Press.

de Tocqueville feared what we might today consider historically inevitable, which is the society we have today; a society not of moral communities, but of competing individual pursuits, a society of utilitarian and expressive interests. A bottom line society. In de Tocqueville's uneasy vision, we begin to comprehend the task that community policing sets for itself – to rebuild our shattered sense of community, to somehow salvage our Jeffersonian moral traditions from the junk-heap of history. It is a bold endeavor, and it is what community policing is about.

Common Good and Individual Rights

Some scholars perceive the array of constitutional "due process" protections to be a threat to community order. By overfocusing on individual rights, it is argued that we overlook the common good and inadvertently allow public-order conditions to emerge that damage community life and viability. Public-order problems that endanger communities may not technically be against the law, or if they are may seem not to warrant a large investment in police services. Yet, it is suggested, a failure to deal with these problems will lead to more profound crime problems in the future. The police should be encouraged to become involved even in seemingly unimportant public-order problems, for these problems can lead to community deterioration and serious crime.

We have a different view of the relationship between the common good and individual rights. We take a historically republican view that such protections provide the primary bulwark against the growth of central state power in the United States (see Klockars, 1995). By focusing on the responsibilities of individuals – the police and the policed alike – to participate in the civic life of their communities, and by empowering local and community institutions to deal with their problems, we can deal meaningfully with the crime and public-order problems that tear at the fabric of community life.[24] The question is: what police tactics and strategies contribute to the common good of communities and what tactics detract from it?

Some aggressive policing tactics, particularly those associated with drug suppression – intensive use of arrest to deal with public-order problems, or the use of battering rams to break into suspected drug houses, for example, may carry in them the seeds of long term neighborhood destruction rather than revitalization. Other tactics that fall into this category include sting operations and stakeouts (Bouza, 1990). It is not that these police tactics are ineffective or illegal – they frequently are seen by the police as the only reasonable way to deal with entrenched drug and/or crime problems. But they can alienate many citizens in precisely those neighborhoods that police are trying to "save." As Bouza observed, stakeouts sometimes end in a deadly force incident, which may be viewed by the surrounding community as an "execution." Street-sweeps are seen as blatant harassment. Community members often view stings as unfair entrapment, even when conducted legally. These kinds of tactics empower police while weakening the policed. If the reader doesn't believe that, watch one sometime. You will not walk away from the experience believing that the community somehow benefits or is empowered, regardless of the rhetoric supporting such police actions.

Tactics such as these are consistent with an individual-level crime-control perspective – remember the crime-control due process model. They may look good, but in practice they undermine the very foundations of policing in a democracy – they undermine support from the communities they are intended to protect.

It is difficult to see the long-term good in police tactics that, in some of our cities, has resulted in as much as 50 percent of the African-American youths currently under correctional control or sought by the police on warrants. The focus on individual-level crime has led us away from an understanding of crime's environmental roots (Felson, 1994). Without understanding how crime is rooted in everyday life, the police are and will continue to be ill-equipped to adapt to the profound changes that are occurring in the economic and social lives of citizens today.

Community policing, by focusing on neighborhood enabling process rather than suppressive crime control tactics that alienate the police from the policed, provides the conditions for organized neighborhood involvement in the political life of cities, a condition essential for the long-term well being of democratic society. When we organize citizens into community groups, we are harkening to the traditions and mythologies of grass roots democracy in the United States. Community policing, done right, adapts that tradition to the emergent needs of the twenty-first century.

Ethical Problems Posed by Community Policing

Community policing poses unique ethical problems for police officers. These dilemmas involve the empowerment of the police and how empowerment is shared with the community. These ethical dilemmas are significant at all levels of the organization. We will review four of these problems here.

Figure 9.8

Problem 1: The Creative Customized Police Work Problem

Community policing empowers officers to take a greater role in fixing crime and public-order problems that they encounter. Officers may be assigned permanently to particular areas, and may be responsible for the development of crime prevention plans. This poses a particular dilemma for managers. Should managers assign individuals to community policing assignments based on traditional departmental criteria, or should they seek particular officers that are more "people oriented?" If managers seek individuals with special aptitudes, they are likely to violate departmental assignment traditions and alienate older, more seasoned officers. However, they may be more likely to successfully assign an individual who will be able to work in a less structured occupational setting.

This is a variation of the means-ends problem. Should a manager go for the good end – place an individual with a strong aptitude for creative, customized policing? Or should a manager go for the means – use the standards already present in the department for giving assignments – even if an officer is placed into a community policing assignment that seems to have little aptitude for, and may in fact resist, the community policing concept?

Our recommendation is to favor the traditional officer. As we have argued before (Crank, 1997), if change is to be effective, it must gain the support of the traditional rank and file. Without their support, community policing changes will be seen as secondary to the primary purposes of the police, law enforcement and territorial control. Commanders, seeking internal reform, have sometimes concluded that reform can only come about from hiring a new kind of officer. This sort of perspective marginalizes real change. It creates resistance on the part of traditional police and may alienate police labor representatives. Commanders have to take an active role, to roll up their sleeves and get out in the field with experienced officers. If an officer resists change, then there is a need to spend some time working with him or her, showing them how community policing tactics can also contribute to good police work. Creative customized police work is not only for line officers working with citizens. It is for managers working with line personnel as well.

Figure 9.9

Problem 2: The "I Smell a Joint" Dilemma

Imagine that you are assigned to a crime prevention unit. You go door to door in a neighborhood meeting with citizens. At one of the residences, when the resident answers, you smell marijuana. If you decide to investigate further for the presence of illegal behavior, you can easily produce an arrest. The inclination of police is to make an arrest. It is morally consistent with a traditional perspective on police work. There may be no dilemma here for you. For many officers, there is no better police work than a good pinch.

Or it may be that you simply don't recognize the dilemma. If you make the arrest, the people in the neighborhood may be afraid to open their doors to you. Your assignment may be ruined. By viewing the arrest as a morally right "end," you have damaged your credibility in the neighborhood. However, by viewing neighborhood relations as the "right end," you may have violated what you consider to be your fundamental responsibility as a police officer.

There is an answer to this dilemma. The answer is that the individual officer must be permitted the discretion to make this decision. The lesson here is twofold. First, a line officer should be permitted to talk about this kind of incident to his duty commander without fear of reprisal, and be allowed to make a decision based on criteria other than arrest production. Second, this example points to the importance of having intelligent, educated, emotionally centered officers who can think through problems and see how their behavior fits into the big picture – community well-being. If community protection is the good "end," then the means, arrest, should be considered in the context of other means to achieve that end.

Figure 9.10

Problem 3: The Use of Citizen Intelligence

This is another means-ends problem. The question is – what is the relationship between the police organization and citizen groups that have mobilized for purposes of crime prevention? This is a command problem, but it also is important for officers who have crime prevention assignments.

Sometimes police departments organize citizen groups and use them primarily in order to develop intelligence about local neighborhood activities. Some commanders view the role of citizens as adjuncts of the police mission. From this perspective, the primary purpose of the public is to act as the "eyes and ears" of the police. This means that

Figure 9.10, *continued*

elements of the public provide information and surveillance in areas where the police cannot. For example, some departments use citizen band patrols, whose purpose is to keep an eye on selected locations – particularly so-called "crack houses" – in their neighborhood.

The dilemma is this. If the police are using the public primarily as intelligence, the public is little more than an auxiliary tool of traditional police decisionmaking. When the public acts as intelligence, the police are sustaining their lead role as the "professional" with the public in a supportive, secondary role. This kind of relationship tends not to endure. As Skolnick and Bayley (1986) point out, when the public is not provided a role as an equal partner, public interest languishes. Promising police-citizen relationships, unsustained, fade.

On the other hand, if police provide citizens not only with the opportunity to be involved but also with the authority in deciding how to respond, police may be providing justification for citizen vigilante actions. What if a citizens group wants to burn down a crack house? As Mike puts it, *What if one of the people in the crack house sold drugs to your kid? What if one of the people in the crack house was your kid?* It would be sad indeed if the courts ended up prosecuting those same citizens the police had enlisted to help control crime.

There is no clear answer to this dilemma. Our inclination is to provide citizens with the opportunity to make reasoned decisions about what course to take. For community policing to work, citizens have to be more than adjuncts of a crime control machine. They must have some say over the way the power of the state is authorized in their neighborhood. The key term in our response, though, is *reasoned*. Vigilante action conjures up images of citizens acting on their own behalf. It also harbors the image of hasty, emotional action.

How can citizens make reasoned decisions about topics traditionally left to the police? We believe that education is the key to an informed citizenry. Training and education in problem solving provides the critical ingredients in dealing with crime problems. We would particularly recommend Goldstein's (1979) problem-solving model as a tool for the education of citizens with voluntary crime prevention responsibilities.

Figure 9.11

Problem 4. What if the Community Group You Are Working with Has Racist (or Religious or Ethnic) Intentions?

One of the dilemmas many critics of community policing have described has to do with the motivations of the leadership of community organizations. A community group may mobilize, for example, because they are concerned about in-migration of another group into the neighborhood, and they fear that property values are going to go down or they fear change. In such instances, community policing can be a mask for discrimination (Mastrofski, 1991).

We're not going to tell a community police officer to jump on the podium and immediately denounce racism in all its forms. Though the reader may be personally opposed to racist or ethnic or religious stereotyping (and we hope you are), such tactics will be counterproductive and futile. On the other hand, if an officer withdraws from the group, what little influence they may have in the group is lost. Given the tendency for racial stereotyping to degenerate into vigilante actions, the police may find themselves unpleasantly surprised by violent vigilante behavior and, after suffering inevitable media humiliation, watch their community policing programs disintegrate.

Our recommendation is to continue to work with the group, even when the group is moving in directions you think are, for whatever reason, wrong or inappropriate. Use skills and training on behalf of non-violent resolutions. But stay engaged with the group.

As we will discuss at length in the next chapter, the future faced by the United States is one that will see continued internal and external migration. We are a polyglot country and, like it or not, will become much more so in the coming century. Yet, all our research on human cultures suggests that the greater the degree that ethnic, religious, and racial groups come into contact with each other, the more important their cultural identities become to them (Huntington, 1996; Robertson, 1987). Intergroup conflicts will follow. The role of the police will increasingly be to facilitate and negotiate order among competing groups.

As the reader might have noted, the scenarios had different outcomes, depending on the values carried by individual officers. The reader might also have noticed that we selected solutions to the dilemmas described above by focusing on "means" rather than "ends." By using means-oriented solutions, we believe that decisions can be made that are sustainable and viable over the long term. What is good for police also is good for the community. In each instance discussed above, short-sighted decisionmaking, aimed at the achievement of a particular end carried enormous potential to make problems worse. Long-term program viability in the community policing arena requires that we consider the means by which decisions are made, and only then do we strive for ends that are worthy.

The Craft of
Public Order:
A Vision for the
Twenty-First Century

10

Key Terms

broken windows perspective	incivility
coin rubbing	mass private property
disorder	melting pot
distinctiveness theory	Neutral Zone
globalization theory	order negotiation

To be both viable and practical, ethics have to make sense in the everyday world inhabited by police officers. Today, that everyday world is in a state of dramatic change. The challenges confronting the police are daunting. The impact of international economics and internal and external migration on local communities are principal forces that will shape who we are and how we live together in the twenty-first century. And the police, like it or not, will be in the thick of it.

In this chapter, we contend that the police, to adapt to the demands of the twenty-first century, will confront new challenges. These challenges will be particularly keen in the area of public order, where increasing racial, ethnic, and religious differences will complicate our ability to find common ground – to get along. The pressures on the police to mediate differences between groups will be among the keenest challenges confronting our democratic traditions. To successfully meet this challenge, a means-related ethic should be a central pillar in a community policing enterprise.

In the first part of this chapter, we will review contemporary perspectives on American demographic changes. In the second part we will consider the impact of population changes on public-order policing.

What We Are and What We're Becoming

The United States is in the midst of dramatic population transformation, both in terms of the kinds of people emigrating to the United States, and in the way various groups are distributing themselves across the American landscape.

Population Internationalization

Consider the changing population makeup. We're witnessing a broad change in general migration patterns. In the 1980s, one-half as many people emigrated from Europe to the United States as in the 1960s. More than five times as many came from Asia, twice as many from Mexico, the Caribbean and central America, and nearly four times as many from Africa (Roberts, 1994:73). These general geographic identities themselves mask astonishing ethnic diversity. The current census counts 179 ancestry groupings for the "Hispanic" category alone (Roberts, 1994:73). And the most recent wave of immigration has seen the numbers of Asians more than double. In Minnesota today, Asians number more than 77,000, triple what they were on the last census. Diversity in some places is remarkable. In Los Angeles, more than 80 languages are spoken (Kaplan, 1998). The long-term implications are clear. By the year 2000, the proportion of whites among the children of America will drop to two-thirds of the total population. By the middle of the coming century, no racial or ethnic group will constitute a majority (Roberts, 1994:246).

What we believe is occurring in the current era is a dramatic internationalization of the population in the United States and throughout much of North America. Kaplan (1998) argued that the United States is in the process of becoming the first true international civilization. The century of European intellectual and financial domination is fading. The United States is "shedding its skin," becoming truly multicivilizational. Increasingly, the intellectual capital of the world centers its activity in the United States. Consider Kaplan's (1998) description of Los Angeles in Figure 10.1.

Figure 10.1

Kaplan and the Internationalization of the American Population

Immigrant dynamism coupled with Asian as well as Latino mestizo-ization are the central facts of late twentieth century Los Angeles. And the reality is richer still, as Indian Immigrants buy up Artesia, next to Cerritos, and Iranian immigrants, after buying many properties in Beverly Hills, buy now in nearby Westwood. (Kaplan, 1998:42)

Walking down streets in Vancouver, Kaplan observed:

I saw many signs in Punjabi, Hindi, Farsi, Arabic, and Khmer – but almost none in French, an official Canadian language. (1998:52)

And in Portland, Kaplan cites another informant:

"The early settlers here recreated the New England village," Seltzer explained. "Since then we've been good at space arrangement and streetscapes. Our next challenge will be to get along with each other." The white population is aging, and twenty years hence Portland will be like greater L.A. in terms of ethnicity. (1998:61)

The driving factor behind these changes is the dramatic internationalization of the economy that has occurred over the past 30 years. Vancouver, one of Kaplan's examples, is not in the United States, yet its changes herald the demographic trends occurring across the Pacific Northwest. It is cheaper, Kaplan observed, for companies to hire educated immigrants than to educate them in the United States. Weak national standards in the United States and low taxes have intellectually and financially impoverished many local school systems, making it far easier to import intellectual capital needed to compete internationally and lessening the Anglo-European influence over the economy. The United States is consequently internationalizing, united not by a common morality but by its commitment to its economic system.

Kaplan suggests that regional economies will become more unified, while at the same time centralized federal control will weaken. The influence of centralized control in Washington will decline as local governments increasingly assert their economic independence. However, regional and local interdependence may carry a price – taxes will be used to reinforce local economic infrastructure, and poorer areas will receive increasingly scant support. There is a chance that poverty, and all the social ills associated with it, could become more pronounced than it is today.

Mass Private Property and Policing

What are the implications of a decline in federal control for policing? Bayley and Shearing (1998) suggested that policing is undergoing a restructuring in the United States. Increasingly, well-heeled suburban communities and large public access facilities make use of private security. Driven by the growth of mass private property, private security is replacing public police in many areas. Mass private property refers to areas of private enterprise that are designed for large-scale public use. These areas include shopping malls, education campuses, residential communities, high-rise condominiums, banks, commercial facilities, and recreation complexes. These enterprises are central to the economic viability of many urban and suburban areas, and will increase their demands on urban space. Market-based private security will inevitably follow as the primary form of security. The use of municipal police officers to provide security for mass private properties will gradually disappear, and indeed has already disappeared in many places.

What of the poor? Bayley and Shearing are concerned that they will be barricaded in urban ghettos, excluded from the economic well-being enjoyed by the rest of society. "Civil society," they argue, "for the poor disappears in the face of criminal victimization and governmental repression" (Bayley & Shearing, 1998:164). The public budget for the poor will shrink, together with that portion will be spent on police efforts aimed at segregating them from public view. Declining opportunities, an economy stagnant in income growth among unskilled labor, and segregation of the poor into urban ghettos will lead to frustration and despair. Indeed, this process is already well underway. In response, collective violence is likely to become commonplace in many large cities. The likely outcome of such violence is repressive police intervention in poor areas.

Community policing, Bayley (1996) suggested, may be the only reasonable way police departments can deal with the continued disenfranchisement of the poor. Only by bringing the police and the policed together can the police adapt their work to the particular needs confronted by the poor in a changing and unpredictable economic climate. Any other police response is likely to further alienate already alienated sectors of the population and increase violence.

Rural and Suburban Changes

The demographic changes in the United States today are not limited to the populated states and big cities. Many areas historically rural are also experiencing the culture shock of in-migration. The states recording the fastest growth are Nevada, Alaska, and Idaho, states most people think as predominantly rural. In urban areas, growth has "deconcentrated" from the inner cities to outlying regions. These outlying areas have been called edge cities, strip cities, and urban "pods." In some places rural sprawl – home tracts emerging next to small communities, with commuters traveling elsewhere for employment – is redefining rural identity with urban meanings. An increasingly frequent characteristic of growth at the turn of the twenty-first century is that formerly rural areas are neither traditionally rural nor dependent on center cities.

Change and Conflict

Growth and demographic change is occurring among many types of people. We tend to think of migration in terms of foreign in-migration. Yet this is a proportionally small aspect of overall migration. Blue-collar workers tend to migrate at a much higher rate than white-collar. City dwellers relocate to the ex-urbs or rural hinterland seeking a more comfortable lifestyle. Religious groups seek divine meaning through rural settlement. All of these are groups on the move in the United States today. Will they "melt" together, as suggested by the melting pot idea? Or will they conflict?

Our history books have described the pattern of ethnic assimilation in the United States groups in terms of a **melting pot** idea. This means that groups are assimilated after immigrating to the United States, their distinctiveness and cultural uniqueness gradually disappearing. Over time, immigrants share common values and beliefs. Yet the opposite may in fact occur. Huntington (1996) observed that cultural identities become more important with increased interactions between groups. He described this as **distinctiveness theory** (McGuire & McGuire, 1988) which means that people define themselves by what makes them different from others. Ethnic self-consciousness is intensified as diverse ethnic and cultural groups become more interdependent, a phenomenon Huntington called **globalization theory** (Robertson, 1987).

Both globalization and distinctiveness theory describe a very un-melting-pot notion – that groups become more different as they interact with each other. Core cultural identities are based in religious beliefs, and increased contact has resulted, Huntington argues, in the rise of fundamentalism in and conflict between many of the world's major religions. A global religious revival marks the onset of a "return to the sacred," in response to people's perception of the world as a single place (Huntington, 1996:68). If this is the case, there is a possibility that ethnic, religious, and cultural diversification will similarly result in internal conflicts in the United States.

Figure 10.2

> ### Conflict or Harmony? The Case of the Hutterites
>
> Consider the following case. Montana has about 54 Hutterite colonies, with approximately 5,000 members. One of these colonies settled near the small town of Ledger. They were not warmly received by some of the local residents. In 1998, they were victimized by arson and vandalism, including damage to vehicles and to their grain bin. The arson caused more than $100,000 in damage. Of particular concern were the attitudes of local non-Hutterite residents toward the crimes. Local residents accused the Hutterites of not paying taxes and competing unfairly in their religious basis for division of labor. The FBI is investigating the arson as a hate crime (Hanson, 1998). In this case, we can see how religious differences better describe the conflict between these two groups better than ideas of a "melting pot" notion of assimilation.

What should the role of the police be in dealing with the frictions between the Hutterites and local residents? Should they, as some advocates of community policing might suggest, try to reinforce or to enact that traditional community's local standards of order? Let's present this question in a different way. What if the police were to adopt the position that they were responsible for reinforcing the will of the "traditional" community? Would they then encourage further acts of violence against the Hutterites? The notion is, of course, offensive, and reveals a fundamental flaw in contemporary ideas of public-order policing. The very presence of public order problems stands as stark proof that the idea of public order is itself an open question. When we ask the police to carry out some idea of "underlying order" we may be unintentionally asking them to take sides in conflicts. This is an inappropriate role for the police, especially in a democracy increasingly polyglot in every religious and ethnic sense of the term.

The police will be best served by an ethic that will promote internal security during the current age of demographic transition and social change. As the American people become more diverse, the police may be the critical mechanism that enables us to get along. It will fall to them to decide how and whether we get along. If they seek balance through negotiation in our complex cultural relationships, we just might succeed. If they view their task as the imposition of morality, we will not.

The Problem of Community Order

The previous example captures a dilemma central to public order. One of the problems police must negotiate has to do with the way in which a highly segmented and diverse society lives, works, and recreates. How will groups coexist, where will the fault lines of conflict and dissent be, and in what constructive way can the police contribute?

Mastrofski and the Problem of Shared Order

Mastrofski has studied the problems of shared order in communities and in neighborhoods. The following discussion is adapted from his analysis of these problems. His findings are insightful (1991:517):

> A basis for police action requires a demonstration that a group of people
> – say a neighborhood – shares a definition of what constitutes right
> order, threats to it, and appropriate methods for maintaining it. . . .
> There are undoubtedly neighborhoods that possess to a high degree this
> value homogeneity and group attachment, but it is in precisely the most
> afflicted areas that community is problematic in the sense required by
> the reform.

In other words, in those areas where we want the police to enforce some standard of existing public order, we are least likely to find it. Isn't it inevitable that the police, if they have the responsibility for carrying out some community standard of order in these communities where no standards exist, will retreat to their own moral standards? Problems of noble-cause corruption can only intensify in such circumstances.

Even the presence of a common ethnicity and shared customs does not guarantee common interest. Reviewing Horowitz (1984), Mastrofski described an old Chicago neighborhood that, by all appearances, looked like it would share a common heritage of values. It in fact did not. Neighborhood residents held widely differing views on two concerns important to public-order policing – what constituted public disorder, and gang membership.

Rieder's (1985) study of Canarsie similarly revealed stark disagreement in residents' assessments of public order. This case was marked by overt racial conflict. Jewish and Italian residents mobilized in order to resist African-American in-migration. They used confrontational strategies such as arson and vigilantism to keep African-Americans out of their community. Block associations and crime patrols were employed to resist African-American in-migration – a lesson in human relations for community policing advocates. In this case, any effort by the police to support traditional community norms would have resulted in openly discriminatory practices.

Block organizations, like other organizations that community police are supposed to work with, may not represent broad-based community interests. As Bohm (1984) observed, block organizations are heavily influenced by the distribution of power and influence in their community, particularly married homeowners with children. Nor do the views of block organization participants necessarily correspond to the interests of a representative population of residents. Research has shown that the attitudes of people active in neighborhood associations are not closely associated with the views of the larger neighborhood. They are, however, significantly correlated with those who have wealth and status (Rich, 1986).

What should be the police responsibility in places where the idea of order is itself problematic? We believe that the police role is to negotiate public order, not superimpose it based on some ill-defined notion of informal community norms. The distinctive mark of neighborhoods where public order problems are the worst is that they are often places of high population mobility and where residents carry diverse notions of acceptable order. Common ground for order will itself change as migration patterns change. There is not a common level of public order that an officer can use as a standard for behavior. Contending and competing notions of order, changing over time, may be the standard with which the police must deal. The best contribution that an officer can make is to act as an arbiter among contending groups and work to negotiate an acceptable resolution to problems. That contribution, however, is truly democratic. It is order derived from within, not imposed from outside.

Skogan and the Limits of Police Authority

In compelling research, Wesley Skogan (1990) examined the causes and consequences of disorder. His work is valuable for anyone trying to understand the many facets of disorder, and we will review it at length here.

Skogan assessed residents' perceptions of public-order problems in 40 neighborhoods in six major American cities. His team interviewed 13,000 residents on topics of disorder, crime, satisfaction, victimization, and neighborhood stability between the years of 1977 and 1983. He defined **disorder** as both individual behaviors that threatened the public order, and signs of physical decay to neighborhoods. To assess disorder, he examined *individual behaviors* such as public drinking, corner gangs, street harassment, drugs, and noisy neighbors, and *signs of physical decay* such as vandalism, dilapidation and abandonment, and rubbish.

Skogan found that neighborhood residents tended to agree on what constituted disorderly conditions. Renters as well as homeowners were likely to see the same sorts things as disorderly. Interracial agreement was also observed: "Blacks and Whites agreed in their views of their communities to a surprising extent" (Skogan, 1990:57).[25]

In what sort of communities was disorder a problem? Skogan conducted several analyses to determine where disorder was most likely to occur. His findings indicated that the best predictors of disorder were poverty and instability, that is, the extent to which the neighborhoods had more long-term residents, more owner-occupied residents, and higher levels of employment. What was the best predictor of poverty and instability? As Skogan notes, "The 'bottom line' is that racial and linguistic minorities in these 40 areas report the most significant disorder problems" (Skogan, 1990:61).

Skogan reviewed several evaluations of efforts to deal with disorder. His assessment of the capacity of community policing to do something about disorder was pessimistic. In Houston, the police had started programs aimed at citizen contacts, storefronts, and community organization. Disorder of all kinds went down after the programs were put into place. However, program successes were reported only for whites and homeowners. Blacks, Hispanics, and renters were unaffected by the program. In other words, "the better off got better off, and the disparity between area residents got deeper" (Skogan, 1990:107). The implications of the findings are bleak:

> The police are likely to get along best with the factions that share their outlook (Morris & Heal, 1981). The "local values" they represent are those of some of the community, but not all. In heterogenous neighborhoods, some residents can easily become the targets of the programs, and are not likely to be happy about that. . . . Equitable community policing may depend on a degree of homogeneity and consensus that does not exist in many troubled neighborhoods. (Skogan, 1990:109)

In other words, police officers who were carrying out community-based ideas of policing tended to find justifications for viewing public-order problems through the lens of their own morality.

Could communities confront disorder on their own, without police assistance? Consider Skogan's review of community efforts to control disorder in Chicago. The Ford Foundation paid 10 community organizations $550,000 to organize block watches and other crime prevention measures. These were dubbed by Skogan as disorder reduction projects. Like the community policing experiment in Houston, evaluators found that those who were already better off were most likely to take advantage of the programs. More disturbingly, evaluators identified very few positive and many negative outcomes. Interaction and solidarity among community members either remained the same or declined. More troubling, residents' perceptions of social disorder, physical disorder, and fear of crime either remained the same or went up. In short, efforts aimed at reducing disorder seemed to be equally unsuccessful whether it was accomplished by the police or by the community itself.

If the community cannot deal with disorder by itself, what could the police have contributed? Very little, suggested Skogan. He concluded that the most the police can hope for is to make their best case to community groups. The police can appeal to the wisdom of community members, but their ability to assert their views on neighborhoods is severely constrained. In the United States where diversity and freedom are highly regarded values, the voice of the police is unlikely to be "automatically accepted as authoritative" (1990:160).

> When it comes to a great deal of disorder, police and community organizations are just additional interest groups jockeying for attention. Order is more likely to be negotiated than imposed. (Skogan, 1990:160)

Skogan identified three limits on the policing of disorder.

1. Can legislators write constitutional statutes concerning disorderly behavior? Our traditions of rights and limited governments suggest fundamental limits on the ability to legislate away disorderly behavior.

2. The use of discretion in controlling disorder is a problem. Officers are free to act upon their prejudices or stereotypes in virtually unchecked fashion when they are the upholders of order who must be satisfied. (Skogan, 1990:164)

The use of discretion to control disorder in a community policing context can inadvertently justify the kinds of violence that are consistent with our ideas of noble-cause corruption:

3. Limits on policing disorder are imposed by other elements of the criminal justice system. It is, Skogan observes, difficult to sustain the interests of judges and prosecutors in disorder cases. If arrest does not lead to prosecution, then disorder arrests are simply an extralegal form of harassment. And if they are not prosecuted, then they provide the basis for legal actions against the police.

In short, there are limits on what the police can hope to accomplish by taking an active role in disorder reduction, even if and when a local community agrees on disorder's root causes. Police efforts to reduce or contain disorder are particularly likely to be ineffective when they try to assert their standard of morality to determine what acceptable order is. It puts them out of touch with other elements of the criminal justice system, it threatens to undermine their legitimacy in the community, and it does not reduce disorder.

Mastrofski and Uchida: The Limits of Government

The migration of diverse human groupings across the American landscape is today paralleled by an increasingly limited capacity of central government to take a major role in the lives of its citizens. There are two reasons for the declining role of federal government intervention.

First, the American public seems to have become disenchanted about the ability of central government to mitigate hardships faced by ordinary people. Social solutions are increasingly defaulted to private, non-profit organizations. Glazer (1988:192), discussing the limits of social policy, observed that the United States is today more dependent on a great variety of private, voluntary, ethically and religiously sponsored, nonprofit and profit agencies to maintain the public welfare.

It may be that citizens have a tolerance for disorder. It certainly appears that there is a preference for low levels of disorder over government intervention aimed at disorder reduction (Glazer, 1988). Though Glazer was referring to social policy when he described government intervention, his comments in the quote below apply to all forms of governmental intervention at the local level, including the police.

> The present mood of the United States does not favor a fully developed national system of social policy; the mood seems to be based more on economic exigency. It reflects the considered judgment by many Americans that despite the cost of social disorder that prevails in their society, they prefer it that way. (Glazer, 1988:192)

Second, even if we wanted government to solve our social problems (and by all indications we do not), it might be unable to provide the solutions we seek. Earlier we suggested that a decline in federal authority might be matched by increases in local and regional economic development and independence. However, this does not lead to greater local and county investment in municipal programs, including the police as well as schools and social services. To the contrary, public policing is likely to receive an increasingly meager slice of the municipal tax pie. Mastrofski and Uchida noted this governmental dilemma and its political implications in Figure 10.3.

These arguments have a direct bearing on police efforts to intervene in public-order problems. We may have to concede that there is a limited capacity of the police to control the urban environment. Neither the resources, nor policy effectiveness, nor the will of the public will be able to muster the artillery needed to achieve such control. Mastrofski and Uchida suggested that the proper role of the police in this urban environment is one of coordination and negotiation rather than control: "Police chiefs must lead, exhort, organize and negotiate with diverse interest groups, the general public, and other government actors (Mastrofski & Uchida, 1997:201). This is also our recommendation. Police must lead through the power of voice and of self. With the power of voice, they can exhort change. With the power of self, through the relations they establish with a diverse population, they are a model for our ability to live together.

Figure 10.3

The Limits of Government

There is, of course, the liberal's concern about the concentration of power in one institution, especially one that has near monopoly on the legal use of force. One can make a counter-argument, however, that the ability to control local urban governments to address worsening problems has deteriorated to such an extent, and the mechanisms of control have become so diffuse, that there is no great danger of the police chief becoming the new urban "boss."

Source: Stephen Mastrofski and Craig Uchida (1997). *Transforming the Police*, pp. 200-201.

Learning the Right Lessons from the Past

How should we police our urban and rural environments in light of the possibility of sharp declines in resources and public support for government intervention? When we think about the right way to do police work, we are inclined to look to the past for models. It is foolish to ignore the lessons of the past. Unfortunately, sometimes we learn the wrong lessons.

Broken Windows

What image of policing is appropriate to the future of the United States? Some advocates of community policing would have us look to America's past to find a model for the police. Consider Wilson and Kelling's "Broken Windows." Published in 1982, this paper argued cogently that we needed to re-think the relationship between public-order problems and crime problems. The paper wisely recognized that fear of disorder and crime ran high in neighborhoods confronting incivility, and provided an important contribution to our understanding about how migration can undermine social institutions.

The broken windows perspective viewed fear of disorder as a critical variable, intervening between public-order problems and the onset of serious crime. Concern with "fear of disorder" has emerged as a popular area of study in contemporary research (see Lewis & Salem, 1986). The literature on disorder and crime is wide, and the government regularly contributes to research through federal granting programs. We believe, however, that there are three issues important to the "broken windows" model that might inadvertently lead us *away* from shared order: the causes of incivility, the capacity of the police to do something about disorder, and the changing and unstable demography of local communities where order problems are the most significant.

Figure 10.4

The Broken Windows Perspective

Wilson and Kelling present an important argument about the relationship between disorderly behavior and serious crime. In simplified form, the **broken windows perspective** is as follows. When neighborhoods experience increasing levels of disorder, residents become increasingly fearful. Disorder is characterized by incivility and physical decay. Once disorder reaches a certain intensity, residents change their behavior, avoid strangers and stay off the streets. This change in residents' activities marks a loss of traditional control over public places – the parks, the streets, shopping, and parking areas in their neighborhood. Residents' loss of social control results in further declines in the quality of life and the onset of serious criminal activity. The way to stop this is to have the police aggressively intercede in public-order problems before citizens become fearful and avoid public areas. Interceding at an early point is the best means to preserve natural, informal social controls.

In the following discussion we will consider (1) what incivility means, (2) the implications of demographic changes for "broken windows" and (3) the role of the police in the maintenance of public order. This discussion will provide the basis for our vision of the future of public-order policing.

Incivility and Commonly Shared Order. First, let us consider the notion of incivility. What does incivility tap? What is uncivil to people? Certainly rudeness, though rude behavior in and of itself is not against the law. Incivility can cover a wide variety of things. Lewis and Salem (1986) suggest that **incivility** is an indication of

> a variety of circumstances which suggest to neighborhood residents that all is not well in their neighborhood . . . They may include unacceptable behavior by teenagers; physical deterioration in homes, commercial areas or public spaces, the intrusion of "different" population groups into the area, or an increase in marginally criminal behaviors such as drug use and vandalism. Although the events or conditions captured in

> the incivility term may vary in each neighborhood, they elicit the same
> concern among area residents that the mechanisms for exercising social
> control are no longer effective, and the values and standards that in the
> past characterized the behavior of local residents are no longer in force.
> (Lewis & Salem, 1986:10)

This long quote can be simplified to some basic ideas. People tend to
fear change. When they are in changing environments, they react by
withdrawing or by becoming hostile toward outsiders, recognizing that
the ways of the past are not going to guide the future. In-migration is a
symbol of that change. Yet, American history tells us that migration is
inevitable. Indeed, American history is in large part written by patterns
of migration.

It is precisely a common notion of order, what people might regard
of as uncivil, that will become increasingly problematic in the coming
years. If the police assert their idea of order or align themselves with like-
minded community "respectables," they will contribute to social friction
and disorder over the long term.

The Role of the Police in the Preservation of Order. Can the
police control public order? In our review of pertinent literature presented in the previous section, it appeared that they could do very little. They
lack the resources to prevent neighborhood deterioration. Broad economic factors determine the fate of neighborhoods, and if the economics
are not there, the physical condition of the neighborhood will decline.
The police can't, and we think shouldn't, control who moves into the
neighborhood. Migration patterns also stem from broad economic conditions. Put simply, people follow jobs. When people are moving into a
neighborhood they are pulled by economic opportunity. If they are moving out, they are being pushed by employment's absence. If people
remain in an area in spite of an absence of jobs, then they are likely
encountering racist barriers in education, housing, or employment that
prevent them from migrating to more prosperous areas. Finally, research
suggests that the public probably doesn't want the police to intervene in
public-order problems on any significant scale. As Glazer (1988) observed
earlier in this chapter, there are limits to which the public tolerates governmental intervention.

What is the proper public-order role of the police? Wilson and Kelling
(1982) described order maintenance policing as:

> The essence of the police role in maintaining order is to reinforce the
> informal control mechanisms in the community itself. [431]

This colorful phrase suggests to us that the police should assess the
kinds and levels of order that local residents find tolerable. With this information in hand, police should then act in an official capacity to preserve
or reassert that idea of order. Put simply, police public order activity

should be shaped by the standards of the neighborhood. They suggested that a model taken from America's past, the "watchman," provided a way to model police behavior. Under the watchful surveillance of the "watchman," communities kept public order, thus preventing a downward spiral of physical decay that began with uncivil behavior and ended in criminal activity.

The idea that there is a common notion of public order simply does not fit many neighborhoods very well. Arguably, it may have been an appropriate policing model for the beginnings of the twentieth century (although, see Walker, 1984). Today, however, we need a model for the twenty-first century. And the present and the future of the United States is a polyglot society, with mixed and blended neighborhoods, high mobility, religious diversity, and contending ideas of public order. The police will be needed for their ability to negotiate order, not assert it.

The community policing model holds that policing is a neighborhood-based phenomenon. It is an organizing principle through which we can describe the responsibility of the police to the maintenance of a common vision of order. The strength of the model lies in its ability to link the legitimacy of the police to the "middle institutions," particularly local communities. In this we are strongly in agreement, as we indicated in Chapter 9. Yet the places most likely to develop public-order problems, our inner cities and their proximate environments, are zones of high mobility. There is rarely enough long-term residential stability to develop a publicly shared idea of order. Residents' notions of disorder management may be no more than a vague hope that the police will fix problems that get out of hand. What, then, can the police contribute to public order?

This may be our most far-reaching recommendation, and it is philosophical as well as practical in its implications. It is that, in the practice of the craft of public order, the responsibility of a police officer is *emphatically not* to reinforce the informal norms of communities and neighborhoods. Neighborhood residents infrequently share a common vision of orderly relations. This is especially the case in our hardest hit inner cities, areas characterized by high crime and high population mobility, where we see diverse groups seeking to improve their quality of life with scant resources and where life's problems are the most deeply entrenched.

Consider this. We ask officers to "reinforce a community's informal sense of order" or the "political will of the community" (Kelling, 1987). We then provide her or him with responsibility for maintaining law and order in a community that may be diversified by religion, age, income, culture and ethnicity. We give that officer wide discretion to act on behalf of community order and to protect its traditions. But where's the order? The order is not in the neighborhoods – that's the problem. No, the order is in the officer's sense of morality. Officers will use public order as a justification for value-based decisionmaking and for carrying out the noble cause.

We believe that the police should view themselves as peacemakers. They shouldn't distribute morality in the name of public order or law enforcement, as we've argued that they do today. How can the police assert or enforce a shared vision of order where none exists? They can't. They can, however, facilitate the ability of people to work together, to get along, to negotiate problems. They can **negotiate order**, which means that they can provide a constructive environment and practical people-skills to negotiate solutions to commonly occurring people problems – relations between landlords and tenants, between youth and oldsters, different ethnic and religious groups, the homeless and business, and traditional locals and recent arrivals.

The promise and danger of negotiating order can be seen in Kelling and Coles (1996; See also Kelling, 1998) recommendations for *fixing broken windows* (also the title of their book). The authors recognize the critical role the police play in negotiating order among diverse community groups. The role is briefly described in Figure 10.5.

Figure 10.5

Fixing Broken Windows and Negotiating Order

Kelling and Coles argue that the preservation or restoration of order requires an integrated effort involving many agencies and social service providers. The role of the police is integral to this effort. They note that:

> A real police presence in neighborhoods, one that persists over time and is intimately familiar with the community and its strengths and problems, will be crucial to this consensus-building process, for good policing will help shape, identify, and give legitimacy to neighborhood standards. Newark police officers negotiated informally with local residents during the 1970s over neighborhood standards; the same informal process took place in Somerville, Massachusetts, when officers negotiated with youths and neighborhood residents over how parks could be used on warm summer nights. Negotiation of standards can also be highly structured and formal, as they were in Dayton in the late 1970s and in New York's subways during the early 1990s.

The key to restoring order, they argue, is a "problem-solving process" in which the authority of the police and community resources are brought to bear on problems, and in which the police use their authority to maintain order once established.

Source: George Kelling and Catherine Coles (1996) *Fixing Broken Windows*, p. 249. New York, NY: The Free Press.

Kelling and Coles provide a conception of the police as negotiators of order. In it we see the promise – problems confronted by local neighborhoods can under some circumstances be mediated by the police. What we consider to be the danger in negotiation of order lies in how order is maintained after it is negotiated. Kelling and Coles, for example, suggest that "Those who absolutely refuse to cooperate and violate both the informal standards and the law may be arrested" (Kelling & Coles, 1996:250). We are troubled by aspects of this statement. Police should not use the power of coercion, as Muir (1977) so aptly described it, to enforce informal notions of order. The coercive authority of the police ends at the boundaries of the criminal law. This is how it must be if democracy is to prevail. In the realm of order under democracy, the authority of the police lies in the powers of voice, of self, and of the purse (See Chapter 2). Through the power of voice, they exhort for the ends they seek. Through the power of the purse, they connect people who have problems with social services or other means that can help them. Through the power of self they lead by example. These skills will be essential if the police are to assist us in the complex and troubling public-order problems that we will confront in the twenty-first century. But the circumstances permitting the use of coercive force must be defined by a criminal code, and never by informal notions of community order.

Kelling's work on the dilemmas confronting police who seek to maintain public order in a democratic environment is increasingly nuanced. In recent work he suggests that the police must focus on their law enforcement role and in the provision of support for citizen groups that have mobilized in the name of crime prevention. It is a vision based in the development of a practical understanding of crime problems – regardless of where that inquiry leads – and acting in a lawful way to resolve those problems. As he notes (1998:18), "Policing and criminal justice practice must be legal and constitutional." Nor is his vision a call for hard-nosed policing: Kelling believes that order is a negotiated outcome. He observes that

> The old role of police as discussed in "Broken Windows" – roughing up "undesirables" – is now unacceptable to police as well as to citizens. The new role of police and other criminal justice agencies is to back up the activities of citizens and social institutions . . . (Kelling, 1998:16)

Kelling's work today is practically grounded in the enforcement of the law and the thoughtful solution of problems, and it recognizes the central role of democratic traditions in peacekeeping.

Immigration and Broken Windows. Perhaps it is in the police-immigrant relationship that we can see the central flaw in the "Broken Windows" idea of police and public order.

The broken windows perspective is too often interpreted as a need to enforce local customs against outsiders with a different idea of public order. In the current age, the avoidance of outsider influence is not an option that we have. When we look at the history of police in the United

States, we find that they have been intertwined in profound ways with immigrant populations. The true lesson of our immigrant past lies not in thinking we can protect ourselves from the world around us, but in the importance of engaging the citizenry of the world in which we live. We need to learn the right lesson from the past: that we are an international people, and we must embrace – not fight – our diversity. In the following section, we will more closely look at the new demographics of the United States and its implications for public-order policing.

Taft: The New Demographics of Policing

Taft (1991) wrote about the dilemmas posed to police by contemporary demographic changes. The "new immigrant ghettoes," as Taft colorfully called them, are a demographic characteristic of the United States today. They present difficult problems for traditional police officers. Taft identified three kinds of problems faced by police: language, customs and traditions, and fear of the police.

Language

One of the problems increasingly confronted by the police in the new immigrant ghettoes is that they do not understand the language they hear on the streets. The ability of the police to communicate with citizens is enormously complicated when the policed speak a different language from the police. Taft describes an encounter between a police officer and a Cuban crowd in Miami Beach. A Russian and an Orthodox Jew were just in a minor car accident with a Cuban national. The police officer, Rick Mendoza, sought an explanation of the accident from the Cuban. A young Cuban woman offered services as a translator. A crowd formed and became agitated with the officer.

> Frustrated, Mendoza turns his back on the crowd and begins to talk to the translator again. With that, a tall, mustachioed man in the crowd mutters under his breath "Que lastima que el no hable español" (what a pity that he doesn't speak Spanish.)
> Mendoza understands this much Spanish. "Estamos en America! Yo no necesito español." (We are in America. I don't need Spanish.), he snaps, his face reddening. Some of the Cubans shake their heads and walk away.
> "They are offended," explains the translator.
> "You tell them I am offended because they don't speak English," Mendoza tells her perfunctorily, writing a summons before he leaves. (Taft, 1991:306-307)

Police-citizen misunderstandings can have deadly consequences. Another incident reported by Taft was as follows:

> in New York City in July 1980, two police officers answered a call to a Brooklyn supermarket. From inside the store, a Korean man holding a gun shouted something to the officers in his native tongue. The officers, neither of whom spoke Korean, shot him dead. The man turned out to be a security guard, a newly arrived immigrant who had just found a job. (Taft, 1991:311).

These examples hint at the futility of imposing some "informal" idea of normative values in a hypothetical community. How can a police officer enforce, or even identify, commonly shared norms when he or she can't even speak the language? Language skills would be far more useful to a police officer in these circumstances described above than ill-defined ideas of community norms. Facile political responses like "Why don't they learn to speak English" are no more than platitudes that disguise the need to find meaningful solutions to language problems faced by the police in the everyday practice of their work. Perhaps politicians can ignore problems caused by language barriers by hiding them behind a wall of immigration rhetoric, but the police have to deal with language issues on a day-to-day basis.

Customs and Traditions

A second type of problem in the new immigrant ghettoes is the ability of the police to adapt their work to the customs and traditions of new immigrant groups. Consider the following example.

> Many Indochinese parents practice **coin-rubbing**, a medicinal technique in which coins are scraped against a child's neck to drive away evil spirits. Sometimes teachers or nurses see the marks and call the police. "It sure looks like child abuse, and it is, by our standards," Says Maj. Noreen Skagen of the Seattle Police Department. "But for them, it's folk medicine." (Taft, 1991:311)

The police cannot simply invoke traditional ideas of morality in order to deal with coin-rubbing (and by extension similar problems). Were coin-rubbing to be treated as child abuse, police officers would find themselves quickly alienated from the community that they are obligated to police. One can see in this example the need of the police to account in some way for the morality of the policed, be it in a change in enforcement practices or in preventive, educational programs.

Fear of the Police

A third problem is the fear of police sometimes displayed by immigrants, many of whom leave their native countries in order to escape harsh repression carried out by the police. Taft reported that:

> When Los Angeles police made felony arrests of Southeast Asians, suspects frequently would flee or become overly anxious, causing police to consider drawing their weapons. Later, police discovered that the arrest position – kneeling, back turned to the officer, hands clasped behind the head – recalled the position used for executions used by the police in Vietnam. (Taft, 1991:311)

Police practices, based on a logic of officer safety, thus may exacerbate frictions of police citizen encounters and inadvertently increase the dangers to police officers. Taken-for-granted police practices, such as arrest procedures, may need to be reconsidered in light of their effects on citizens, not simply in terms of the safety they may (or may not) provide police officers.

These examples reveal the way in which the police have had to adapt to the changing demographic face of America. And this is how we must continue to adapt. We are entering a world in which the idea of enforcing a traditional idea of morality, or maintaining some common notion of public order, is increasingly quaint and badly out of date. "We can't just sit back smugly," stated one of Taft's respondents. "We have to work with them. If we don't then they withdraw and that causes us more problems than reaching out and giving them a hand" (Taft, 1991:314).

Police and Youth

The new American demographics are not only about recently arrived immigrants and citizens whose traditions encompass a history in the United States. They are also about the way in which different status groups mix. Status differences refer to differences between young and old, renters and owners, businesses and homeless, and the like. When police enforce some "informal" notion of public order, they tend to enforce the perspective of groups with greater status. Public-order policing can consequently be repressive for lower status groups already suffering from scant community resources, especially lower-class youth. In this section, we will consider an area of status conflict in which the police frequently take sides: between juveniles and oldsters.

Curfews

A variety of polls have shown that oldsters are fearful of juveniles. It is unclear whether their fear stems from real acts of crime or simple fear of strangers, though increasing evidence suggests that it is from a fear of strangers and a concern over juvenile rowdiness (Kelling, 1985).

The tendency of police in many jurisdictions has been to take a repressive legalistic posture toward juvenile behavior in order to control anticipated misbehavior. Consider California's use of curfews to keep juveniles off the streets during night-time hours. Many cities in California have been implementing curfews for teenagers. Early anecdotal evidence suggested that juvenile crime decreased when curfews were stringently enforced. Monrovia's (CA) curfew program, an exemplar of curfew efforts, has drawn praise from both the Governor of California and President of the United States.

A comprehensive study of California curfews, conducted by Dan Macallair of the Justice Policy Institute at the Social Ecology Program at the University of California, revealed that successes were overstated. Using a variety of controls and closely examining crime data, the study found that curfews in no instance resulted in lower crime. In some instances, curfews were associated with increased juvenile crime. Youth crime actually jumped 53 percent during the school year when it was in force, and dropped 12 percent during the summer when it was suspended. As a suppressive measure of youthful activity, it appeared from this report that curfews were ineffective and at times counterproductive. Let's look at a different way to deal with juvenile crime, one which uses the police as negotiators of order rather than as order enforcers.

The Neutral Zone

If we look at some of the more effective experiments in the community policing movement, we find that the police are acting more as negotiators or mediators of public order than as purveyors of it. Consider the **Neutral Zone**, an experiment in gang control and cooperation put into place in Mountlake Terrace, Washington (Mueller & Heck, 1997).

Mountlake Terrace, a small community on the outskirts of Seattle, Washington is typical of many of the new, high-growth communities in the United States. From 1988 to 1992, it experienced a 63 percent increase in arrests for juvenile violent crime. The Mountlake Terrace police department held a series of public meetings to deal with related crime problems, and the issue of juveniles out after curfew became a central topic of discussion. Data collected by the police department had suggested that suppressive police tactics wouldn't work. The police held community meetings. These meetings produced a new idea: involve area youth in a sports related programs to keep them busy and off public streets when juvenile-related crime was the most frequent.

A collaborative program called the Neutral Zone was established. Its purposes were to:

1.   Reduce youth involvement in crimes of violence.

2.   Make inroads into gang culture.

3.   Provide an arena where recreation and services were available to high-risk youth.

4.   Allow youth, community volunteers, police, and other community professionals to work together.

The Neutral Zone was organized for juveniles, aged 13-20. It opened Fridays and Saturdays from 10:00 p.m. to 2:00 a.m. It became a preferred place for area youth to play basketball, though a service providing hot and cold meals was also popular. Eventually, a food and clothing bank were established at the Neutral Zone. The program seems to have had a substantial impact on crime. By one estimate, juvenile violent crime, the principal target of the program, dropped by 63 percent (Thurman, Giacommazi, Reisig & Mueller, 1996). The Neutral Zone has since been touted as a community policing success, and indeed, its authors should be proud of their accomplishments. Important to our ideas is the way in which the police were involved in the program.

The police had their rules. They were not "informal" rules but basic, clearly understood rules of law enforcement aimed at keeping the peace. No weapons were permitted inside the Neutral Zone. Gang members and other participants were patted down for weapons prior to entry. Nor was violence permitted inside. The police closely enforced peacekeeping among this group of potential rowdies.

They also negotiated order. This doesn't mean that they were "asking" participants to "get along." They created a set of conditions for mutual interaction, and they used their influence to minimize confrontation between the various groups.

What the police did not do was superimpose some vague community-based notion of informal order on the juveniles. The police, working with the Mountlake Terrace Community Action Program, provided a forum for previously violent groups to compete in common activities. This is order negotiation, not order imposition.

Guyot expressed the spirit of negotiating order in her 1991 book titled *Policing as Though People Matter*, and we will conclude this section with one of her quotes.

Figure 9.1

To Keep Different Moral Worlds from Colliding

"To keep different moral worlds from colliding" is the phrase of Police Chief David Couper of Madison, Wisconsin (Couper, 1979). The larger the city, the more likely it is to be the home of people with diverse life-styles, some of whom will take offense at the life-styles of their neighbors. For the most part, Americans accommodate each other's diverse ways, but when tolerance wears thin, police have a crucial role in building bridges between citizens.

Source: Dorothy Guyot (1991). *Policing as Though People Matter,* p. 281.

The United States is becoming an inter-ethnic, international nation-state, diversifying on religious, ethnic, and status fault lines. If police continue to be drawn from the ranks of the ideologically pure, we will encounter increasing friction between them and the public in our changing society. An ends-based police ethic will increasingly be at odds with the problems confronted by American society.

Many police departments today share a common path. They recruit individuals with a fixed, narrow moral view of their world, individuals who believe that it is right to impose their definition of morality on the rest of us. They encourage that narrow view in training practices. These departments will be morally underequipped to deal with America's future. This path will only contribute to division and confrontation. A wider vision is needed. Adaptation of the police to tomorrow's world will be facilitated by a peacekeeping philosophy, based in the negotiation of order and enforcement of law, by cultivating the skills of voice and of self, to lead through reason and by example.

Recommendations   *11*

In this section we will provide recommendations whose purpose is to balance ethical decisionmaking. Our recommendations are grounded in the belief that values are central to decisionmaking and cannot be removed from police work. The question we have addressed throughout this book is not whether police should be value-based decisionmakers, but rather, what values should inform their craft. We consequently do not provide recommendations that favor expanding administrative supervision. We believe that supervisory strategies tend to be punitive and alienate line officers. We focus instead on an ethical balance in the decisionmaking process and discuss recommendations that we think will add balance to the current overemphasis on the noble cause.

Our recommendations are based on the idea that the behavior of the police should reflect values characteristic of the middle of the due-process crime control continuum. The middle of the continuum characterizes the center of American political and moral life – a concern for victims and a need to do something about bad people, and at the same time a commitment to insure that fairness is a cornerstone of public service. Excess in either direction – toward the noble cause, or toward just means – may make good politics, but either can lead to its own types of corruption.

We discussed just means in Chapter 2. It will be recalled that, by **just means**, we mean an overemphasis on legal and administrative process, to the point where ends are not valued or seen as important. Just means is as potentially corrosive as the noble cause – anything can be justified if one claims that they were "just following rules." International crime tribunals have rejected the excuse that a soldier is "following orders" when charged with crimes against humanity, for example.

We have focused on corruption of the noble cause variety because noble-cause corruption is a problem in police departments today. This does not mean that we advocate an abandonment of the noble cause. We believe in the noble cause – in balance with its opposite on the continuum, the pursuit of just means. The kinds of judgments made at the middle of the continuum represent what we believe is a balanced, thoughtful perspective, and must enable the police to carry out their work in a demographically diverse society.

In this chapter we present recommendations that we believe will strengthen middle ground perspective and behavior. Recommendations are offered in the spirit of balance – the noble cause balanced with just means. Some of the recommendations are practical, while others may seem a bit far-fetched. Yet all recommendations, in one way or another, serve the goal of balance.

Teach 'em Ethics!

In the introduction to this book we recommended ethics instruction, though the recommendation was presented in a somewhat facetious way. Here we convey the recommendation with more gravity. We believe that ethics instruction, properly conferred, can lead to greater judgmental balance and more thoughtful police decisionmaking.

What is the proper form for ethics preparation? This is a seemingly simple question with many different facets, masking complex issues. Below, we will review elements of Kleinig's (1990) fine discussion on teaching and learning police ethics, with an eye to how his recommendations match our ethical concerns about noble-cause corruption.

To Whom Should Police Ethics Be Taught?

Ethics should be taught at police academies. Kleinig noted that many officers do not enter police work prepared for its moral demands. Officers face ethical problems daily, problems to which they are often poorly equipped to respond. Ethics preparation in all "introductory" training levels is needed. Instruction should be practical, and should include discussions of problems faced by TOs and senior officers in the organization. This discussion should not be rule-oriented but should constantly endeavor to make recruits aware of the complexity of real-life situations.

However, there is also a role for ethics in college settings. Individuals will understand the moral rigors of police work better, and they will learn about ethics in an environment that will not simply reinforce the common-place self-serving view that "the police have to bend the rules in order to do something about bad guys."

Ethical education in a college environment provides other advantages:

> Reflection on ethical issues relatively free from the constraints of time, tiredness, temptation, and peer pressure allows for a better appreciation of relevance and weightiness than the exigencies of the "street." The rookie police officer, thus prepared, can bring to those critical circumstances a mind that is already informed, even if not yet made up. (Kleinig, 1990:5)

Kleinig also suggests, and we wholeheartedly agree, that there is a need to provide mid-career teaching of police ethics. Ethical issues for managers and experienced street officers are different from those facing recruits, primarily because they involve supervisory activity, and also because public and organizational responsibilities tend to become more complex. TOs are central to a recruit's adaptation and socialization into a police organization. Mid-level managers confront circumstances involving broad tactical decisions. Commanders and chief executives must make fundamental decisions about long-range forecasting and its impact on officers in their command and on the public and civic groups. We consequently support ethical training at all organizational levels.

What Should Police-Ethics Training Achieve?

Kleinig identifies three ethics training goals.

Figure 11.1

Goal 1: The Reinforcement of Moral Resolve

By **moral resolve**, Kleinig means that ethics training should try to offset weaknesses of the will, the susceptibility to temptations and the loss of self-control. Officers will find themselves under pressures to compromise, both at the street level and in the departments. Ethics should seek to reinforce their moral resolve. This goal might seem inconsistent with our admonition to avoid noble-cause corruption, which we have described as an excess of resolve. However, corruption is encouraged by police cultural, departmental, and environmental pressures. Ethics training will be useless if officers cannot find in it intellectual and moral reasons to resist occupational pressures toward corruption.

Figure 11.2

> ### Goal 2: Moral Sensitization
>
> **Moral sensitization** is the nurturing of moral breadth and depth. Kleinig suggests that it too is an important part of ethics instruction. If officers are not sensitized to perspectives other than their own, their behavior is likely to be awkward and uninformed, at best. A broad ethical perspective can contribute to officers' awareness of the implications of their behavior, the circumstances in which they may find themselves, and the impact of their actions on individual citizens, colleagues, administrators, and the overall community they police.

Figure 11.3

> ### Goal 3: Imparting Moral Expertise
>
> **Moral expertise** is the ability to systematically think through ethical issues as they emerge in police work. Police, he contends, need to be able to recognize the ethical complexity in the encounters in which they find themselves. He provided the following example:
>
> > A police officer who is offered a small gratuity has to respond. Both unthinking acceptance and brusque rejection pose difficulties, particularly in a department committed to community policing . . . The situation can be further complicated, on the one hand, by regulations or a code that eschews the acceptance of gratuities, and on the other hand, by their common acceptance by members of that agency. (Kleinig, 1990:11)
>
> Police officers that lack the capacity to think through these complex situations are likely to blunder through them or hide behind what Kleinig calls a "culture of defensive conformity." These complex situations need to be discussed by officers, TOs, and managers across the agency. This dimension of ethics preparation is particularly of interest to us because it is similar to our idea that police should be examples, in their words and actions, to the communities they police.

How Should Ethics Be Integrated Into a Curriculum?

This query can be separated into several components. First, should ethics be mandatory or optional? Our position should be clear at this point – ethics preparation in any curricula should be mandatory, both in academic and in academy training environments. Second, should ethics be taught as a separate course or as an ingredient in many courses? As a separate course, ethics today is typically a marginal component in programs heavily weighted toward administrative, regulatory, and managerial components of police work. However, when it is integrated into all courses, instructors tend to skimp on it in favor of traditional course content.

We agree with Kleinig that ethics probably is best taught as a separate course or an integrated block in a training curriculum, so that complex issues can be explored and discussed. However, ethics should not be neglected in other classes. Police work, as Kleinig observes, is ethics-dense. As Kleinig (1990:12) puts it, "There is probably no aspect of police training that is wanting in ethical issues . . ." Preparers of curricula in both college and academy training settings should consequently review curricula for ethical content and insure that instructors appropriately emphasize ethical issues.

Hire Towards the Center of the Continuum

We have argued throughout this book that police officers enter police work already committed to the noble cause, and their commitments are finely tuned through formal and informal training processes. They are hired with predispositions sharply to the crime control side of the due-process crime control continuum. And there is precious little in the work, administration, or environments of the police that pull them back toward the center. Indeed, if one were to design a hiring process and work setting that emphasized the corruption of noble cause, it would be difficult to design a more effective system than American policing today. What is needed is a way to moderate the powerful influence of the crime control side over the work of police. Efforts to encourage a balanced perspective needs to be initiated in the hiring process.

We encourage departments to hire toward the center of the continuum. Recruits will tend to be ideologically committed to crime control. This is not bad, and only becomes a problem when excessive crime control shades into corruption. Departments can counter the tendency toward excessive crime control by emphasizing the importance of just means at each stage of the hiring process. This can be carried out in a way that does not undercut the importance of the noble cause (a doomed effort were it to be undertaken). It is unlikely that departments could be, or unclear that they should be, staffed with those whose sentiments aren't mobilized by noble-cause considerations. However, if just means are emphasized at each step of the hiring process, officers will learn that their parent organization encourages a balanced perspective, grounded in concern for fair play and democratic process as well as sympathetic to the plight of victims and determined to serve and protect.

The key to balanced hiring is for administrators to recognize that officers are easily corrupted by the current overemphasis on the noble cause, and that they (administrators) carry the responsibility for embedding balance into the hiring process. Administrators must set the ethical tone of the department. Recognizing that recruits will likely be committed to the noble cause, the hiring process at every step should encourage officers to consider the ways in which just means are important to their work. Consider the following elements of the hiring process.

Figure 11.4

Knowledge Testing

Police departments prefer to hire technically efficient officers – as long as they are not too intelligent. Some departments do not hire officers that test too highly on knowledge examinations. They fear that high-scoring officers will think about police work in too complicated a manner, will become too easily cynical about police work, or will be frustrated by the long wait for eligibility for promotion to sergeant, typically six years in most departments.

Hiring practices that reject the most intelligent applicants should end. Officers should be hired that are intelligent enough to think through the complex human issues confronting them. Ethical problems are the most complex that police face, and they are sometimes confronted on a daily basis. If recruits lack the intellectual capacity to make thoughtful decisions in the complex ethical environment inhabited by the police, either they should not be hired or detailed attention should be provided for their ethical training. We recommend that departments cease using broad-based intelligence tests and incorporate into their pre-employment testing jobs and skills-based tests that also include ethical decisionmaking as a component. Recruits should be presented with non-solvable ethical dilemmas to see if they can recognize their complexities.

Figure 11.5

Background Check

Too often a background check is used only to determine if the candidate has a criminal history. We agree with this goal, but also recommend that the breadth of a candidate's previous experience also be examined. Has the candidate been exposed to a variety of experiences, or does he or she have a culturally limited background? Has the candidate demonstrated a capacity to get along with many different kinds of people? A breadth of experience in diverse human situations will increase the capacity of the police to identify with the problems of the policed. Officers with limited life experience will have to learn how to get along in a diverse society "on the job," where mistakes will be made and an officers too easily can retreat to force to hide a lack of people skills.

Figure 11.6

> ### Polygraph
>
> Like a background check, a polygraph tends to look for criminal history. Testers, we believe, should also probe for an officer's racial and ethnic predispositions. It is our belief that noble-cause corruption is easier to justify when recruits have predispositions or prejudices against the police. If departments adopt a community policing approach, they should make sure that recruits aren't going to undermine their efforts with biases toward the policed. Recall that recruits will carry out the will of the department on the street, in public view. Probing questions should assess whether a recruit's attitudes toward ethnic or religious minority group members are consistent with the department's official position.

Figure 11.7

> ### Oral Interview
>
> Commanders skilled in oral interview techniques will use the interview to probe for stress points. Can the recruit make reasoned decisions in conflicting situations? How do recruits respond when commanders make conflicting requests? We recommend that commanders expand their often considerable oral interview skills to include ethical problems. Ethical problems can be presented that are substantial. Officers can be pressured for their ability to think through ethical problems.

Figure 11.8

> ### POST Academy, TOs, and the Problem of War Stories
>
> Employers must recognize that anecdotal stories told by trainers, TOs, and seasoned officers to new recruits are more than simple war stories or "tales of the wild." All stories involving the department carry in them its traditions and values. Even a single story, told by a trainer in a class on topics such as "due process" or "officer safety," can undercut the importance of just means or encourage noble-cause corruption. The message conveyed in such stories is "don't pay attention to what the class is officially about. Here's what the organization really considers valuable."

Imagine, for example, that recruits are in a four-hour training class on explosives. At the end of the second hour, the instructor describes an incident in which an officer failed to adequately protect himself disarming a small bomb and was injured. The message is clear – always use adequate precaution. Then imagine that the instructor states that the bomber was apprehended, but pled guilty to aggravated assault because an officer had conducted an illegal search of the suspect's house and the prosecutor was reluctant to go forward with more serious charges. Suppose that then the instructor says "you can't tell who's on whose side anymore." What message would such a statement convey? To an outside observer, the message could be either "don't get caught" or "don't commit due process violations." But an outside observer will not understand the power of the noble cause. Our experience tells us that officers are going to hear the message "violate the law but don't get caught" *unless* the instructor uses the incident to emphasize the importance of due process. Stories can "poison the well," as it were, informally encouraging officers to disguise their behavior or to violate the law. Employers must consequently be closely tuned into each stage of the hiring process, to make sure that recruits are receiving the kind of training they are supposed to be receiving.

By including ethical considerations in each step of the hiring process, and then reviewing with recruits how they responded and were evaluated, managers convey the message that just means are as important to organizational well-being as the noble cause. They will be hiring toward the center of the due-process/crime control continuum.

Figure 11.9

Buerger: War Stories and Black Swans

Occasionally, the recollections into past incidents are illuminative, providing practical insight into both situational assessment and tactical response. More frequently, they are **Black Swan** anecdotes that contradict the primary message of the instruction, whether intentionally or inadvertently (the latter usually occurs when the speaker, presenting in "good faith" mode but with no personal investment in the material, fails to recognize that the anecdote undermines the primary purpose of the lesson.

Buerger cites the following anonymous quotation from a West Coast police academy:

> [trainers] . . . were just spouting the official [agency] line on everything, all the while strongly suggesting that it was all bullshit and that we would learn the real stuff out on the street – 'ya know, we can't tell you to slap the shit out of those punk gang-bangers back in the alley here, but don't worry about that, you'll learn soon enough.

Source: Michael Buerger (1998). "Police Training as a Pentecost." *Police Quarterly*, 1-1:31.

Make Pre-Service College Education of the Police a Priority

The idea that police officers should be educated has been around for many years. College education has been available since Vollmer founded the first college program at Berkeley, California, in 1919 (Carte, 1986). Since then, college education in the areas of criminal justice has expanded dramatically. Today, there are more than 1,000 programs and departments of criminology or criminal justice in the United States.

Our needs are perhaps even greater in the current era than they were in the 1920s. The dramatic diversification of the American population has created a working police environment that requires intelligence, quick thinking, and breadth of human experience. As Garner (1999:91) notes, "Policing is an occupation that demands the education and skills of a teacher, lawyer, counselor, social worker, doctor, psychologist, and minister. Yet it is interesting that all of these professions long ago required a college degree." We need officers with the capacity to think through problems in a multi-ethnic, multi-religious society. We believe that a four-year college education is a minimal requirement for the complex ethical demands on police in the coming century.

Figure 11.10

The Value of the College Experience

As Goldstein (1986) observed, the college experience not only provides substantive course content, but college experience will provide a better officer. Departments that recruit college-educated officers benefit. The following are ways in which the experience contributes to the police, independent of the specific content of particular courses.

1. A greater share of intelligent young people.

2. Individuals with a wider view of the people with which they must deal.

3. Degree-carrying officers will bring greater confidence to citizen interactions.

4. The field as a whole will gain in status and dignity.

5. Officers are older and more mature when they begin their police careers.

6. Highly motivated youth.

Carter, Sapp, and Stephens (1988) describe eight ways in which college education can enhance decision-making skills. These ways are pertinent to ethical decisionmaking and are included here. They are reproduced from Palmiotto's (1999:73-74) discussion of police education in Figure 11.11.

Figure 11.11

Advantages of College Education for Decision-Making Skills

1. College education develops a broader base of information for decisionmaking.

2. Course requirements and achievements inculcate responsibility in the individual and a greater appreciation for constitutional rights, values, and the democratic form of government.

3. College education engenders the ability to flexibly handle difficult or ambiguous situations with greater creativity or innovation.

4. Higher education develops a greater empathy for diverse populations and their unique experiences.

5. The college-educated officer is assumed to be less rigid in decisionmaking and more readily accepts and adapts to organizational change.

6. The college experience will help officers better communicate and respond to crime and service needs of a diverse public in a competent manner with civility and humanity.

7. College-educated officers exhibit more "professional" demeanor and performance.

8. The college experience tends to make the officer less authoritarian and less cynical with respect to the milieu of policing.

Source: D. Carter, A. Sapp, and D. Stephens (1988). Reproduced in Palmiotto (1999). "Should a College Requirement be Required for Police Officers." Sewell (ed.) *Controversial Issues in Policing.* Allyn and Bacon.

It is our belief that only college-educated officers will be able to grasp the social complexities of the working environment they will encounter in the twenty-first century. It is preposterous that we continue debating the merits of college education for the police. A four-year degree is the minimum intellectual capital needed to participate in public life. Failure to educate the police is simply another mark of declines in the quality of public education in the United States. Officers with only a high-school education will be psychologically unprepared and intellectually ill-equipped for all but the most parochial of police jobs – and probably even those. Police without four-year degrees – uneducated by the world's standards – will be relegated to second-class citizen status in their own country.

Our recommendation: Abandon the practice of hiring officers with less than a college degree. Replace chiefs that don't actively seek out educated officers for employment in their organization with those who will.

Evaluate All Agency Tactical Practices

Police departments do not have a good grasp of the consequences of their tactical practices, from routine patrol to detective work. They rarely know if what they do works. Consider Skolnick and Fyfe's (1993) comments:

> The incapacity of police departments to evaluate their own effectiveness is a . . . significant impediment to innovation. With hardly any exception, police departments don't know whether the innovations they are trying are preferable to the old ways . . . Rarely have traditional practices been subjected to rigorous evaluation. When they have, they have usually been found wanting.

How does the evaluation of police tactics foster a balanced perspective? In public organizations, habitual practices take on a life of their own. If not periodically examined, they can become valued in themselves. In short, they become institutionalized. Through evaluations, taken-for-granted practices can be rationally examined and their consequences assessed in terms of organizational goals and strategies.

Lawrence Sherman and his colleagues (1997) published a comprehensive overview of what works, what doesn't, and evaluational criteria across a wide breadth of research in policing. It is beyond the scope of this book to review Sherman et al.'s findings. The document, however, may be the most important academic contribution to criminal justice policy to date. Agencies are advised to obtain a copy of it, and to continue its tradition: evaluate the effects of what they do. This applies equally to new and to taken-for-granted traditional practices.

It is possible that efforts to systematically evaluate programs will default to commanders, who are responsible for forecasting and budgeting in their respective areas of command. Most commanders are already busy, dealing daily with their unique blend of structured (long-term) and unpredictable (short-term) elements of command. The notion of expanding existing workload for commanders will be received as unfair and burdensome, and may consequently be carried out haphazardly. Where possible, we recommend a reallocation of budget priorities so that evaluation can be carried out by a department's research and development unit.

Also, we suggest that police agencies contact local colleges to see if faculty in criminal justice departments are interested in undertaking evaluations. Although evaluations tend to be expensive, sometimes police departments can barter with local college programs. For a modest expense, college students can be hired to carry out much of the evaluational activity. Agencies can encourage the use of college-based interns for some of the work as well.

Use Performance Evaluations to Provide Feedback for All Officers

Police departments are increasingly using **performance evaluations** to assess the work of police officers. Performance evaluations are instruments that assess the nature of the work process, specific accomplishments of police officers, and public attitudes about the performance of the department in general. Thoughtful performance evaluations can provide suggestions for work improvement and direction in an unstructured environment. And they can be a managerial tool for directing officers how to adapt to innovation in their departments.

The evaluation of individual-level performance in police departments is complicated for two reasons. First, managers can unintentionally turn evaluation into a hostile process. Personnel systems in police departments tend to be oriented toward punishment more than reward. Officers who are not performing up to some formal level of expectations may face reprimand or find that their chances of promotion are diminished. Consequently, poorly constructed or misused performance evaluations can have an alienating effect on line officers and encourage more secretive elements of line-level culture.

Second, performance evaluations confront an **importance/usefulness dilemma**. The dilemma can be stated as follows: The more important the performance evaluation is for a candidate's career, the greater the likelihood that evaluators are not going to provide useful distinctions among candidates. Chief executives often want to use performance evaluations for purposes important to line officers – promotion or salary, for example. Commanders who actually carry out the evaluations, and who have to work with both the promoted and the unpromoted, tend to give similar scores to the candidates competing for promotions. Even if they prefer a particular candidate, they may not want to hurt the feelings (or make enemies of) other candidates or offend colleagues that support other candidates. The problem is a genuine pickle.

We recommend that evaluations be used as "feedback" instruments rather than as tools to assess officer's competency or performance. By **feedback**, we mean that they provide useful and practical information to officers taking the evaluation, rather than turning the information over to commanders or to personnel units. First, evaluations can be used for constructive feedback for employees while abandoning their use for differentiating among employees (Oettmeier & Wycoff, 1997; Gabor, 1992). If the purpose of the evaluation is to provide constructive feedback to police officers, there is little gained by incorporating them into the department's promotional system. Secondly, evaluations should not become a part of an officer's permanent file. If they do, they will always be controversial. Third, evaluations can be conducted of officer teams as well as individuals. This further distances evaluations from the departmental reward system while at the same time integrates them more effectively with the team assignment nature of community policing.

Performance Evaluations in a Community Policing Environment

Community policing poses unique problems for the evaluation of line-officer performance. Community policing carries with it the notion that police work requires discretionary decisionmaking and flexibility in street judgments. If this is the case, how can officers be evaluated and held accountable for tasks that cannot be clearly defined? The development of performance evaluations for community policing confront two problems, one having to do with community policing and the other having to do with the performance evaluation process itself.

Performance evaluations play an important role in organizational innovation in a police organization – precisely the kind of issue that departments undergoing transition to community policing face (Oettmeier & Wycoff, 1995). Evaluation can enhance the innovative process by providing line officers with job expectations consistent with sought changes. The adoption of innovative police procedures and tactics, to be successful, requires changes throughout the organization's infrastructure. A performance evaluation process can be a critical element of the adoptive process:

> . . . a personnel performance measurement process designed to reflect and reinforce the functions that officers are expected to perform can provide structural support for a philosophy of policing and can be a valuable aid in the implementation of organizational change. (Oettmeier & Wycoff, 1995:136)

Performance measures should be tied to organizational purposes. This is particularly important for agencies adopting a community policing model of service delivery. It should be clear that evaluation is not to be used to punish but carries other organizational purposes.

In this context, evaluation is not simply a process of discipline and punish, but serves other important organizational objectives. It allows officers to assess their success in implementing community policing objectives. It provides commanders with an opportunity to see if their innovations are viable. It enables problem-solvers to reflect on their successes and failures.

Figure 11.12

Performance Evaluation in a Community Policing Environment

The following purposes can be accomplished by performance evaluation in a community policing environment (Oettmeier & Wycoff, 1977):

1. *Socialization.* The evaluation should "convey expectations content and style of (an officer's) performance" and reinforce the mission and values of the department.

2. *Documentation.* Evaluations should record the types of problems and situations officers encounter in their neighborhoods and their approaches to them. This also allows for officers to have their efforts recognized.

3. *System improvement.* What organizational conditions impede improved line-officer performance?

Finally, performance evaluation, we think, should be implemented throughout the organization. Put simply, what's good for the goose is good for the gander. Managers can demonstrate through example that evaluational procedures are not a punitive tool to extend autocratic control over line officers.

Re-Evaluate the Purposes of Peace Officer Standards and Training

We believe that there is a training imbalance in per-service police academies. There is an overemphasis on the preparation and use of deadly force skills in police work. An emphasis on deadly force skills, together with training scenarios that rapidly translate uncertainty in routine encounters into deadly force situations, can create a predisposition to view uncertainty first in terms of deadly force, thus escalating encounters to levels of danger they might not otherwise reach.

Consider the following quote from Delattre (1996:212):

Beginners are likely to look for simple rules when they are taught, to paraphrase Edmund Burke, "to make the extreme medicine of human life its daily bread." When this happens, Burke observes, people tend to become weak, because they develop the bad habit of thinking and speaking lightly about profoundly demanding matters, both before and after the fact. This is as true in law enforcement as elsewhere.

We think that this observation has important implications for police training, particularly pre-service academy training. Today, police training is intensely focused on officer safety. Officer safety training is important for the police. But it is, we believe, sharply out of balance with the kind and quality of training that is needed to prepare officers for the practical needs of day-to-day police work.

Deadly force is a central focus of training today. We are not advocating its abandonment. Yet we need to recognize that, when we train our young officers to think in terms of deadly force encounters, their natural tendency will be to use their training – to make a situation into a deadly force encounter so that they can apply their training. If we train them in deadly force, they will always approach situations from the perspective of deadly force resolutions. We fear that, by such intensive deadly force training, we are "knocking on wood." We are inadvertently contributing to the emergence of precisely those situations that we most dread.

The answer? It is not to abandon deadly force training. It is to put it into the perspective of the rest of the police craft. As many observers of the police have noted (see Wilson, 1968), it is the order maintenance function – not the law enforcement function – that best describes the daily routine of police work. We need to provide training for the ordinary events of police work, instead of turning it over to TOs to train officers by their esoteric, culturally specific standards. Officers need to be trained to deal with ordinary situations as well as extraordinary. The vast majority of situations never reach levels of deadly force. Moreover, many of the encounters police find themselves in will require their ability to work with people – not adopt a defensive posture. If the police are to negotiate order, a significant part of their training should lie in developing verbal skills, in learning about their public constituency, and in insuring that sentiments remain low key and channels of discussion remain open among citizens and citizen groups. They need to develop skills to use the power of voice and of self.

Commanders, let us ask you a question. Do your officers know how to *talk* to citizens? Or are they limited to "command voice" techniques. If the latter is true, your officers are being trained for war making, not peacekeeping.

We've brought this up with command officers before, and sometimes we hear "well, we were having some problems, but we started giving classes in 'verbal judo'." *Verbal judo*? What are you trying to do, verbally outfight the public? A class in simple verbal courtesy would go a long way. It might give your officers the idea that police work is a public service. Wouldn't that be a good thing?

Make Police Departments Smaller

Anyone who has thoughtfully read Felson's (1994) discussion of the relationship between large schools and crime can't help but cast an inquisitive eye toward large police organizations. Like the large urban school, the large urban police organization may create unsolvable problems of accountability by virtue of its size. Anyone watching the endless rounds of talented leadership and inspired reform inevitably breaking on the shoals of corruption in New York City, for example, must begin to wonder if large departments are manageable. It may be that they're not. The New York Police Department has many, many officers. By one estimate it has 21,000 patrol officers (Strawberry & Strawberry, 1990). That's 21,000 officers on the street, making decisions that convey to the public what the purpose of the department is. The answer, we think, is to break super-large departments into smaller agencies, provide governance at the precinct level, and make them autonomous to each other and to the communities they serve.

A reader might be tempted to respond "yeah, we can just break up our large cities into smaller political units while we're at it." In fact, most large cities are already separated into smaller units. Perhaps our contemporary deceit has been in thinking that we could effectively govern departments so large and consolidated over such densely crowded precinct areas – that bigger was better. We recognize that it is not reasonable to rush out and carve up America's largest police departments. That doesn't mean that we shouldn't recognize the pathogenic effects of size on governability, accountability, and quality of service delivery.

Research has suggested that consolidation of police services over large metropolitan areas may not be efficient or effective. Agencies distributed across the urban metroplex may provide services more effectively tuned to the needs of local communities than a single, overarching public safety department can. Ostrom's (1974) research on smaller police organizations in metropolitan areas concluded that smaller departments could better manage the problems confronted by their representative districts. Where political divisions allow for smaller jurisdictional boundaries, policing has the potential to be more efficient and effective – and accountable. Moreover, forecasts of the likely direction of large urban environments describe a breaking into smaller economic federations loosely tied together in economic confederations. Public services – the police included – will have to do the same to survive. Like big schools, big police departments don't work well. In the current age, we're rethinking what we want the police to do. We want them to be responsive to the middle institutions of American life. We should think about the scale of size that can get us there. Smaller might be better.

Conclusion: The Noble Cause

12

The noble cause is the heart of police culture: it inspires the values that officers carry and animates their daily work routines. If police officers are so moved by the noble cause that they are willing to do anything to achieve so-called good ends, they have corrupted their craft. They have learned all the wrong things about policing and doing good things. They have become part of the problem, not the solution. There will be a price to pay, and they will pay it as surely as their department will, and as will the citizens they police.

Mike tells a story about perspective. *You will be tempted to pop some asshole with your PR 24. It happens. It's a bad idea. What if you kill him? It happens. You can never control the outcome – don't forget that. You'll think you can – until something goes wrong. Then it's too late. Someone really gives you a hard time. You put a carotid choke-hold on him, to inflict a little extra punishment. That's wrong.*

You have to learn to keep your moral center inside you. Never let someone take it from you. If someone is pushing your buttons, that's their problem. How you react is your problem. Don't let them direct the action. Never use somebody else as a justification for what you do. Don't blame the courts, the public, some asshole for your behavior. It's your behavior. Never forget that. It's your moral center, and you can lose it. You can lose it forever.

A Hispanic song, popular in 1995, carried the theme "no somos verbos somos sustantivos." It translates as "we're not verbs, we're nouns." It's perhaps not the most elegant translation, but the meaning is important.

The message it contains is that we should not use people to achieve material or ideological goals. We should focus our efforts on getting along with each other. The ends we seek are us, our ability to get along. And that is the end that justice should serve as well.

Kleinig captures the spirit of ethics that we share in this book. He observes that:

> Morality is concerned essentially with humans in their relations with each other, whether those relations are interpersonal, collective, or structural. Aspirationally, the "we" of morality is first and foremost a *human* we – not an American or European or Black or capitalist or police "we." Morality is concerned with being and doing at the most basic level, with people's common standing as human beings. For that reason there can be no distinctive police ethic but only a human ethic applied to police situations. (Kleinig, 1990:2)

Sometimes we get it backwards. We use people to achieve ends personally meaningful to us. When people don't conform to our way of thinking, we might feel a need to punish them, to make them behave. There are real problems with thinking about people as means to an end, rather than as ends in themselves. Noble-cause corruption makes the cause the ultimate end, with people the means to achieve that end.

Consider Silberman's (1978) description of ends and means. His words, printed in Figure 12.1, were written about the courts, but they apply equally well to the police.

Figure 12.1

The Substantive Importance of Procedure

If Watergate taught us anything, it is what the legal historian Willard Hurst calls the substantive importance of justice – the recognition that means shape ends, that how people do things may be as important as what they do. All the more so in criminal court, for the criminal law is an instrument of education as well as coercion, shaping behavior through its moral influence as well as through fear of punishment. When the law is educating effectively, people conform to it because they want to; law-abiding behavior becomes a matter of habit, of voluntary (if unconscious) choice, rather than a means of avoiding punishment. In a large and complex society such as ours, respect for law – the willingness to obey the law because it is the law – is a more effective instrument of social control than is fear of punishment.

Source: Charles Silberman (1978). *Criminal Justice, Criminal Violence,* pp. 345-346.

Mike continues. *I want to share something with you I recently came across, in Silberman's book on criminal justice* (Silberman, 1978:418). *It's from Through the Looking Glass, by Lewis Carroll. You remember this book? In this part of the book, everything is happening backwards. The quote goes as follows:*

> ". . . there's the King's messenger. He's in prison now, being punished; and the trial doesn't even begin till next Wednesday: and of course the crime comes last of all." "Suppose he never commits the crime?" said Alice. "That would be all the better, wouldn't it?" the Queen said.

What's the problem here? Mike asks.

One of the officers responds "well, punishment comes before the trial, and there's not even a crime yet."

Is it a good way to run a criminal justice system?

"It could be," one of the officers replies. The others chuckle. It's a normal response. Another hesitates and responds. "Oh, I get it. We have to put everyone in jail."

Mike smiles and holds his arms out, as if holding up the idea for all to see. *Exactly. We have to put everyone in jail. It's the only way we can really control the outcome. Why don't we want to do that?*

The commanders give him reserved looks.

Okay. Good. Let's go back to the beginning. I've got this loud-mouthed asshole. He hangs with bad company, and I know he's selling drugs. I know it. I catch him drinking beer in the park. So I pat him down, all legal, and feel a small bag. Then, voila, it just slips out of his pocket, onto the ground, a small bag containing a powdery white substance. I got him. I use my super-duper magic pencil, and he's got five years. I sleep better tonight, knowing another asshole is off the street. He knows the truth, but who's going to believe him?

Justice is reversed. I've arrested and booked this guy. Pure noble-cause corruption. He's already in jail serving time. There's no trial. I got him before he hurt someone. It's beautiful. But it's Alice in Wonderland justice.

Mike pauses for a moment, to collect his words carefully. *And the crime this guy committed. What's the crime? What's the crime?*

"Possession," one commander responded.

What was the crime? Possession? Wasn't the crime created by the officer?

"The guy was in possession of drugs."

Mike turns to face the commander squarely. *Are you sure? Are you absolutely certain of that? You already know that the officer uses the law to act out his values on the street. You already know that the officer acted illegally. Can you be absolutely certain that the officer didn't take one more step?*

The commander blushes. It had not crossed his mind that the officer might have planted the drugs. The room is quiet.

This is the problem with confusing means and ends. Humans are the ends, not the means. Law and order are the means, not the ends. We have law and order in the service of humans. When we reverse them, we have *Alice in Wonderland* justice. For one commander, the lesson is learned.

A captain speaks out, miffed by the example. "I know that I did not carry drugs when I was a street officer. Run your example another way." Cops often ask questions by making direct statements.

OK. Let's think about a partner you had. You had a pretty good idea how he thought about things. Sometimes he's your best friend, sometimes he's a real asshole. Right? Now how would you feel about having to do everything the way he wanted to do it?

"When I was a patrol officer my partner was a female," the officer responds. Everyone laughs.

I'll take that. Your partner was a woman. How would you feel about living in that world? Did she ever say anything about your diet? About how you drive? How you dress? Your drinking habits? Your range skills? You didn't have to listen to her, did you?

"Sometimes." They laugh again. Nervously. Boisterous laughter is no longer permitted on this topic.

But you didn't have to. But what happened when she was dealing with someone on the street? Did they have to listen to her? You didn't have to put up with her bullshit, but I bet they did. If they blew her off, then what happened to them?

No comment.

What happened?

"COC" one commander replies.

Exactly. Contempt of cop. They went to jail. But that's Alice in Wonderland justice. Mike smiles. Now they understand. Finally, they've got it. Justice reversed, in the name of the noble cause. It seems normal, but it's not justice at all. It's just order.

If people are your means to achieve order, you don't have a society. You have a prison. It's the only way you can be sure. It's the only way you can control the outcome. You want to be a prison guard? Is that what you want?

Today, officers are taught to think like warriors. They believe that they're in a "war" against crime and drugs. They are increasingly heavily armed, often with a minimum of a 9mm and shotgun, they wear body armor, and they carry a variety of sub-lethal weapons. They are the young Centurions, and they occupy the streets like warriors. They generate fear in bad guys. And they don't recognize the extent to which they cause fear in ordinary citizens. They are trained for battle, and they dream warrior dreams.

This is wrong. The police in America are not about making war. All the metaphors are cockeyed. Warriors search out and destroy the enemy.

But this is not how the police can maintain order. How can they accomplish this important goal?

They can use the powers of voice and of self in the name of peace. Peace is, after all, the visible, social expression of our ability to get along. To insure that we somehow, and against some pretty long odds, survive as a democratic people. For neighborhood groups in conflict, to negotiate order when we disagree, so that we don't settle our differences with violence and the politics of exclusion. To find the middle ground. For the disenfranchised and the poor, to help them reclaim the middle institutions of American life. For victims, to help them find critically needed community services to heal their minds, bodies, and souls so that they can move forward with their lives, not backward into despair and vengeance. These tasks are the burden of a democratic police, of a police force that leads by the power of self as well as authority of law. To return all citizens the station to which they rightfully belong – as the true ends of policing. And finally, as a police officer, to know that you are an inspiration to others, and for that, respected.

Endnotes

[1] See Barker (1996) for a thorough and practical discussion of the Law Enforcement Code of Ethics. His discussion is aimed at a practical explanation of ethical issues for police recruits.

[2] Both dilemmas have been separately addressed in a wide literature. Our concern is that they have not been looked at in a systematic way with regard to each other. It is their interplay that makes accountability among the police profoundly difficult.

[3] Consider the following quote from Muir (1977:49).

> Coercion creates a situation in which what is effective is at odds on every point with what Lord Acton called "the inflexible integrity of the moral code." The gap between being a good man and a good practitioner of corruption appears unbridgeable.

Muir is not seeking to discover a way to permit corruption. To the contrary, he is looking for a counterbalance, a morality to limit the corrosive effects of coercive power. Passion, or responsibility, is for him that counterbalance.

[4] Testilying is a term that describes police lying when giving sworn testimony.

[5] For a street cop, saying that we need to balance passion with perspective is too close to suggesting that strength should be balanced with weakness.

[6] Weber in his writings developed the notion of Charismatic authority. This authority, however, resonates with Muir's development of the power of voice, to exhort, and not what we call the power of self.

[7] The actual score that the Tacoma officers gave for "freedom" was actually lower than it was in the Rokeach sample of police officers.

[8] Representativeness of findings is an important issue not developed in this book. It should be noted that there are more than 18,000 police agencies in the United States, and a small sample can hardly be considered representative.

[9] The authors observe that "The comparison of three groups (Tacoma, Spokane, and the original Rokeach survey) concerning the ranking of values . . . shows that only one item – "Mature Love" – featured a difference large enough to reach the .05 statistical level."

[10] We are familiar with two other researchers that have recently collected data using the Rokeach value inventory. We have not seen and do not know their findings.

[11] Mark Furman was the detective in charge of the case, who was accused by the defense of racial bias in his investigation of the case.

[12] We tend to view police work as difficult to bring under administrative control. However, others have argued that the unpredictable nature of police work is more of a self-serving doctrine of police work than fact. See, for example, Fyfe's discussion of the "split-second syndrome."

[13] To be made the object of a practical joke; to be fooled or made to look like a simpleton.

[14] Release-on-recognizance is the practice of releasing arrestees while they await trial. Arrestees are "trusted" by the courts to appear for their court hearing. This practice is used for offenders who have committed non-serious offenses.

[15] In the language of institutional theory, the municipal system refers to the organizational environment of police departments. The environment is made up of groups whose opinions can influence the well-being of the department (Crank & Langworthy, 1992). Police organizations, as institutionalized organizations, face "out" to their institutional environment in order to determine the well-being of the organization. This distinguishes them from business organizations, who face "inward" to their technological core and survive by being more efficient and effective than competitors.

[16] Joycelyn Pollock (1998:34) distinguishes between act and rule utilitarianism as follows: "in act utilitarianism, the basic utility derived from an action is alone examined. We look at the consequences of any action for all involved and weigh the units of utility accordingly. In rule utilitarianism, one judges that action in reference to the precedence it sets and the long-term utility of the rule set by the action."

[17] Line officers have a social environment that is both cultural and subcultural. It carries cultural elements because many of its values and beliefs are the product of adaptation to its occupational setting (Crank, 1998). It also has subcultural elements because there are many values that are imported from a broader institutional context (Martin, 1980). The interested reader is recommended to Manning's (1989) discussion of police culture in the *Encyclopedia of Police Science*.

[18] Wolf-packing means that multiple patrol vehicles respond to routine traffic stops.

[19] Police can intervene in a limited way under conditions of reasonable suspicion, if they think a law is about to be broken. Oregon recently passed a law allowing the police to seize a vehicle, a probable cause standard, if they think a law is about to be broken.

[20] Assholes, for the police, represented "all those persons who would question, limit, or otherwise attempt to control the police" (Van Maanen, 1978:235).

[21] *Mapp v. Ohio*, 367 U.S. 643 (1961).

[22] Jeffrey Bils. "State Troopers Filling Out Patrols in Cicero," *Chicago Tribune*, May 4, 1998. Internet.

[23] This, of course, is not true for African-Americans. See Williams and Murphy, 1995.

[24] The embeddedness of local institutions in international economies is a mark of the inter-dependence of people in the world today. Without a doubt, lack of economic supports can have a profound effect on the ability of local communities to deal with quality of life issues. Our position is that economic conditions are only one of a host of factors, though certainly a very important one, affecting neighborhood quality of life. Local actors, if orga-nized, can in fact have a positive quality of life impact on their communities even when economic conditions are bleak.

[25] The correlation between renters and homeowners on disorder was .90. The correla-tions between Blacks and Whites on disorder was .87. These are strong correlations, well above what would be expected by chance alone.

Bibliography

Ahern, James (1972). Police in Trouble: Our Frightening Crisis in Law Enforcement. New York, NY: Hawthorne Books.

Armstrong and Possley (1999). "Break Rules, Be Promoted." Chicagotribune.com/news. January 14.

Barker, Thomas (1996). *Police Ethics: Crisis in Law Enforcement*. Springfield, IL: Charles Thomas Publishers.

Barker, Thomas (1994). "An Empirical Study of Police Deviance Other Than Corruption." Pp. 123-138 in T. Barker and D. Carter (eds.) *Police Deviance*, Third Edition. Cincinnati, OH: Anderson Publishing Co.

Barker, Thomas and David Carter (1999). "Fluffing up the Evidence and Covering Your Ass: Some Conceptual Notes on Police Lying." Pp. 342-350 in L.K. Gaines and G.W. Cordner (eds.) *Policing Perspectives: An Anthology*. Los Angeles, CA: Roxbury Publishing Company.

Barker, Thomas and David L. Carter (1994). "Police Lies and Perjury: A Motivation-Based Taxonomy." Pp. 139-153 in T. Barker and D. Carter (eds.) *Police Deviance*, Third Edition. Cincinnati, OH: Anderson Publishing Co.

Barker, Thomas, Rodney Friery, and David Carter (1994). "After L.A., Would Your Local Police Lie?" Pp. 155-168 in T. Barker and L. Carter (eds.) *Police Deviance*, Third Edition. Cincinnati, OH: Anderson Publishing Co.

Bayley, David H. (1996). "The Best Defense." Police Executive Research Forum.

Bayley, David H. (1988). "Community Policing: A Report from the Devil's Advocate." Pp. 226-237 in J.R. Greene and S.D. Mastrofski (eds.) *Community Policing: Rhetoric or Reality*. New York, NY: Praeger.

Bayley, David H. and Clifford D. Shearing (1998). "The Future of Policing." Pp. 150-168 in G. Cole and M. Gertz (eds.) *The Criminal Justice System: Politics and Policies*, Seventh Edition. Belmont, CA: West/Wadsworth Publishing Company.

Bellah, Robert N., Richard Madsen, William M. Sullivan, Ann Swidler, and Steven M. Tipton (1985). *Habits of the Heart: Individualism and Commitment in American Life.* Berkeley, CA: University of California Press.

Belluck (1999). "Convict Freed After 16 Years on Death Row," New York Times National Report. Saturday, February 6.

Berman, Jay S. (1987). *Police Administration and Progressive Reform: Theodore Roosevelt as Police Commissioner of New York.* New York, NY: Greenwood Press.

Bittner, Egon (1991). "The Functions of Police in Modern Society." Pp. 35-51 in C. Klockars and S. Mastrofski (eds.) *Thinking About Police: Contemporary Readings,* Second Edition. New York, NY: McGraw-Hill, Inc.

Bittner, Egon (1970). *The Functions of Police in Modern Society.* Washington, DC: U.S. Government Printing Office.

Black, Donald J. (1980). *The Manners and Customs of the Police.* New York, NY: Academic Press.

Black, Donald J. (1973). "The Mobilization of the Law." *Journal of Legal Studies.* The University of Chicago Law School, Volume II: 125-144.

Bohm, Robert M. (1984). "The Politics of Law and Order." (Book Review). *Justice Quarterly,* 3-1:449-55.

Bordua, David and Albert Reiss (1986). "Command, Control and Charisma: Reflections on Police Bureaucracy." Pp. 31-36 in M.R. Pogrebin and R.M. Regoli (eds.) *Police Administrative Issues; Techniques and Functions.* Millwood, NY: Associated Faculty Press.

Bouza, Anthony (1990). *The Police Mystique: An Insiders Look at Cops, Crime, and the Criminal Justice System.* New York, NY: Plenum Press.

Braswell, M., B. McCarthy and B. McCarthy (1996). *Justice Crime, and Ethics,* Second Edition. Cincinnati, OH: Anderson Publishing Co.

Buerger, Michael (1998). "Police Training as a Pentecost: Using Tools Singularly Ill-Suited to the Purpose of Reform." *Police Quarterly,* 1-1:27-63.

Camus, Albert (1974). *Resistance, Rebellion, and Death.* Trans. Justin O'Brien. New York, NY: Vintage Books.

Caldero, Michael (1997). "Value Consistency Within the Police: The Lack of a Gap." Paper presented at the (March) 1997 annual meetings of the Academy of Criminal Justice Sciences, Louisville, KY.

Caldero, Michael (1995). "Community Oriented Policing Reform: An Evaluation and Theoretical Analysis." Doctoral dissertation. Washington State University.

Cao, Liqun, James Frank, and Francis T. Cullen (1996). "Race, Social Context, and Confidence in the Police." *American Journal of Police,* 15(1):3-22.

Carte, Gene (1986). August Vollmer and the Origins of Police Professionalism." Pp. 3-9 in M. Pogrebin and R. Regoli (eds.) *Police Administrative Issues: Techniques and Functions.* Millwood, NY: Associated Faculty Press.

Carte, Gene and Elaine Carte (1975). *Police Reform in the United States: The Era of August Vollmer, 1905-1932.* Berkeley, CA: University of California Press.

Carter, David L. (1999). "Drug Use and Drug-Related Corruption of Police Officers." Pp. 311-323 in L.K. Gaines and G.W. Cordner (eds.) *Policing Perspectives: An Anthology.* Los Angeles, CA: Roxbury Publishing Company.

Carter, D., A. Sapp, and D. Stephens (1988). "Higher Education as a Bona Fide Educational Qualification (BFQ) for Police: A Blueprint." *American Journal of Police,* 7(2):16-18.

Casey, R. (1996). "Cop Wins One Million in Whistleblower Appeal." In *The Ethics Roll Call*, 4:6.

Cohen, Howard (1996). "Police Discretion and Police Objectivity." Pp. 91-106 in J. Kleinig (ed.) *Handled with Discretion: Ethical Issues in Police Decision Making*. New York, NY: Rowman and Littlefield Publishers, Inc.

Cordner, Gary (1999). "Elements of Community Policing." Pp. 149 in L. Gaines and G. Cordner (eds.) *Policing Perspectives: An Anthology*. Los Angeles, CA: Roxbury.

Coser, Lewis (1956). *The Functions of Social Conflict*. New York, NY: The Free Press.

Couper, David (1979). "Police: Protectors of Peoples Rights." *Law Enforcement News*, 5(12 March):8.

Crank, John (1998). *Understanding Police Culture*. Cincinnati, OH: Anderson Publishing Co.

Crank, John (1997). "Celebrating Agency Culture: Engaging a Traditional Cop's Heart in Organizational Change." Pp. 49-57 in Q. Thurman and E. McGarrell (eds.) *Community Policing in a Rural Setting*. Cincinnati, OH: Anderson Publishing Co.

Crank, John, Bob Regoli, John Hewitt, and Robert Culbertson (1993). "An Assessment of Work Stress Among Police Executives." *Journal of Criminal Justice,* 21-4:313-324.

Crank, John and Robert Langworthy (1991). "An Institutional Perspective of Policing." *The Journal of Criminal Law and Criminology*, 83:338-363.

Crank, John and Michael Caldero (1991). "The Production of Occupational Stress Among Police Officers: A Survey of Eight Municipal Police Organizations in Illinois." *Journal of Criminal Justice*, 19(4):339-350.

Cullen, Francis, Bruce Link, Nancy Wolfe, and James Frank (1989). "The Social Dimensions of Police Officer Stress." *Justice Quarterly*, 2:507-533.

Davis, Kenneth Culp (1969). *Discretionary Justice: A Preliminary Inquiry*. Baton Rouge, LA: Louisiana State University Press.

Delattre, Edwin J. (1996). *Character and Cops: Ethics in Policing,* Third Edition. Washington, DC: American Enterprise Institute.

Dombrink, John (1994). "The Touchables: Vice and Police Corruption in the 1980s." Pp. 61-100 in T. Barker and D. Carter (eds.) *Police Deviance*, Third Edition. Cincinnati, OH: Anderson Publishing Co.

Donahue, Michael and Arthur Felts (1993). "Police Ethics: A Critical Perspective." *Journal of Criminal Justice*, 21-4:339-352.

Felson, Marcus (1994). *Crime and Everyday Life*. Thousand Oaks, CA: Pine Forge Press.

Ferguson, Kathy E. (1987). "Male-Oriented Politics: Feminism and Political Science." In T. Ball (ed.) *Idioms of Inquiry: Critique and Renewal in Political Science*. New York, NY: State University of New York Press.

Festinger, Leon (1957). *A Theory of Cognitive Dissonance*. Evanston, IL: Row, Peterson.

Fletcher, Connie (1991). *Pure Cop*. New York, NY: St. Martin's Paperbacks.

Fletcher, Connie (1990). *What Cops Know*. New York, NY: Pocket Books.

Fogelson, Robert (1977). *Big-City Police*. Cambridge, MA: Harvard University Press.

Frank, James R., Cory Watkins, and Steven Brandl (1997). "The Content of Community Policing: Does It Really Differ from Traditional Policing?" *Policing: International Journal of Police Strategy and Management*, 20(4):716-728.

Frank, James, Steven Brandl, Robert Worden, and Timothy S. Bynum (1996). "Citizen Involvement in the Coproduction of Police Outputs." *Journal of Crime and Justice*, 12(2):1-29.

Frazer, Donald M. (1985). "Politics and Police Leadership: The View from City Hall." Pp. 41-47 in W.A. Geller (ed.) *Police Leadership in America: Crisis and Opportunity*. New York, NY: Praeger.

Fyfe, James (1989). "The Split-Second Decision and Other Determinants of Police Violence." Pp. 465-479 in R. Dunham and G. Alpert (eds.) *Critical Issues in Policing: Contemporary Readings*. Prospect Heights, IL: Waveland Press, Inc.

Gabor, Andrea (1992). "Take this Job and Love It." *New York Times*. 26 January.

Garner, Randall (1999). "College-Educated Cops: Is the Time Now? Yes." Pp. 89-97 in J. Sewell (ed.) *Controversial Issues in Policing*. Boston, MA: Allyn and Bacon.

Geller, William (1985). *Police Leadership in America: Crisis and Opportunity*. New York, NY: Praeger.

Geller, William and Guy Swanger (1995). *Managing Innovation in Policing: The Untapped Potential of the Middle Manager*. Washington, DC: Police Executive Research Forum.

Glazer, Nathan (1988). *The Limits of Social Policy*. Cambridge, MA: Harvard University Press.

Goffman, Erving (1967). *Interaction Ritual*. Garden City, NY: Anchor Books.

Goldstein, Herman (1986). "Higher Education and the Police." Pp. 243-256 in M. Pogrebin and R. Regoli (eds.) *Police Administrative Issues: Techniques and Functions*. Milkwood, NY: Associated Faculty Press.

Goldstein, Herman (1979). "Improving Policing: A Problem Oriented Approach." *Crime & Delinquency*, 25:236-258.

Goldstein, Joseph (1998). "Police Discretion Not to Invoke the Criminal Process: Low Visibility Decisions in the Administration of Justice." Pp. 85-102 in G. Cole and M. Gertz (eds.) *The Criminal Justice System: Politics and Policies*, Seventh Edition. West/Wadsworth: Belmont, CA.

Goolkasian, G., R. Geddes, and W. DeJong (1989). "Coping with Police Stress." Pp. 498-507 in R. Dunham and G. Alpert (eds.) *Critical Issues in Policing*. Prospect Heights, IL: Waveland.

Greene, Jack R. and Stephen D. Mastrofski (1991). *Community Policing: Rhetoric or Reality?* New York, NY: Praeger.

Guyot, Dorothy (1991). *Policing as Though People Matter.* Philadelphia, PA: Temple University Press.

Guyot, Dorothy (1979). "Bending Granite: Attempts to Change the Rank Structure of American Police Departments." *Journal of Police Science and Administration*, 7:235-284.

Hanson, Amy Beth (1998). "Neighbors Stay Cool to Sect Hit by Crime." *Oregonian*, May 10:A20.

Harmon, Michael M. (1995). *Responsibility as Paradox: A Critique of Rational Discourse on Government.* Advances in Public Administration Series. Thousand Oaks, CA: Sage.

Harris, Richard (1973). *The Police Academy: An Inside View.* New York, NY: Wiley.

Hopkins, Ernest (1931). *Our Lawless Police.* New York, NY: Viking Press.

Horowitz, R. (1984). *Honor and the American Dream: Culture and Identity in a Chicago Community.* New Brunswick, NJ: Rutgers University Press.

Hudnut, William H. III (1985). "The Police and the Polis: A Mayor's Perspective." Pp. 20-29 in W. Geller (ed.) *Police Leadership in America: Crisis and Opportunity.* New York, NY: Praeger.

Human Rights Watch (1998). *Shielded from Justice: Police Brutality and Accountability in the United States.* New York, NY: Human Rights Watch.

Huntington, Samuel (1996). *The Clash of Civilizations and the Remaking of World Order.* New York, NY: Simon & Schuster.

International Association of Chiefs of Police (1989). *Building Integrity and Reducing Drug Corruption.* Arlington, VA: International Association of Chiefs of Police.

Jefferson, Tony (1987). "Beyond Paramilitarism." *British Journal of Criminology,* 27:47-53.

Johnson, Kevin (1998). "New Breed of Bad Cop Sells Badge, Public Trust." *USA Today.* April 16. Internet.

Kaplan, Robert (1998). "Travels into America's Future." *Atlantic Monthly,* August 1998.

Kappeler, Victor E., Richard D. Sluder, and Geoffrey P. Alpert (1994). *Forces of Deviance: The Dark Side of Policing.* Prospect Heights, IL: Waveland Press.

Kappeler, Victor E. and Peter B. Kraska (1998). "A Textual Critique of Community Policing: Police Adaptation to High Modernity." *Policing: An International Journal of Police Strategies and Management,* 21(2):293-313.

Kelling, George (1998). "Crime Control, the Police, and Culture Wars: Culture Wars and Cultural Pluralism." Pp. 1-19 in Kelling, George, Randall Kennedy, David Musto, Joan Petersilia, and Philip Cook (eds.) *Perspectives on Crime and Justice: 1997-1998 Lecture Series.* Washington DC: U.S. Department of Justice.

Kelling, George (1987). "Acquiring a Taste for Order: The Community and the Police." *Crime & Delinquency,* 33:90-102.

Kelling, George (1985). "Order Maintenance, the Quality of Urban Life, and Police: A Line of Argument." Pp. 296-308 in W. Geller (ed.) *Police Leadership in America: Crisis and Opportunity.* New York, NY: Praeger.

Kelling, George and Katherine Coles (1996). *Fixing Broken Windows: Restoring Order and Reducing Crime in Our Communities.* New York, NY: The Free Press.

Kelling, George and William J. Bratton (1993). *Implementing Community Policing: The Administrative Problem. Perspectives on Policing* 17. Washington, DC: National Institute of Justice.

Kerner, Otto, and the National Advisory Commission on Civil Disorders (1968). *Report of the National Advisory Commission on Civil Disorders.* Washington, DC: U.S. Government Printing Office.

Kilborn, P.T. (1994). "Police Profile Stays Much the Same: A Try for Diversity Meets Old Patterns. *The New York Times*, B1, B3. October 10.

Klein (1999). "A Free Woman, Finally." ABCNEWS.com, February 8.

Kleinig, John (1996). "Handling Discretion with Discretion." Pp. 1-12 in J. Kleinig (ed.) *Handled with Discretion: Ethical Issues in Police Decision Making*. New York, NY: Rowman and Littlefield Publishers, Inc.

Kleinig, John (1990). "Teaching and Learning Police Ethics." *Journal of Criminal Justice*, 18-1:1-18.

Klockars, Carl (1995a). "The Legacy of Conservative Ideology and Police." Pp. 349-356 in V. Kappeler (ed.) *The Police and Society: Touchstone Readings*. Prospect Heights, IL: Waveland Press.

Klockars, Carl (1991a). "The Rhetoric of Community Policing." Pp. 530-542 in C. Klockars and S. Mastrofski (eds.) *Thinking About Policing*, Second Edition. New York, NY: McGraw Hill.

Klockars (1991b). "The Modern Sting." Pp. 258-267 in C. Klockars and S. Mastrofski (eds.) *Thinking About Policing*, Second Edition. New York, NY: McGraw-Hill.

Klockars, Carl (1985a). "The Idea of Police." *Law and Criminal Justice Studies*, Vol 3. Beverly Hills, CA: Sage.

Klockars, Carl (1985b). "Order Maintenance, the Quality of Urban Life, and Police: A Different Line of Argument." Pp. 309-321 in W. Geller (ed.) *Police Leadership in America: Crisis and Opportunity*. New York, NY: Praeger.

Klockars, Carl (1983). "The Dirty Harry Problem." Pp. 428-438 in C. Klockars (ed.) *Thinking About Police: Contemporary Readings*. New York, NY: McGraw-Hill.

Knapp Commission (1972). *Report on Police Corruption*. New York, NY: George Braziller.

Kraska, Peter B. and Victor E. Kappeler (1995). "To Serve and Pursue: Exploring Police Sexual Violence Against Women." *Justice Quarterly*, 12:15-112.

Kraska, P. and D. Paulsen (1996). "Forging the Iron Fist Inside the Velvet Glove: A Case Study of the Rise of U.S. Paramilitary Units." Paper presented at the annual meeting of the Academy of Criminal Justice Sciences, Las Vegas, NV.

Launay, G. and P. Fielding (1989). "Stress among Prison Officers. Some Empirical Evidence Based on Self Reports." *Howard Journal of Criminal Justice*, 28-1:38-47.

Lewis, Dan and Greta Salem (1986). *Fear of Crime: Incivility and the Production of a Social Problem*. Oxford: Transaction Books.

Lyng, Stephen (1990). "Edgework: A Social Psychological Analysis of Voluntary Risk Taking." *American Journal of Sociology*, 95-4:851-886.

Maguire, K. and A. Pastore (eds.) (1995). *Sourcebook of Criminal Justice Statistics*. Washington, DC: U.S. Government Printing Office.

Maguire, Kathleen and Ann L. Pastore (1984). *After Virtue: A Study in Moral Theory*, Second Edition. Notre Dame, IN: Notre Dame University Press.

Manning, Peter K. (1997). *Police Work: The Social Organization of Policing*, Second Edition. Prospect Heights, IL: Waveland Press.

Manning, Peter K. (1989). "The Police Occupational Culture in Anglo-American Societies." In. L. Hoover and J. Dowling (eds.) *Encyclopedia of Police Science*. New York, NY: Garland.

Manning, Peter K. (1979). "Metaphors of the Field: Varieties of Organizational Discourse." *Administrative Science Quarterly*, 24:660-671.

Manning, Peter K. and Lawrence Redlinger (1977). "Invitational Edges of Corruption: Some Consequences of Narcotic Law Enforcement." Pp. 279-310 in P. Rock (ed.) *Drugs and Politics*. Rutgers, NJ: Society/Transaction Books.

Martin, Susan E. (1980). *Breaking and Entering: Policewomen on Patrol*. Berkeley, CA: University of California Press.

Mastrofski, Stephen (1999). "What Does Community Policing Mean for Daily Police Work?" Pp. 100-104 in C.W. Eskridge (ed.) *Criminal Justice: Concepts and Issues: An Anthology*, Third Edition. Los Angeles, CA: Roxbury Publishing Co.

Mastrofski, Stephen (1991). "Community Policing as Reform: A Cautionary Tale." Pp. 515-529 in C. Klockars and S. Mastrofski (eds.) *Thinking About Police: Contemporary Readings*, Second Edition. New York, NY: McGraw-Hill, Inc.

Mastrofski, Stephen and Craig Uchida (1997). "Transforming the Police." Pp. 196-219 in B.W. Hancock and P.M. Sharp (eds.) *Public Policy: Crime and Criminal Justice*. Upper Sadler River, NJ: Prentice Hall.

Mayo, Louis A. (1985). "Leading Blindly: An Assessment of Chiefs' Information About Police Operations." Pp. 397-417 in W. Geller (ed.) *Police Leadership in America: Crisis and Opportunity*. New York, NY: Praeger Publishers.

McCoy, C. (1987). "Police Legal Liability Is Not a Crisis." *Crime Control Digest*, January:1.

McDonald, Cherokee Paul (1991). *Blue Truth*. New York, NY: St. Martin's Paperbacks.

McGuire, William and Claire McGuire (1988). "Content and Process in the Experience of Self." *Advances in Experimental Social Psychology*, 21:102.

Meadows, Robert J. (1996). *Legal Issues in Policing*. Pp. 96-115 in R. Muraskin and A. Roberts (eds.) *Visions for Change: Crime and Justice in the Twenty-First Century*. Upper Sadler River, NJ: Prentice-Hall.

Meyer, John W. and Brian Rowan (1992). "Institutionalized Organizations: Formal Structure as Myth and Ceremony." Updated Version. Pp. 13-21 in J. Meyer and W. Richard Scott (eds.) *Organizational Environments: Ritual and Rationality*. Newbury Park, CA: Sage.

Miller, Mark R. (1995). *Police Patrol Operations*. Placerville, CA: Copperhouse Publishing Company.

Morris, P. and K. Heal (1981). *Crime Control and the Police*. London: Her Majesty's Stationery Office, Home Office Research Study # 67.

Mueller, David and Cary Heck (1997). "The Neutral Zone as One Example of Police-Community Problem Solving." Pp. 115-121 in Q. Thurman and E. McGarrell (eds.) *Community Policing in a Rural Setting*. Cincinnati, OH: Anderson Publishing Co.

Muir, William Ker Jr. (1977). *Police: Streetcorner Politicians*. Chicago, IL: University of Chicago Press.

Murphy, Patrick (1985). "The Prospective Chief's Negotiation of Authority with the Mayor." Pp. 40-40 in W. Geller (ed.) *Police Leadership in America: Crisis and Opportunity*. New York, NY: Praeger.

Niederhoffer, Arthur (1967). *Behind the Shield*. New York, NY: Doubleday.

Ostrom, Elinor (1974). "The Design of Institutional Arrangements and the Responsiveness of the Police." In L. Reiselbach (ed.) *People vs. Government: The Responsiveness of Institutions*. Bloomington, IN: Indiana University Press.

Oettmeier, Timothy and Mary Ann Wycoff (1997). *Personnel Performance Evaluations in the Community Policing Context*. U.S. Department of Justice, Washington, DC: Community Policing Consortium.

Oettmeier, Timothy and Mary Ann Wycoff (1995). "Police Performance in the Nineties: Practitioner Perspectives." Pp. 131-156 in G.W. Cordner and D.J. Kennedy (eds.) *Managing Police Organizations*. Cincinnati, OH: Anderson Publishing Co.

Packer, Herbert (1968). *The Limits of the Criminal Sanction*. Stanford, CA: Stanford University Press.

Palmiotto, Michael J. (1999). "Should a College Degree Be Required for Today's Police Officer? Yes." Pp. 70-75 in J. Sewell (ed.) *Controversial Issues in Policing*. Boston, MA: Allyn and Bacon.

Pollock, Joycelyn M. (1998). *Ethics in Crime and Justice: Dilemmas and Decisions*, Third Edition. New York, NY: West/Wadsworth.

Pomeroy, Wesley A. Carroll (1985). "The Sources of Police Legitimacy and a Model for Police Misconduct Review: A Response to Wayne Kerstetter." Pp. 183-186 in W. Geller (ed.) *Police Leadership in America: Crisis and Opportunity*. New York, NY: Praeger.

Powers, Mary D. (1995). "Civilian Oversight Is Necessary to Prevent Police Brutality." Pp. 56-60 in P.A. Winters (ed.) *Policing the Police*. San Diego, CA: Greenhaven Press.

Punch, Maurice (1985). *Conduct Unbecoming: The Social Construction of Police Deviance and Control*. London: Tavistock Publications.

Regoli, Robert (1976). "An Empirical Assessment of Niederhoffer's Cynicism Scale." *Journal of Criminal Justice*, 4:231-241.

Regoli, Robert and John Hewitt (1996). *Criminal Justice*. Englewood Cliffs, NJ: Prentice Hall.

Regoli, Robert and Eric Poole (1978). "Specifying Police Cynicism." *Journal of Police Science and Administration*, 6:98-104.

Reuss-Ianni, Elizabeth (1983). *Two Cultures of Policing: Street Cops and Management Cops*. New Brunswick, NJ: Transaction Books.

Rich, R. (1986). "Neighborhood-Based Participation in the Planning Process: Promise and Reality." Pp. 41-73 in R. Taylor (ed.) *Urban Neighborhoods: Research and Policy*. New York, NY: Praeger.

Rieder, J. (1985). *Canarsie: The Jews and Italians of Brooklyn Against Liberalism*. Cambridge, MA: Harvard University Press.

Roberg, Roy, John Crank, and Jack Kuykendall (2000). *Police in Society*, Second Edition. Prospect Heights, IL: Waveland Press.

Roberg, Roy R. and Jack Kuykendall (1993). *Police & Society*. Belmont, CA: Wadsworth Publishing Company.

Roberts, Sam (1994). *Who We Are: A Portrait of America Based on the Latest U.S. Census*. New York, NY: Random House/Times Books.

Robertson, Roland (1987). "Globalization Theory and Civilizational Analysis." *Comparative Civilizations Review*, 17:22.

Rokeach, Milton (1973). *The Nature of Human Values*. New York, NY: The Free Press.

Rokeach, Milton, Martin Miller, and John Snyder (1971). "The Value Gap Between Police and Policed." *Journal of Social Issues*, 27-2:155-171.

Sachs, Susan (1998). "2nd Trial in Killing of Officer Ends With Acquittal." The New York Times on the Web, 7/28/98, [www.nytimes.com/yr/mo/day/news/national/regional/nj-landano-trial.html]

Shearing, Clifford and Richard V. Ericson (1991). "Culture as Figurative Action." *British Journal of Sociology*, 42:481-506.

Sherman, Lawrence (1999). "Learning Police Ethics." Pp. 301-310 in L. Gaines and G. Cordner (eds.) *Policing Perspectives: An Anthology*. Los Angeles, CA: Roxbury.

Sherman, Lawrence, Denise Gottfredson, Doris MacKenzie, John Eck, Peter Reuter, Shawn Bushway in collaboration with members of the Graduate Program (1997). *Preventing Crime: What Works, What Doesn't, and What's Promising*. Washington, DC: U.S. Department of Justice.

Sherman, Lawrence (1985). "Becoming Bent: Moral Careers of Corrupt Policemen." Pp. 253-265 in F. Elliston and M. Feldberg (eds.) *Moral Issues in Police Work*. Totowa, NJ: Rowman & Littlefield Publishers, Inc.

Silberman, Charles E. (1978). *Criminal Violence, Criminal Justice*. New York, NY: Vintage Books.

Skogan, Wesley (1990). *Disorder and Decline: Crime and the Spiral of Decay in American Cities*. New York, NY: The Free Press.

Skolnick, Jerome (1994). *Justice Without Trial*, Third Edition. New York, NY: Wiley.

Skolnick, Jerome (1994). "A Sketch of the Policeman's Working Personality." Pp. 41-68 in *Justice Without Trial: Law Enforcement in Democratic Society*, Third Edition. New York, NY: Wiley.

Skolnick, Jerome (1988). "Deception by Police." Pp. 75-98 in F. Elliston and M. Feldberg (eds.) *Moral Issues in Police Work*. Totowa, NJ: Rowman & Littlefield Publishers.

Skolnick, J. and D. Bayley (1991). "The New Blue Line." Pp. 494-503 in C. Klockars and S. Mastrofski *Thinking About Police: Contemporary Readings*, Second Edition. New York, NY: McGraw-Hill.

Skolnick, Jerome and David Bayley (1986). *The New Blue Line: Police Innovation in Six American Cities*. New York, NY: The Free Press.

Skolnick, Jerome and James Fyfe (1993). *Above the Law: Police and the Excessive Use of Force*. New York, NY: The Free Press.

Strawberry, Peter and Diedre Strawberry (1990). *A Networking Guide to Recruitment, Selection, and Probationary Training of Police Officers in Major Police Departments of the United States of America*. New York, NY: Strawbridge.

Sykes, Gary (1989). "The Functional Nature of Police Reform; The "Myth" of Controlling the Police." Pp. 286-197 in R. Dunham and G. Alpert (eds.) *Critical Issues in Policing*. Prospect Heights, IL: Waveland.

Taft, Philip B. Jr. (1991). "Policing the New Urban Ghettos." Pp. 307-315 in C. Klockars and S. Mastrofski (eds.) *Thinking About Policing: Contemporary Readings,* Second Edition. New York, NY: McGraw, Hill Inc.

Terry, W. (1985). "Police Stress: The Empirical Evidence." Pp. 357-368 in *The Ambivalent Force,* Third Edition. New York, NY: Holt, Rinehart and Winston.

Thomas, R. (1988). "Stress Perception Among Select Federal Probation and Pretrial Services Officers and Their Supervisors." *Federal Probation,* 52:48-58.

Thurman, Quint, Andrew Giacomazzi, Michael Reisig and David Mueller (1996). "Community Based Gang Prevention and Intervention: An Evaluation of the Neutral Zone." *Crime & Delinquency,* 42:279-295.

de Tocqueville, Alexis (1969). *Democracy in America,* trans. George Lawrence (ed.) J.P. Mayer. New York, NY: Anchor, Doubleday.

Trojanowicz, Robert, Victor E. Kappeler, Larry K. Gaines, and Bonnie Bucqueroux (1998). *Community Policing: A Contemporary Perspective,* Second Edition. Cincinnati, OH: Anderson Publishing Co.

Van Maanen, John (1997). "Making Rank: Becoming an American Police Sergeant." Pp. 167-183 in R. Dunham and G. Alpert (eds.) *Critical Issues in Policing: Contemporary Readings,* Third Edition. Prospect Heights, IL: Waveland Press, Inc.

Van Maanen, John (1978). "Observations on the Making of Policemen." Pp. 292-308 in P.K. Manning and J. Van Maanen (eds.) *Policing: A View from the Street.* Santa Monica, CA: Goodyear Publishing Company.

Van Maanen, John (1978b). "The Asshole." Pp. 221-238 in P.K. Manning and J. Van Maanen (eds.) *Policing: A View from the Street.* Santa Monica, CA: Goodyear Publishing Company.

Wagner, Allen and Scott Decker (1997). "Evaluating Citizen Complaints Against the Police." Pp. 302-318 in R. Dunham and G. Alpert (eds.) *Critical Issues in Policing,* Third Edition. Prospect Heights, IL: Waveland Press.

Walker, Samuel (1994). *Sense and Nonsense about Crime and Drugs: A Policy Guide,* Third Edition. New York, NY: McGraw-Hill.

Walker, Samuel (1993). *Taming the System: The Control of Discretion in Criminal Justice, 1950-1990.* New York, NY: Oxford University Press.

Walker, Samuel (1990). *The Police in America,* Second Edition. New York, NY: McGraw-Hill.

Walker, Samuel (1984). "Broken Windows and Fractured History: The Use and Misuse of History in Recent Police Patrol Analysis." *Justice Quarterly,* 1:57-90.

Walker, Samuel (1977). *A Critical History of Police Reform.* Lexington, MA: Lexington Books.

Weber, Max (1981). "Politics as a Vocation." Pp. 426-436 in M. Curtis (ed.) *The Great Political Theories.* Volume 2. New York, NY: Avon Books.

Weber, Max (1946). "Politics as a Vocation," Pp. 77-128 in H. Gerth and C. Wright Mills (ed. and trans.) *From Max Weber: Essays in Sociology.* New York, NY: Oxford University Press.

Westley, W. (1970). *Violence and the Police.* Cambridge, MA: The MIT Press.

White, Susan O. (1986). "A Perspective on Police Professionalism." Pp. 221-232 in M. Pogrebin and R. Regoli (eds.) *Police Administrative Issues: Techniques and Functions.* Millwood, NY: Associated Faculty Press.

Wicklund, Robert and Jack Brehm (1976). *Perspectives on Cognitive Dissonance.* Hillsdale, NJ: Lawrence Erlbaum Associates, Publishers.

Williams, Hubert and Patrick V. Murphy (1995). "The Evolving Strategy of the Police: A Minority View." Pp. 29-52 in V. Kappeler (ed.) *The Police and Society: Touchstone Readings.* Prospect Heights, IL: Waveland Press, Inc.

Wilson, James Q. (1993). *The Moral Sense.* New York, NY: Free Press.

Wilson, James Q. (1968). *Varieties of Police Behavior: The Management of Law and Order in Eight Communities.* Cambridge, MA: Harvard University Press.

Wilson, James Q. and George Kelling (1982). "The Police and Neighborhood Safety: Broken Windows." *Atlantic Monthly*, 249(March):29-38.

Wycoff, Mary Ann and Wesley Skogan (1994). "The Effect of Community Policing Management Style on Officers' Attitudes." *Crime & Delinquency*, 40:371-383.

Zhao, Jihong, Ni He, and Nicholas P. Lovrich (1998). "Individual Value Preferences Among American Police Officers: The Rokeach Theory of Human Values Revisited." *Policing: An International Journal of Police Strategies and Management*, 21:22-36.

Glossary

Act utilitarianism: A form of utilitarianism according to which we look at the consequences of any action for all involved and weigh the units of utility accordingly (Pollock, 1998). Utilitarianism as practiced by the police is more similar to act utilitarianism than rule utilitarianism. See *rule utilitarianism*.

Asshole: A term of disrespect used to describe citizens who question a police officer's authority.

August Vollmer: Frequently referred to as the patriarch of police professionalism, Vollmer (1876-1955) established the first scientific crime laboratory and was appointed full professor at the University of California in 1931.

Avenging angel syndrome: The idea that officers exact their sense of street justice on individuals or groups they personally dislike (Barker, 1996). When citizens acted rudely or disrespectfully, the likelihood that they would go to jail or get citations increased sharply.

Black Swan anecdotes: Stories told by training instructors that contradict the primary message for the instruction, whether intentionally or inadvertently.

Boomerang effect: Efforts to change the behavior of the police that increase the resistance of line offices, making long-term change more difficult.

Boundary spanner: Individuals who represent the interests of an organization to other organizations and agencies in its environment.

Broken windows perspective: A perspective developed by Wilson and Kelling (1982) that described a progressive relationship between public disorder and crime, and argued that the police should intercede early and aggressively before citizens become fearful of crime and avoid public places.

Central ethical dilemma: A two-pronged dilemma. On the one hand, if administrative oversight mechanisms are used to control the behavior of street-level officers, then they will resist, disguise, or obscure their behavior under the secretive protection of line-level culture. On the other, if managers try to control behavior by hiring morally righteous officers, their morality will undermine subsequent administrative efforts to control their behavior.

Coactive function: The police work with citizens on a partnership basis in order to build or reinforce community "self-defense."

Code: See *code of silence.*

Code of silence: The unwritten code among police officers that prohibits them from talking about some aspects of their work to outsiders.

Cognitive dissonance: The psychological state of discomfort that occurs when a person has to contend with two or more cognitions that conflict with each other.

Coin rubbing: A medicinal technique used by some Indochinese in which coins are scraped against a child's neck to drive away evil spirits.

Contingency: In a moral career, each subsequent stage in the moral career is not inevitable, and an officer can decide not to proceed. However, peer pressures make it difficult for an officer to resist advancing to the next stage.

Crevasse: The term has two interrelated meanings, (1) the "official" rank-determined boundary between line officers and everyone with a rank of Lieutenant and above, and (2) the antagonisms and conflicts that occur across that boundary.

Crime control model: One of Packer's (1968) models of justice, according to which the purpose of the justice system is the efficient and effective processing of law violators. Packer compares this model to the *due process model* of justice.

Cynicism: A loss of commitment to the ideals of police work.

Deontological: Deontology is the theory of moral duty. Deontological morality is based in the idea that ethics resides in appropriate behavior and the intent of that behavior, regardless of the consequences.

Dilemma of ends-oriented ethics: A person, committed to achieving a good end, can never know ahead of time that their behavior will produce the end that they seek.

Dirty Harry problem: A situation in which a police officer must commit a dirty act in order to achieve an unquestionably good end.

Disorder: Skogan (1990) described disorder as two related social conditions: (1) individual behaviors that threaten the public order, and (2) signs of physical decay, such as vandalism, dilapidation and abandonment, and rubbish. See also *incivility.*

Distinctiveness theory: Ethnic groups define themselves by what makes them different from others.

Due process model: The other of Packer's (1968) models of justice, according to which individuals are presumed innocent until guilt is proven by the state. The due process model reflects philosophical concerns over the power of the state. Compare to the *crime control model.*

Edge: The point at which turbulence turns into physical danger.

Edge control: Skills carried by police officers that are used to contain turbulence below the *edge* of significant danger.

Ethics: Values related to certain behaviors in a profession or occupational specialization.

Excessive force: Force that occurs when officers use a greater degree of force than is necessary to counter a suspect's resistance. Excessive force happens when force is justified but an officer uses a greater degree than is necessary. If an officer were to use forceful grips, for example, to restrain a suspect when the officer could have accomplished the task with command voice, the officer is using excessive force.

External ethics: These are organizationally based ethical standards. They are administrative codes produced by police managers to inform officers about organizationally correct behavior.

External accountability mechanisms: Mechanisms for holding the police accountable for their behavior outside the police organization, including the courts, citizen review, and newspapers.

Feedback: Feedback is an electrical term that refers to the return of some part of the output to the input stage. In performance testing, the idea of feedback is that officers being evaluated should receive some part or all of the information in the evaluations (the output) rather than turning over the results of the evaluations to commanders for inspection.

General definition of discretion: The ability to choose between alternatives when making a decision.

Globalization theory: Ethnic self-consciousness is intensified as diverse ethnic and cultural groups become more interdependent.

Golden apples: Police officers who are intelligent and committed to the noble cause, and who are highly focused on efficiency and effectiveness in police work.

Gospel of professionalism: The term for the professionalizing creed promoted by August Vollmer. Police departments focused on excellence through hiring standards, and officers were committed to public service and the contribution of police to society.

Grafting subcultures: Groups or cohorts of police officers involved in illegal activity, and who socialize new officers into corrupt practices.

Grass-eaters: Police officers that passively accept graft. For example, an officer that accepts a bribe from a motorist, but does not ask for it, is a grass-eater.

Hypothesis: A statement of relationship between two variables.

Importance/usefulness dilemma: A paradox – the more important a performance evaluation is for a candidate's career, the greater the likelihood that evaluators are not going to make useful distinctions between candidates. The paradox stems from the logic that administrators do not like to make harsh judgments of individuals with whom they will have to work throughout their careers.

Incivility: Incivility is a term that describes passive or active conflict among neighborhood residents. Lewis and Salem (1986) explain incivility in terms of unacceptable behavior by teenagers, physical deterioration in homes, commercial areas or public spaces, the intrusion of "different" population groups into the area, and an increase in marginally criminal behaviors such as drug use and vandalism. See also *disorder*.

Informal norms: The idea that a community or society has unwritten, taken-for-granted standards of appropriate or acceptable behaviors.

Instrumental values: Preferred modes (or means) of behavior. For example, "obedient" is an instrumental value that might be a preferred mode of behavior.

Intentional tort: A civil action based on a police officer's wanton disregard for a person's rights.

Internal ethics: This means that officers carry within themselves a sense of ethical or moral responsibility about what constitutes "correct" behavior.

Internal accountability mechanisms: Accountability procedures within a police organization. These include the chain of command, internal affairs, and written standard operating procedures.

Iron fist: Aggressive law enforcement practices, such as the aggressive enforcement of public order problems and street sweeps.

Just means: The ethical concern that means used to achieve ends should conform to broad considerations of human values, particularly as those values are embodied in legal and administrative due process.

Justice efficiency: The idea that the purpose of justice is to seek efficient outcomes. Efficiency is one of the elements of Packer's (1968) *crime control model* of the justice process, and views due process as an impediment to the efficient running of the justice system.

Legal suspicion: Based on a legal standard of reasonableness, suspicion is determined by an officer's ability to articulate reasons why he or she thinks that a suspect might be a danger to a police officer or might have committed or is about to be involved in a crime.

Legitimacy: A legitimate organization is one whose claim to authority is accepted. Legitimating organizations are organizations who can affect the finances or well-being of the organizations.

Logic of good faith: Members of public sector organizations tend to have "good faith" that their organization acts legally and correctly, and organizational members believe in what they do. It is consequently difficult for organizational members to believe that incidents occur in which the organization (or important organizational members) has acted badly or illegally.

Low-visibility decisionmaking: Police officers do their work mostly out of sight of supervisors, and usually involving only a few citizens.

Magic pencil: A form of police corruption in which police officers write up an incident in a way that criminalizes a suspect.

Mama Rosa's test: A loyalty test that assesses the willingness of a rookie to go along with other officers when they are violating departmental policy.

Management cop culture: According to Reuss-Ianni (1983) this is the perspective of police work held by managers. It is characterized by a belief in principles of scientific management and bureaucratic process.

Mass private property: Areas of private enterprise that are designed from large scale public use. Such areas include shopping malls, college campuses, and recreation complexes.

Matched groups: Two different groups that are made comparable to each other by being matched on important related characteristics. For example, a group of police officers might be compared to a group of non-police citizens by being selected for similarities (matched) in age, gender, political affiliation, and income.

Material reward corruption: Whatever a police officer receives through the misuse of his or her authority.

Maturity: The ability to balance the use of force with a belief in just means.

Means-ends continuum: This refers to Packer's (1968) crime control/due process model of the justice system, in which crime control and due process are viewed as opposite ends on a continuum. Individuals with a focus on ends will tend to be on the crime control side, and individuals with a focus on means will be on the due process side.

Means-ends conflicts: Conflicts that occur when officers encounter situations in which good ends cannot be achieved by legal means. The idea of conflict is that officers must choose between striving for those "good" ends at the expense of legal means, or act legally even if they cannot achieve those "good" ends.

Melting pot: This is the idea that ethnic groups are assimilated after immigrating to the United States, their distinctiveness and cultural uniqueness gradually disappearing.

Middle-ground institutions: Institution that are mid-way between individuals and general government, particularly local neighborhoods and neighborhood organizations.

Moral resolve: The ability to counter weaknesses of the will, susceptibility to temptations and the loss of self-control. Moral resolve, Kleinig (1990) contends, will assist police officers in their efforts to resist pressures to compromise their ethics.

Moral sensitization: The nurturing of moral breadth and depth. Kleinig (1990) argues that this is an important part of ethics instruction.

Moral career: A series of stages an officer goes through when becoming corrupt.

Moral expertise: The ability to recognize and systematically think through ethical dilemmas encountered in the work environment.

Morality: The values related to the "total person," the sum of a person's actions in every sphere of life.

Municipal system: The mutual interdependencies and obligations shared by various members of the city and county businesses and governing organizations.

Negligent tort: Civil actions based on a police officer's failure to protect the public from harm.

Negotiable issues: Issues over which a chief and mayor (or other municipal executive) typically negotiate, including the handling of media relations, and the mayor's role in personnel and organization of the police department.

Neutral Zone: An experiment in gang control and cooperation carried out by Mountlake Terrace, Washington. The Neutral Zone is a collaborative program that provided a variety of activities such as basketball, a food and clothing bank, and hot and cold meals.

Noble cause: A moral commitment to make the world a safer place, or simply put, "getting bad guys off the streets."

Non-negotiable issues: Issues over which a chief should not have to negotiate with a mayor (or other municipal executive), such as police salaries and promotions. Even with non-negotiable issues, an astute chief will sometimes take the mayor's counsel.

Occupational socialization: The process by which a recruit learns the values, habits, beliefs, and norms of the organization into which he or she is hired.

Order maintenance: The peacekeeping role of police, in which police intervene in disputes between two people or between a citizen and a neighborhood (Regoli & Hewitt, 1996).

Order negotiation: The use of practical people-skills to develop solutions to commonly occurring people-problems, such as relations between landlords, youth and oldsters, the homeless and businesses, and traditional locals and recent arrivals.

Pascal's wager: This is the idea that it is impossible to know with certainty the existence of God. However, the wise man won't take the chance and live a sinful life. The chance of spending an eternity in Hell offsets any possible reason for taking the chance that God doesn't exist.

Passion: A commitment to the ends of policing. Officers with too much passion, Klockars (1991a) stated, tended to ignore just means.

Patronage: The personnel system according to which hiring and continued employment depend on loyalty to the political party holding office.

Performance evaluations: Instruments and tests that assess the nature of the work process, specific accomplishments of police officers, and public attitudes about the performance of the department in general.

Perspective: A wide vision of the human condition. Too much perspective, Klockars (1991a) argued, interfered with a police officer's need to use force in some encounters.

Police accountability: Generally, accountability refers to all types of efforts to control police behavior.

Police brutality: Police brutality is more severe than excessive force. It represents a gross imbalance between citizen non-compliance and level of police force. The use of a baton to strike a compliant handcuffed suspect, for example, is an example of police brutality.

Police community reciprocity: Police and community members work together to solve crime problems and to develop crime prevention tactics.

Police culture: The accepted practices, rules, and principles of conduct that officers apply according to particular situational needs. It also includes their generalized beliefs about police work (Manning, 1989).

Power of self: The power to show others right behavior through example, to pass values on to others because one acts as a representative of particular values.

Pre-hiring procedures: Procedures that assess the qualifications of recruits for police work.

Proactive function: Law enforcement and crime prevention activities initiated by the police. These include directed patrols, the use of undercover police officers, and police-initiated investigations.

Quality of life: Quality of life commonly has two meanings: (1) subjectively, it refers to citizen attitudes about the well-being of their lives and more specifically their fears of crime, and (2) objectively, quality of life refers to the physical condition or well-being of neighborhoods.

Reactive function: Traditional policing for victim-centered crime, and is characterized by routine police responses to citizen calls for assistance.

Representativeness: The extent to which the values held by a single group or an individual correspond to the average values of all members from which the group or individual is drawn.

Role stress: Characteristics of an organization's role that produces adverse consequences for an individual.

Rule utilitarianism: This form of utilitarianism means that a person judges their actions in terms of the precedents they set and the long-term utility of the rules set by their actions (Pollock, 1998).

Scandal cycle: A department becomes involved in a scandal, the city holds hearings, and the department then passes through a "professionalizing" period under the guidance of a new chief. After a period of external calm, a new scandal sometimes emerges, suggesting that scandals go through cycles in some departments.

Scientific management: The belief that a police department should be organized hierarchically, and employment and advancement should be based on merit. Managerial practices should be rationally organized so that all employees perform their work efficiently and effectively.

Sixth-sense suspicion: The ability to identify criminal wrongdoing from the most trivial of clues. It is based on intuition, not fact, though when it is highly honed it will produce solid evidence.

Slippery-slope model of economic corruption: The theory that the first illegal acts committed by a police officer are minor and easy to justify. However, subsequent, more serious acts of wrongdoing are easier to justify.

Slippery-slope model of noble-cause corruption: A series of stages of noble-cause corruption that an officer goes through, in which each previous stage makes increasingly serious noble-cause violations easier to commit.

Social distance: The degree of friendliness and sense of comfort between two people or groups. The greater the social distance, the lower the comfort.

Specific definition of discretion: The decision by a police officer not to make an arrest when the requisite conditions for an arrest are present.

Standard operating procedure: The body of all departmental policies officers are expected to know and to use as behavioral guides.

Station-house sergeants: Police sergeants who tend to see their work in terms of controlling the conduct of the officers assigned to them.

Stealth driving: The practice of turning off the lights of a squad car and driving through dark areas unseen.

Street cop culture: According to Reuss-Ianni (1983) this is the perspective of police work held by line officers. The organizing ethos of the police is the "good ole days" when police were respected by the public, officers could count on each other, and managers were part of the police family.

Street justice: Violent or rude behavior carried out by police officers against citizens in order to assert police authority or control.

Street environment: The romantic term for the public working environment of line officers and detectives.

Street sergeants: Sergeants who are more "street" oriented, and take an active role in their officer's assignments.

Stress: Any condition that has adverse consequences for an individual's well-being.

Subcultural traits: Values that are imported from broader American life and accentuated in police work.

Teleological: Teleology is the study of final causes. Teleological ethics are based in that idea that desired end-states determine a person's behavior.

Terminal values: Preferred end-states. For example, the value "family security" is a terminal value that might be a preferred end-state for some individuals.

Title 42, section 1983: A U.S. code defining the basis for legal action against the police. It states that *Every person who, under color of any statute, ordinance, regulation, custom, or usage, of any State or Territory, subjects, or causes to be subjected, any citizens of the United States or other person within the jurisdiction thereof to the deprivation of any rights, privileges, or immunities secured by the Constitution and laws, shall be liable to the party injured in an action at law, suited in equity, or other proper proceeding for redress.*

Turbulence: Turbulence has two meanings: (1) the speed with which activity happens during police-citizen interactions, (2) the degree of unpredictability in police-citizen interactions.

Type II drug corruption: Carter's (1999) definition of drug corruption, which happens when officers commit corrupt activities in the pursuit of legitimate goals.

Value-based hiring: According to the idea of value-based hiring, assessments of a recruit's values occur at every stage of the hiring process. These assessments are a formal part of the hiring process, as when officers are tested for their willingness to back other officers up, and informally, and informally according to local cultural standards.

Value-based decisionmaking: The values carried by police officers determine their decisions to intervene in the lives of citizens, what they do when they intervene, and the way in which they bring interventions to a conclusion.

Value-neutral hiring: According to this perspective, officers are not screened for their values, except for honesty, psychological stability, and criminal history. Officers should not carry or act out predispositions about social rights or wrongs.

Value predisposition perspective: Recruits are hired with their values already in place, and these values are selectively highlighted and finely tuned during academy and on-the-job training.

Value systems: Enduring organizations of beliefs concerning preferable modes of conduct or end states of existence.

Value transmission: The process by which values are carried from society to the occupation of policing.

Values: Enduring beliefs that specific modes of conduct or end-states of existence are preferable to their opposite

Values are learned on job perspective: Values held by police officers are learned on the job and stem from the unique characteristics of the occupation of policing.

Velvet glove: Non-aggressive community-based police strategies and tactics, such as community watch groups and block meetings.

Victim-centered: refers to information about crime is obtained from crime victims or related individuals who report crimes to the police.

Wall of silence: The inability of outsiders, including police managers, to find out information about incidents involving line officers. The existence of a "wall of silence" is controversial, with many observers arguing that it is pervasive and protects officers from external inspection, and many police representatives contending that it does not exist. See also *code of silence*.

Warping effect: Reforms are assimilated by the police according to the cultural values carried by individual officers, thus shifting the effects of planned changes in unpredictable ways.

Name Index

Subject Index